ORACLE® PL/SQL: EXPERT TECHNIQUES FOR DEVELOPERS AND DATABASE ADMINISTRATORS

LAKSHMAN BULUSU

COURSE TECHNOLOGY
CENGAGE Learning™

Australia, Brazil, Japan, Korea, Mexico, Singapore, Spain, United Kingdom, United States

COURSE TECHNOLOGY
CENGAGE Learning™

Oracle® PL/SQL: Expert Techniques for Developers and Database Administrators

Lakshman Bulusu

Publisher and General Manager,
Course Technology PTR:
Stacy L. Hiquet

Associate Director of Marketing:
Sarah Panella

Manager of Editorial Services:
Heather Talbot

Marketing Manager: Mark Hughes

Acquisitions Editor: Mitzi Koontz

Project/Copy Editor: Kezia Endsley

Technical Reviewer: Aneesha Bakharia

CRM Editorial Services Coordinator:
Jen Blaney

Interior Layout: Jill Flores

Cover Designer: Tyler Creative Services

CD-ROM Producer: Brandon Penticuff

Indexer: Valerie Haynes Perry

Proofreader: Laura R. Gabler

For product information and technology assistance, contact us at
Cengage Learning Customer & Sales Support, 1-800-354-9706

For permission to use material from this text or product,
submit all requests online at **cengage.com/permissions**
Further permissions questions can be emailed to
permissionrequest@cengage.com

Library of Congress Control Number: 2007939371

ISBN-13: 978-1-58450-554-9

ISBN-10: 1-58450-554-0

Course Technology
25 Thomson Place
Boston, MA 02210
USA

Cengage Learning is a leading provider of customized learning solutions with office locations around the globe, including Singapore, the United Kingdom, Australia, Mexico, Brazil, and Japan. Locate your local office at: **international. cengage.com/region**

Cengage Learning products are represented in Canada by Nelson Education, Ltd.

For your lifelong learning solutions, visit **courseptr.com**

Visit our corporate website at **cengage.com**

Printed in the United States of America
1 2 3 4 5 6 7 11 10 09 08

To the loving memory of my father-in-law Mr. G.V.S.J. Somayajulu,
who will always remain as a shining light to me.

Acknowledgments

I thank my wife, Anuradha, for her patience and my lovely kids Pranati and Pranav for not giving me a hard time during the course of my entire writing period.

I thank my brother, Visweswar Kasi Bulusu, for his suggestions on various programming language concepts that really proved invaluable.

I thank the publisher; the Acquisitions Editor, Mitzi Koontz; and the various editors at CRM and Cengage Learning for their help in making this book see the light of day.

About the Author

Lakshman Bulusu is an experienced Oracle professional with 15 plus years of extensive experience in software management, design, and development using Oracle and its related technologies, including PL/SQL and Java. He's the author of *Oracle Developer Forms Techniques* (published by SAMS) and *Oracle and Java Development*, (published by SAMS and translated into Polish and Japanese), *Oracle9i PL/SQL: A Developer's Guide* (published by Apress), and *Oracle Programming FAQ* (published by NetImpress), all of which have been popular in the market. He also holds an Oracle Masters credential and an OCP certification from Oracle Corporation, and is a double honors graduate in computer science and engineering and mathematics. He has presented at numerous international and national conferences on Oracle and its tools and published articles in various technical magazines and journals in the United States and the United Kingdom. Currently, as a Technical Manager for Software Development, employed by Delaware-US-based Genex Technologies, he oversees the management, design, and development of mission-critical Oracle projects for major clients across the U.S. Europe, and Asia.

Contents

Introduction

Welcome aboard the first book focusing exclusively on PL/SQL techniques, through Oracle 11g, that cover "how-to" and "when-to," and are tried-tested-true without compromising on performance. The book's techniques encompass *all* technical scenarios, starting from design to coding to testing to debugging and tuning, thus proving the fact that PL/SQL is more than just a 3GL sequel to SQL. Instead, this book can be used as a methodology for application development using Oracle. The use of these techniques has a broader scope, in applications ranging from OLTP to OLAP and data warehousing and business intelligence. The world of PL/SQL is exciting and this book provides a repository of these techniques for PL/SQL developers and DBAs that caters to all types of needs, starting from developers mining for "tricks-of-the-trade" to the on-the-go consultant looking for pluggable code to the all-concerned DBA working to enhance performance while working on issues related to "lot-of-time," "lot-of-code," and "lot-of-data."

This book takes its readers one level above the existing ones including professional and reference texts and online docs; a majority of these techniques have been implemented successfully in real-world projects involving Oracle and PL/SQL.

The author appreciates all comments and suggestions to make these "tried-tested-true" techniques "trusted" through more and more successful PL/SQL code implementations.

What This Book Covers

This book covers the most effective solutions to the problems encountered in practical programming using the PL/SQL language through version 11g of Oracle. It covers these techniques in an easy-to-follow style that enables you to quickly pick up the content. Each topic presented is explained by means of a distinct style specifying "how to use it" and "when to use it."

Starting from PL/SQL Internals that include PL/SQL program structure, internal representation, compilation, and execution, it takes the readers through a variety of techniques that explore core PL/SQL concepts that take PL/SQL beyond SQL such as data structure management, error management, data management, application management, and transaction management. An exclusive section on "Applying PL/SQL in the Real World" details the practical how-to techniques of applying PL/SQL in live projects and elaborates on various PL/SQL frameworks, the integration of PL/SQL with Java, and Web-enabling PL/SQL.

The last two chapters on PL/SQL tuning and debugging and PL/SQL coding standards contain comprehensive coverage of performance-enhancing techniques and PL/SQL coding standards and make this book an asset for any PL/SQL programmer and a stand-out from other titles in the market.

The numerous techniques described with examples and hands-on code in each chapter as well as the tips and coding standards included in this book make it ideal for an academic course as well as for corporations using Oracle and PL/SQL for their application development or those who are migrating from earlier versions.

How This Book Is Organized

This book is divided into three parts containing 13 chapters, as follows.

Part I: Introductory Concepts

This part consists of Chapters 1, 2, and 3. Chapter 2 describes the internal architecture of a PL/SQL program and its workings starting from coding to compilation to execution. Chapter 3 focuses on the new features of PL/SQL introduced in versions 10g and 11g of Oracle from an application development perspective.

Part II: Techniques for PL/SQL Programming

This part consists of Chapters 4 through 8, which describe the PL/SQL techniques involved in core areas of database development, starting from data structure and error management to data and transaction management and application construction. It covers techniques pertaining to records, associative arrays, nested tables, and multi-dimensional arrays in Chapter 4; techniques regarding error management in Chapter 5; data retrieval and data manipulation techniques using array processing and dynamic SQL and PL/SQL in Chapter 6; techniques involving the use of procedures, functions, user-defined operators, packages, application contexts, and database triggers and that of sharing data between applications in Chapter 7; and techniques for transaction management, particularly those for using autonomous transactions and auditing queries, in Chapter 8.

Part III: Applying PL/SQL in the Real World

This part contains five chapters, spanning from Chapter 9 through Chapter 13, that explain the application of PL/SQL techniques in real-world projects with special reference to application development frameworks, extending the use of PL/SQL with Java and the Web, as well as tuning, debugging, and standardization. Chapter 9 describes application development frameworks using PL/SQL that can be adopted as a methodology for application development using Oracle and PL/SQL. Chapter 10 highlights techniques for extending the use of PL/SQL to Java and Web environments. Chapter 11 describes miscellaneous but powerful techniques pertaining to simulating datasets, auto-generating statically and dynamically executable code, and hiding PL/SQL source code. Chapter 12 is all about performance-centric PL/SQL and the framework for debugging PL/SQL. Chapter 13 deals with the standardization of PL/SQL in terms of code design and development.

Prerequisites and Intended Audience

This book is targeted toward two audience types. First, Oracle developers programming in PL/SQL in the database. They need not have any prior 3GL experience. All it assumes is a working knowledge of SQL and PL/SQL. Also, Oracle database professionals targeted toward the DBA line will benefit from this book because it describes the techniques of constructing PL/SQL methodologies for live application development projects.

Secondly, students and teachers in the academic field pursuing a course in database programming involving server-side Oracle will find this book handy in answering the many problems involved in both theory and practical programming.

Part I

Introductory Concepts

1 Introduction to PL/SQL

In This Chapter

- Why use PL/SQL?
- When not to use PL/SQL
- PL/SQL Overview

For any programming language, the journey from concepts to code is a challenging one, and PL/SQL is no exception. The design of the code is an important factor that contributes to the reusability, maintainability, and performance of the same. The bottom line is the inability to break the code without the code breaking. What this means is that the code should be unbreakable by anyone starting from newbies to experts and regardless of the environment in which it runs. For this to happen, you need to use the best techniques for coding. And better techniques lead to better code. This is what this book is all about. Good code design reduces the chance of errors and leads to effective maintenance. It adheres to the use of coding standards that pertain to standard practices for formatting, documentation, and use of effective control, as well as data and application structures and modularization of code. The benefits derived are many:

- Better readability and understandability resulting from better formatting and documentation (and hence easy maintenance that also helps in debugging)
- Better performance resulting from use of effective control, and data and application structures (because of optimal code and fewer errors)
- Better organization and reusability resulting from modularization (and hence reduced errors, which means less debugging and more effective maintenance)

PL/SQL is the primary procedural component of Oracle server-side programming and is regarded as the primary language for developing Oracle applications on the database and application tiers. PL/SQL has incorporated many new features that take the programmer to a higher level of coding in terms of practicality and efficiency. Also, Oracle provides for support of Java in the database. PL/SQL provides this capability by means of Java stored procedures and their new functionality, to build highly scalable applications.

The subject matter of this book comprises the PL/SQL internals and a variety of techniques and frameworks that relate to core PL/SQL concepts, such as data structure management, error management, data management, application management, transaction management, and performance management.

Before elaborating on these techniques, let's take a quick peek at the pros and cons of using PL/SQL.

WHY USE PL/SQL?

PL/SQL as a programming language has several firsts that leverage its use as a 3GL (a third generation language, which includes procedural capabilities) component for Oracle. Remember this rule of thumb: if you are running applications using Oracle, use PL/SQL. It is the simplest and best option. The reasons are many; the primary ones are as follows:

■ The design and development of applications in Oracle call for data querying and manipulation using SQL that is a 4GL (a fourth generation language, which is purely nonprocedural). PL/SQL as a procedural language is tightly integrated with SQL and shares the same datatypes. This makes it optimal for SQL-intensive processing in regard to writing less code and execution speed.

■ PL/SQL facilitates the moving of application logic to the database tier, thus making the database an active one. This makes the code reusable in addition to reducing network traffic. Furthermore, the code can be natively compiled, resulting in still faster execution.

■ PL/SQL offers cross-platform portability as long as Oracle is the database you use, no matter at what tier and which operating system.

■ Enhanced features of PL/SQL, such as packages, error management, dynamic SQL, array processing, and object support, provide for greater flexibility and efficiency.

WHEN NOT TO USE PL/SQL

PL/SQL is not suitable in the following situations:

■ When your code needs to be RDBMS independent. Java is a better choice in this case. RDBMS independent means the code can run one of the existing commercial relational database management systems, such as Oracle, Microsoft SQL Server, IBM DB2, or Sybase, without making portability changes pertaining to the particular RDBMS.

■ When a direct interface to the end user is required. A customized user interface is needed that in turn calls stored PL/SQL code.

PL/SQL OVERVIEW

As the lingua franca of Oracle, PL/SQL (with its tight integration with SQL) is the language of choice for developing Oracle applications in terms of reliability, scalability, maintainability, and efficiency. PL/SQL supports both traditional procedural as well as object-oriented features. Using a combination of these features, you can build powerful and optimal techniques that enable you to develop real-world applications. From an application-development perspective, these techniques can be broadly classified into the following categories:

■ Data structure management (covered in Chapter 4)
■ Error management (covered in Chapter 5)
■ Data management (covered in Chapter 6)
■ Application management (covered in Chapter 7)
■ Transaction management (covered in Chapter 8)

Each of these categories determines the completeness of a PL/SQL application and hence the correct and optimal implementation of each is indispensable for the successful running of the same.

DATA STRUCTURE MANAGEMENT

Data structure management refers to the proper and effective use of PL/SQL program structures (and/or SQL schema level structures) to hold the data for functions such as intermediate transformation, data I/O, and/or performance enhancements. Examples include PL/SQL records, collections, and objects. Chapter 4 touches upon the techniques for using records, associative arrays, nested tables, VARRAYS, and multi-dimensional arrays.

ERROR MANAGEMENT

Error management refers to the elegant exception handling, tracking, and customization of server-side errors. Every PL/SQL program should have at least one exception handling section to trap server errors and handle them as required. Multiple exception handlers pertaining to specific sections of code should be programmed to take care of intermediate sections of code. Care should be taken when letting exceptions fall through the code. Chapter 5 details techniques for obtaining complete error information, including the line number where the error occurred. It also covers how to customize the error information returned and how to halt further processing on error occurrence.

DATA MANAGEMENT

Data management refers to the retrieval of data from the database using SQL, processing it using PL/SQL, and inputting it back to the database using SQL DML (Data Manipulation Language) statements. The output and input of data might consist of using advanced techniques like dynamic SQL when the SQL used needs to be constructed at runtime. The use of array processing using static and dynamic SQL can speed up this process. Chapter 6 details techniques for data retrieval and management, for using dynamic SQL and/or PL/SQL, and for array processing using static and dynamic SQL.

APPLICATION MANAGEMENT

Application management refers to building logic for application implementation in the form of stored PL/SQL code. Examples include using standalone and packaged procedures and functions, sharing data between applications, and so on. PL/SQL packages play a major role in this area and can be used to globalize or localize data and privatize code. Chapter 7 elaborates on techniques such as coding packages and the benefits of doing so, reading and writing package variables dynamically, and passing data between applications using collections and REF CURSORS. This chapter also compares procedures versus functions, packages versus contexts, and packages versus objects.

TRANSACTION MANAGEMENT

Transaction management refers to the process of properly committing and rolling back transactions from PL/SQL. There are situations when normal transaction processing isn't enough. For example, when you are logging errors, the actual transaction needs to be rolled back but the error information needs to be committed. The use of autonomous transactions circumvents this limitation. Chapter 8 describes techniques such as using asynchronous COMMIT, using autonomous transactions, and auditing queries.

USING PL/SQL IN THE REAL WORLD

Using PL/SQL in the real world calls for pre-designed prototypes that can be utilized in application development. These templates can be implemented using frameworks that can be used to develop applications. The frameworks can be so designed that changes made to them are transparent to the applications using them. A PL/SQL framework consists of pre-tested code that provides standardized API and can be used in application code to achieve the desired functionality. All the application needs to do is to make the API calls providing proper parameters or return values. Examples include frameworks for error logging, DML auditing, ETL (Extract, Transform, and Load) processing, file I/O, and performance tuning. All of these techniques are described in more detail in Chapter 9.

PL/SQL as a procedural extension to SQL has evolved in its support for 3GL features since its inception in Oracle V6. Oracle 10g and 11g bring in a host of enhancements to the language in addition to the ones incorporated in Oracle 8i and 9i. Also the object-relational nature of Oracle has introduced certain object-oriented programming features in PL/SQL. However, there are certain areas where PL/SQL still lacks in its capabilities. Examples are interaction with the OS from within the database and true multiple inheritance. To circumvent these limitations, Oracle has allowed PL/SQL interaction with 3GLs such as C and object-oriented languages like Java and C++. By means of external procedures, PL/SQL can call C and C++ programs. Also, by means of Java stored procedures, PL/SQL can call Java programs.

The Internet has played a major role in Web-enabling software applications, thus providing seamless access over the Web. Extending PL/SQL to use HTML has opened the gateway for using PL/SQL in HTML for HTML-intensive applications and using HTML in PL/SQL for PL/SQL-intensive applications, making them Internet-based. This, coupled with email support from within the database, provides a powerful solution to running PL/SQL applications over the Internet. These aspects of PL/SQL are described in Chapter 10.

PL/SQL is fun to program and, as long as the code runs in production without any complaints from the users, the fun is well-intended. As the number of users increases and volume of data increases, chances are that the code runs slower or breaks before completion. This cost in performance results in a lower overall rating score. Proper tuning of the code, augmented by tuning of system resources, helps in boosting the performance, finally resulting in a quality deliverable.

If coding PL/SQL is fun, debugging PL/SQL is more fun. However, this task is easier said than done. Runtime system and server-specific errors require immediate attention and at times it becomes a nightmare to figure out what is going on. However, PL/SQL has certain powerful debugging techniques that make the task easy. In fact, debugging is as important when testing as when fixing live errors. The book devotes a complete chapter to tuning and debugging techniques—Chapter 12.

Just coding PL/SQL isn't enough. Code adhering to standards is globally acceptable, more reliable, more readable, and easily maintainable. Standards can be defined for data structures as well as application logic. Starting from defining variables and specifying parameters to writing executable logic and exception handling to coding application-specific packages, PL/SQL standards redefine the way code is written. Chapter 13 concentrates on PL/SQL standards.

PL/SQL is a well-structured language with an optimized compiler and built-in features like compile-time warnings, conditional compilation, and native compilation add to the productive use of the language. Through Oracle 11g, PL/SQL is optimized for SQL as well as in its internal structure, compilation, and execution. The best way to use PL/SQL is to analyze the application-specific requirements and design the code accordingly. This design decides the way the enhanced features can be leveraged.

Table 1.1 summarizes the techniques presented in the book, categorized under the headings of data structure management, error management, data management, application management, transaction management, applying PL/SQL in the real world, and miscellaneous.

TABLE 1.1 SUMMARY OF PL/SQL TECHNIQUES

Category	Sub-Category	Description of Technique
Data structure management	Records	Data I/O using records
		Using functions to perform record comparison
	Associative arrays	Performing data I/O
		Caching look-up data
	Nested tables	Passing resultsets between PL/SQL programs
		Transforming collection resultset into a cursor
		Pipelined table functions
		Manipulating stored nested tables using SQL
	VARRAYS	
	Miscellaneous	Simulating multi-dimensional arrays
		Simulating datasets using pipelined table functions
Error management		Obtain complete error information
		Customize error information returned
		Halt further processing on error occurrence
Data management		Data retrieval
		Data manipulation
		Using dynamic SQL and PL/SQL
		Array processing using static SQL
		Array processing using dynamic SQL
		Transforming DBMS_SQL cursor to REF CURSOR

Continued

Application management	Packages	Coding packages to globalize data and code
		Reading and writing package variables dynamically
		Coding packages to localize data and privatize code
		Coding packages to break dependency chain
		Coding packages to pass data between applications
		Sharing data using collections versus sharing data using REF CURSORS
Transaction management	Transaction control	Performing asynchronous COMMIT
	Autonomous transactions	Auditing queries
		Performing DML in functions called from SQL
		Circumventing mutating table errors
		Performing error logging
Applying PL/SQL in the real world	Application development frameworks	Error logging framework
		DML auditing framework
		ETL framework
		File I/O framework
		Performing tuning framework
	Integration with 3GLs	Using Java stored procedures
		Using external procedures

Continued

	Integration with Web	Using PL/SQL in HTML
		Using HTML in PL/SQL
		Emailing from PL/SQL (with and without attachments)
Miscellaneous		Auto-generating code using dynamic SQL and/or PL/SQL
		Hiding statically written and dynamically generated PL/SQL code
		Batch scheduling of OS command jobs

PL/SQL, with its set of enhanced features, enables development of powerful applications and APIs by employing expert techniques. Its applications are scalable across a large number of users and at the same time perform efficiently. When to use what technique depends on what the requirement is and the size of the dataset that is being worked on.

This book exposes the many how-tos and gotchas involved in programming and the techniques presented provide the most effective solutions to the problems encountered in practical programming using the PL/SQL language through Oracle 11g.

SUMMARY

This chapter was an introductory one on PL/SQL and its capabilities listed by way of coding techniques. The subsequent chapters detail each of the techniques listed in this chapter and their implementation. The next chapter explains the PL/SQL internals, which include PL/SQL program structure, internal architecture, compilation, and execution.

2 PL/SQL by Dissection

In This Chapter

- Program structure
- Internal architecture
- Program compilation
- Program execution
- Memory usage
- Meta-data for PL/SQL code
- Program debugging
- Protecting source code

This chapter discusses the basic structure of a PL/SQL program and the various phases it goes through before it can be executed from an end-user interface and/or a server-side batch program. The topics covered include typical PL/SQL program structure, internal PL/SQL architecture and memory usage, and the compilation and execution phases. The chapter ends with a discussion on PL/SQL debugging and protecting source code.

PROGRAM STRUCTURE

PL/SQL is a block-structured language with the block as the primary language element. A typical PL/SQL block consists of a declaration section, an executable section, and an exception-handling section. The declaration section is optional. The executable section is enclosed between BEGIN and END statements, is terminated by a semicolon, and is mandatory. The exception section is also optional but it is recommended and it's standard to include an exception-handling section in every PL/SQL program. The exception-handling section is included immediately preceding the END keyword. A PL/SQL program can be an anonymous block, a named block, or one that is stored in the database in the form of procedures, functions, packages, and/or triggers. A stored PL/SQL program unit has its definition and logic stored in the data dictionary views. These are often referred to as *metadata views.*

The executable section is usually a combination of SQL and PL/SQL statements and this embedding of SQL within a PL/SQL block comes with the advantages of reduced network traffic and productivity.

Here's an example of a typical PL/SQL block, also illustrated in Figure 2.1:

```
DECLARE
  v_rate NUMBER;
  v_threshold NUMBER := 100.00;
  v_increase_flag BOOLEAN := FALSE;
BEGIN
  SELECT rate
  INTO   v_rate
  FROM   rate_tab
  WHERE  rate_type = 'Monthly'
    AND  effective_date = TRUNC(SYSDATE);
  IF (v_rate < v_threshold) THEN
    v_increase_flag := TRUE;
  END IF;
  IF v_increase_flag THEN
    UPDATE rate_tab
       SET rate := rate + 2.5*rate
    WHERE  rate_type = 'Monthly'
    AND  effective_date = TRUNC(SYSDATE);
    COMMIT;
  END IF;
EXCEPTION WHEN NO_DATA_FOUND THEN
    dbms_output.put_line('Rate not available, contact FS');
```

```
WHEN OTHERS THEN
  dbms_output.put_line('Server Error as follows, contact MIS ');
  dbms_output.put_line(SQLERRM);
END;
/
```

Typical PL/SQL Block Structure

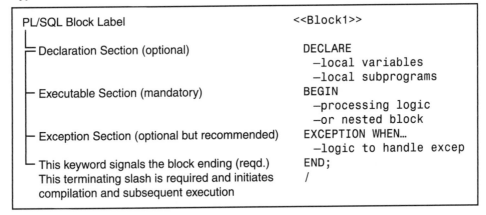

FIGURE 2.1
The typical structure of a PL/SQL block.

Note how some variables are initialized during declaration and how SQL statements are embedded within procedural logic (in this case, conditional statements). Also note how the exception section is used to track particular errors such as NO_DATA_FOUND and generic errors such as other server errors.

Storing code within the database comes with the following advantages:

- The code is easily manageable. For example, you can use SQL to query the data dictionary.
- The code is sharable across applications. With the associated source code being stored in the database, granting authorized access to the meta-data views enables querying the same to retrieve the code and reuse, by applications running on both the same database and separate databases.
- The code gets modular, thus enabling plug-and-play capability in application programs.
- The code is independent of client applications.
- The database manages the dependencies between database objects.

The previously defined PL/SQL block can be converted into a PL/SQL stored program such as a procedure using the CREATE OR REPLACE syntax. Here's the code for the same:

```
CREATE OR REPLACE PROCEDURE p_process_rate(
                 ip_rate_type IN rate_tab.rate_type%TYPE,
                 ip_effective_date IN rate_tab.rate_type%TYPE,
                 ip_threshold IN NUMBER,
                 op_rate OUT NUMBER,
                 op_success OUT VARCHAR2,
                 op_errmsg OUT VARCHAR2)
IS
  v_rate NUMBER;
  v_increase_flag BOOLEAN := FALSE;
BEGIN
  SELECT rate
  INTO   v_rate
  FROM   rate_tab
  WHERE  rate_type = ip_rate_type
    AND  effective_date = ip_effective_date;
  IF (v_rate < ip_threshold) THEN
    v_increase_flag := TRUE;
  END IF;
  IF v_increase_flag THEN
    UPDATE rate_tab
      SET rate := rate + 2.5*rate
    WHERE  rate_type = ip_rate_type
    AND  effective_date = ip_effective_date
    RETURNING rate INTO v_rate;
    COMMIT;
  END IF;
  op_rate := v_rate;
  op_success := 'Y';
EXCEPTION WHEN NO_DATA_FOUND THEN
  op_rate := NULL;
  op_success := 'N';
  op_errmsg := 'Rate not available, contact FS';
  WHEN OTHERS THEN
    op_rate := NULL;
    op_success := 'N';
```

```
        op_errmsg := 'Server Error as follows, contact MIS '
                        ||CHR(10)||CHR(13)||
                     SQLERRM;
END;
/
```

A procedure can have an optional extra header definition, in addition to the declaration, executable, and exception-handling sections, that specifies the input and output parameters. These parameters define the data input and output values that make the procedure sharable across applications. Multiple applications can invoke the same procedure with different input values. The keyword IN signifies an input parameter and OUT represents an output value returned by the procedure to the calling environment. As shown from the previous example, a procedure can return multiple values.

Note how the rate type, effective date, and threshold are defined as input parameters and how the rate is returned as an output value. Also note how the procedure returns a success or failure status along with the appropriate error message in case of failure.

Once a procedure is defined and compiled in the database, its source code along with its header specification is stored in the database. The procedure then needs to be called from a calling program in order to be executed. The calling environment can be another PL/SQL stored program or an anonymous block, a client-side program, or a batch program. Here's how the p_process_rate procedure can be executed from an anonymous PL/SQL block:

```
DECLARE
    v_rate NUMBER;
    v_success_flag VARCHAR2(1);
    v_errmsg VARCHAR2(1000);
BEGIN
    p_process_rate('Monthly',TRUNC(SYSDATE), 100.00,
                    v_rate, v_success_flag, v_errmsg);
    IF (v_success_flag != 'Y') THEN
       dbms_output.put_line('Procedure p_process_rate failed
                with error(s) as follows');
       dbms_output.put_line(v_errmsg);
    END IF;
END;
/
```

Note how a variable of appropriate type is passed as an argument for each OUT parameter.

Programs of other types such as functions, packages, and/or triggers can also be defined to store code inside the database. A function includes a return type in its header specification and a package is created as a group of procedures and/or functions. A package includes a specification part that defines the header of public procedures and functions and a package body that provides implementation of these objects in addition to defining private objects that are accessible only by the defining package. Also, global variables and cursors can be included in the definition of a package specification. The creation of packages offers many important advantages in addition to storing code, including the following:

- Encapsulation
- Information hiding
- Isolation of application programs from implementation details
- Breaking dependency chains to avoid cascading invalidations

INTERNAL ARCHITECTURE

The architecture of PL/SQL processing on the server-side is built into the Oracle RDBMS server and involves the following phases and components:

- PL/SQL compilation—This involves compilation of procedural code and is done by the PL/SQL compiler.
- SQL compilation—This involves compilation of any embedded SQL code and is done by the SQL compiler.
- SQL execution—This involves database interaction to process SQL within PL/SQL and return SQL statement results and is done by the SQL execution engine.
- PL/SQL execution—This involves final (that is, overall) execution of the PL/SQL program. This is done by the PL/SQL execution engine, also called the runtime engine or PL/SQL Virtual Machine (PVM).

Figure 2.2 depicts the typical architecture of PL/SQL processing for a PL/SQL program.

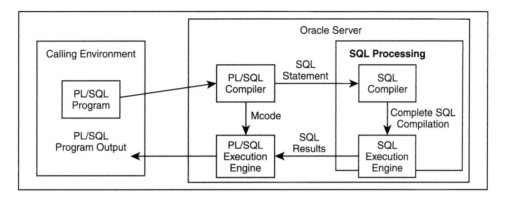

FIGURE 2.2
The typical architecture of PL/SQL processing for a PL/SQL program.

PL/SQL compilation is complemented by any SQL compilation followed by SQL execution and final PL/SQL execution, thus completing the PL/SQL processing cycle. As far as server-side processing is concerned, every component involved is internal to the RDBMS server and each individual phase is carried out within the server.

PL/SQL Compilation

PL/SQL code is "more" interpreted and "less" compiled. This is the default behavior and comes as no surprise. What this means is that PL/SQL source code is compiled by default in the INTERPRETED mode, resulting in machine code that is interpreted during execution.

PL/SQL compilation is typical of early binding. Early binding performs the compilation before the execution process begins. This saves a fair amount of time resulting in faster execution.

PL/SQL compilation is greatly improved in Oracle 10g and 11g with the introduction of an optimized compiler. Here are the steps involved in PL/SQL compilation:

1. Parsing
2. Name resolution, semantics checking, and security checking
3. Byte code generation

The following sections describe these steps in more detail.

Parsing

Parsing involves tokenizing the source program into atomic components such as PL/SQL keywords, identifiers, and so on, and then generating DIANA. *DIANA* stands for Descriptive Intermediate Attribute Notation for Ada and is an abstract syntax tree for the source code. DIANA is required to perform syntactic analysis and automatic recompilation of dependent objects at runtime. DIANA is generated as a tree structure with nodes. The maximum number of nodes is a limitation of the Oracle version. As of Oracle 10g, this limit is 2^{26}, or 64M. This corresponds to approximately 6 million lines of code.

The parse step also interacts with the SQL parse to perform syntax checking of any embedded SQL statements and to resolve any PL/SQL identifiers in them.

Name Resolution, Semantic Checking, and Security Checking

During this phase, namespaces are resolved and dependent objects are determined. Also, embedded SQL statements are checked for semantics.

Code Generation

This is the final phase of compilation where DIANA is used to generate machine code, or Mcode. The *Mcode* is byte code that is stored in the data dictionary along with DIANA to be later used for execution. However, in case of anonymous PL/SQL blocks, DIANA is discarded. Oracle 10g has a new code generator that improves performance significantly as compared to earlier versions.

There are two parameters that determine what happens to the Mcode after generation. These are

- PLSQL_OPTIMIZE_LEVEL
- PLSQL_CODE_TYPE

The former determines whether the byte code generated should be optimized for performance. The default value is 2. Oracle 11g has added a value 3 to this parameter, which performs intra-unit inlining of code for better performance. Setting PLSQL_OPTIMIZE_LEVEL to 2 will optimize the byte code based on source code analysis at compile-time.

The second parameter determines whether the Mcode should be interpreted at execution time or natively compiled into shared DLLs (Dynamic Link Libraries) that require interpretation at runtime. The values are INTERPRETED and NATIVE and can be set globally or at the individual program unit level. In Oracle 11g, if set to NATIVE, the Mcode is directly converted into native shared DLLs that are linked and loaded into Oracle without the need for any third-party C compiler. In Oracle 10g, a third-party C compiler is required to perform the conversion and then the DLL needs to be linked and loaded into Oracle. Additional setup is needed for this to maintain the DLLs on the file system. (The DLL name, its file location, and a copy of the DLL are also stored in the data dictionary in Oracle 10g.) No matter what the version, native compilation improves performance drastically for compute-intensive PL/SQL programs. Native compilation applies to PL/SQL code only and does not affect SQL. This improves performance as natively compiled code is no longer interpreted at runtime.

PL/SQL EXECUTION

Once the byte code (or native DLL) is created and the DIANA tree is stored (in case of stored code), the PL/SQL program is ready for execution. PL/SQL execution occurs in the following steps:

1. The Mcode or native code is loaded into Oracle internal memory (pinned in the shared pool of the SGA in case of the INTERPRETED mode and PGA in case of native compilation).
2. EXECUTE privileges are checked as per definer or invoker rights rules. External references are re-resolved as per invoker rights rules if applicable. Also, automatic recompilation occurs if needed. To do this, Oracle uses dependency tracking results (fine-grained in Oracle 11g).
3. Once loaded, the Mcode is interpreted and executed by the PL/SQL runtime engine in sync with the Oracle server. Native code is simply executed.
4. During step 2, any SQL embedded in the PL/SQL program is processed by the SQL engine. This processing includes syntactic and semantic validation, name resolution, and authentication and authorization checks. If the PL/SQL program is a stored subprogram, the embedded SQL is present in the Mcode in the form of SQL statements with bind variables. Soft parsing can be avoided to save SQL compilation time at runtime. The SQL compiler then prepares the execution plan if required and the SQL execution engine runs the SQL at runtime.
5. The results are passed back to the calling environment.

MEMORY USAGE

Memory usage refers to the runtime memory used by PL/SQL program execution. There are at least four memory areas in the context of PL/SQL (along with embedded SQL) processing, namely:

- System global area (SGA)
- Program global area (PGA)
- User global area (UGA)
- Library cache

Figure 2.3 depicts the typical PL/SQL runtime memory architecture.

Typical PL/SQL Runtime Memory Architecture

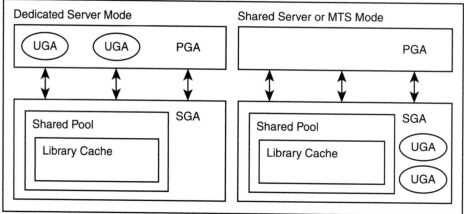

FIGURE 2.3
The typical PL/SQL runtime memory architecture.

Here's a brief description of how these memory areas are related to PL/SQL processing:

1. In a dedicated server, the UGA resides in the PGA. In a shared server or multi-threaded environment, the UGA is located inside the SGA. As described previously, the byte code is placed in the SGA for the INTERPRETED mode of compilation and in the PGA in case of natively compiled

programs. The former works using a place-in/age-out policy in the shared pool, thus freeing the memory after the program call terminates. The place-in/age-out policy works as follows:

■ The called subprogram byte code is loaded into the SGA on demand (only when it is called).
■ When the subprogram byte code is called, room has to be made in the SGA for it to be loaded. If sufficient memory is available there, the byte code is immediately loaded and added to the LRU (Least Recently Used) list. Otherwise, non-executing subprogram code sitting in the memory is aged out (removed), based on the LRU.
■ When the current subprogram has finished executing, it is also aged out in a similar fashion.

2. The library cache is an in-memory structure in the shared pool that stores the byte code in case of the INTERPRETED mode of compilation. During execution, the byte code is loaded into the library of the shared pool once it is read from the disk. This saves some I/O cost required to reread. The library cache also plays a role in SQL processing, because the SQL text embedded in the byte code is parsed and validated here. Each type of program is differentiated by a namespace such as SQL AREA, PROCEDURE, TRIGGER, and so on. These are accessible via the v$librarycache view.

There are ways you can reduce memory usage. Although Oracle has provided ways to automatically free memory in some instances (such as from cursors), the API programmatically does this. Here's a list of methods you can use to reduce memory usage:

■ Use bind variables to facilitate statement-sharing so that more parsed statements are avoided in the shared pool. Bind variables should always be used for dynamic SQL statements because literals are automatically replaced with bind variables in static SQL only. This reduces memory at the instance level.
■ Use packages and pin them in the shared pool. Packages are loaded in their entirety into the shared pool whenever they are first referenced. This is called *package instantiation*. This process saves memory especially in the case of large packages, as multiple instantiations are eliminated. The memory used by the package runtime state can be freed by resetting the package state using the DBMS_SESSION.RESET_PACKAGE procedure. This also includes the memory used by packaged collections.

- Programmatically free unused user memory. You can do this using the DBMS_SESSION.FREE_UNUSED_USER_MEMORY procedure. Executing this procedure frees any unused UGA memory to the parent heap.
- Close open cursors. This allows Oracle to free the session cursor cache. When you also delete arrays after use, the corresponding memory can be freed.

This way of explicitly freeing unused memory allows other sessions to reuse the memory.

META-DATA FOR PL/SQL CODE

PL/SQL source code and other information for stored programs are stored in the data dictionary in views, along with the machine code. This constitutes the meta-data for PL/SQL code. The other information includes the object type, object name, status, and last DDL time (that is, creation/modification time). The status is one of DISABLED, ENABLED, or INVALID. The DISABLED value is new in Oracle 11g. Here's a list of data dictionary views that hold the meta-data for PL/SQL stored programs:

- DBA/ALL/USER_OBJECTS—Stores the stored program name, type (PROCEDURE, FUNCTION, PACKAGE, PACKAGE BODY, JAVA CLASS, and so on), status (whether INVALID, ENABLED, or DISABLED), and last DDL timestamp.
- DBA/ALL/USER_SOURCE—Stores the source code for procedures, functions, packages, object types, and so on.
- DBA/ALL/USER_TRIGGERS—Stores the information about triggers along with their source code.
- USER_STORED_SETTINGS—Stores the compilation related settings like interpreted or native modes of compilation.
- USER_OBJECT_SIZE—Stores the byte code and DIANA size information.
- USER_ERRORS—Stores the most recent error information that occurred during compilation about the stored subprogram, including triggers.
- USER_DEPENDENCIES—Stores information about objects that a particular stored program depends upon. However, dependent objects referenced using dynamic SQL are not revealed in this data dictionary view.
- NCOMP_DLL$—Stores the native DLL created as a result of native compilation in the form of a BLOB (Binary Large Object).

PROGRAM DEBUGGING

PL/SQL debugging deals with identifying the cause of runtime errors in PL/SQL programs. This involves tracking execution steps of PL/SQL programs to help fix these errors. The most common and easiest way to debug is to have the PL/SQL program output trace to the calling environment using the DBMS_OUTPUT packaged procedures. However, this process has certain limitations—it is synchronous and it does not work with batch programs like scheduled jobs. Apart from this method, PL/SQL has provided other methods that make tracing execution a lot better. Here's a list of some other methods you can use:

■ Output to a file or log it in a debug table rather than to the screen. This can be done asynchronously.

■ Use compile-time warnings (new to Oracle 10g) so the PL/SQL compiler can identify code that is most likely to perform badly during execution. This is revealed during compilation. It is a recommended practice to have this feature turned on while debugging and turned off in production environments.

■ Use the DBMS_TRACE package to track specific steps executed by PL/SQL code in a server trace file, accessible via schema tables.

■ Use the DBMS_PROFILER package to monitor execution of PL/SQL code including the time taken for each line to execute and the number of times it executed the line. This helps to track performance bottlenecks.

■ Use DBMS_UTLITY.FORMAT_CALL_STACK to track the execution call stack of a particular program.

■ Use the DBMS_APPLICATION_INFO package that can be called by executing programs to set information about session activities—for example, setting the OS (machine) login username rather than the database login name when multiple users are running the same program.

■ Use the PL/SQL hierarchical profiler (introduced in Oracle 11g) with the DBMS_HPROF packaged procedures (in conjunction with the plshprof utility) to track dynamic execution profiles at a fine-grained level. This hierarchical profiler includes execution statistics for descendent subprograms for the current subprogram (in addition to all the information, as mentioned in the previous bullet listings) and customized profiler report generation based on the profiler output.

Chapter 12 describes a typical debugging framework in detail.

PROTECTING SOURCE CODE

PL/SQL source code needs to be exposed when there are requirements to port applications to different customer sites and maintain them for user-specific customizations. This in turn exposes the application logic that might contain sensitive information. To circumvent this bottleneck, Oracle provides two ways to hide the source code by converting it into a nonreadable hex format. You can use the WRAP utility or the DBMS_DDL package. The following sections describe these two methods in more detail.

WRAP UTILITY

This is a command-line utility that hides the source of statically written PL/SQL except that in triggers. Here's how this utility is invoked:

```
WRAP iname=infile_name oname=outfile_name
```

If the latter parameter is omitted, the resulting PL/SQL binary takes the name of the input file with the extension as plb.

The WRAP executable is located in the $ORACLE_HOME/bin directory.

DBMS_DDL PACKAGE

As of Oracle 10g Release2, there are two new package elements in the DBMS_DLL package, namely, the WRAP function and the CREATE_WRAPPED procedure. These elements enable you to dynamically hide generated PL/SQL code, thus overcoming the limitation of the WRAP utility.

To use the DBMS_DLL.WRAP function, follow these steps:

1. Generate a dynamic PL/SQL string containing the code to be wrapped and assigned to a PL/SQL variable.
2. Simply call the DBMS_DDL.WRAP function to display the wrapped code—for example, using DBMS_OUTPUT.PUT_LINE. Or call this procedure with this variable passed as an argument to the EXECUTE IMMEDIATE statement.

Here's the code to illustrate this process:

```
DECLARE
  v_string VARCHAR2(32767);
BEGIN
  v_string := 'CREATE OR REPLACE FUNCTION get_os_user
```

```
                    RETURN VARCHAR2 '||
                'IS '||
                'BEGIN '||
                '   RETURN (SYS_CONTEXT(''USERENV'', ''OS_USER''); '||
                'END; ';
    EXECUTE IMMEDIATE SYS.DBMS_DDL.WRAP(v_string);
END;
/
```

The function is created and its text can be viewed in DBA/ALL/USER_SOURCE.
To use the DBMS_DDL.CREATE_WRAPPED procedure, follow these steps:

1. Generate a dynamic PL/SQL string containing the code to be wrapped and
   assigned to a PL/SQL variable.
2. Call the DBMS_DDL.CREATED_WRAPPED procedure with this variable
   passed as an argument without using the EXECUTE IMMEDIATE statement.

Here's the code to illustrate this process:

```
DECLARE
  v_string VARCHAR2(32767);
BEGIN
  v_string := 'CREATE OR REPLACE FUNCTION get_os_user
                  RETURN VARCHAR2 '||
                'IS '||
                'BEGIN '||
                '   RETURN (SYS_CONTEXT(''USERENV'', ''OS_USER''); '||
                'END; ';
    SYS.DBMS_DDL.CREATE_WRAPPED(v_string);
END;
/
```

The function is created and its text can be viewed in DBA/ALL/USER_SOURCE.

SUMMARY

This chapter described the internals of PL/SQL processing in terms of its structure, compilation and execution steps involved, debugging the code for troubleshooting errors resulting from execution, and hiding source code for proprietary or other reasons. It also dealt with the memory- and storage-related details of PL/SQL source code and its execution. The next chapter deals with the new features available in Oracle 11g and 10g PL/SQL from an application development perspective.

3   New Features in PL/SQL

In This Chapter

- New features in Oracle 11g
- New features in Oracle 10g

INTRODUCTION

This chapter discusses the top enhancements Oracle has introduced in versions 10g and 11g PL/SQL from an application developer's perspective. These new features include better PL/SQL exception handling, collection improvements, performance-related improvements, and new PL/SQL API packages. Whenever possible, code snippets are provided for implementing these concepts. The use of these features in application-coding techniques will optimize your PL/SQL in terms of both productivity and efficiency.

NEW FEATURES IN ORACLE 11G

Oracle 11g takes the development of PL/SQL to an entirely new level with cool and much-wanted new features that enhance its usability and performance. This section discusses the top new features.

New PLW-06009 Warning When a WHEN OTHERS Clause Does Not Have a RAISE or RAISE_APPLICATION_ERROR

If a PL/SQL stored subprogram has a WHEN OTHERS EXCEPTION section without a RAISE or RAISE_APPLICATION_ERROR, a compile-time warning is issued. The code in Listing 3.1 illustrates this feature.

LISTING 3.1 CODE FOR NEW PLW-06009 WARNING

```
ALTER SESSION SET PLSQL_ WARNINGS = 'enable:all';

CREATE OR REPLACE PROCEDURE p_test (ip_id NUMBER, ip_status VARCHAR2)
IS
BEGIN
    UPDATE test_tab
    SET    status = ip_status
    WHERE  id = ip_id;
EXCEPTION WHEN OTHERS THEN
    NULL;
END;
/
```

Here's the warning that's displayed:

```
PLW-06009: procedure "P_TEST" OTHERS handler does not
        end in RAISE or RAISE_ APPLICATION_ ERROR
```

This feature is an addition to the existing list of compile-time warnings introduced in Oracle 10g. Pre-Oracle 11g, this feature was benchmarked as a PL/SQL error-handling standard that recommends coding an EXCEPTION WHEN OTHERS section with proper handling of the error, in every subprogram, no matter what, to prevent raising of un-handled exceptions (in the executable section).

FINE-GRAINED DEPENDENCY TRACKING

With fine-grained dependency tracking, only database objects that are relevant to the subprogram being executed are validated instead of whole objects. This helps to avoid excessive recompilations (think efficiency). Examples are when columns are added to underlying tables or when the package specification has new cursors or procedures added. In these cases, the dependent objects are not invalidated or re-compiled.

DYNAMIC SQL ENHANCEMENTS

Dynamic SQL is now faster and enhanced with more features. The most asked-for feature was that the 32K string restriction on NDS be lifted—and it has been. Native dynamic SQL (EXECUTE IMMEDIATE) and DBMS_SQL (DBMS_SQL.PARSE) can now accept a CLOB (Character Large Object) input.

A second enhancement in this respect is the interoperability of DBMS_SQL cursors and ref cursors. This means you can code a dynamic SQL SELECT statement using a DBMS_SQL cursor, parse it and execute it using DBMS_SQL, and then process the resultset using native dynamic SQL using a REF CURSOR. Moreover, this interoperability can take advantage of bulk operations. The API transforms the DBMS_SQL to REF CURSOR, using the DBMS_SQL.TO_REF_CURSOR function. Similarly, the reverse is also possible using the API DBMS_SQL.TO_CURSOR_NUMBER.

Finally, DBMS_SQL now supports user-defined types as well as dynamic bulk operations on these types.

PL/SQL TRIGGERS ENHANCEMENTS

Many developers have long wanted a way to specify the order of trigger execution. This enhancement is finally available. In Oracle 11g, the FOLLOWS clause can be used to specify trigger-firing order. Here's a simple syntactical example:

```
CREATE OR REPLACE TRIGGER trg_ai_trans_g
AFTER INSERT ON trans_tab FOR EACH ROW
FOLLOWS trg_ai_trans_l
BEGIN
    /* Some logic */
END;
/
```

Oracle 11g introduced the concept of a *compound trigger*. Instead of defining multiple triggers, each of a separate type, the compound trigger has sections for BEFORE/AFTER and STATEMENT/EACH ROW. This way, the state of the variables can be maintained. For example, any variables that are defined before the BEFORE STATEMENT section persist until the triggering statement finishes. Here's a sneak peek at how such a trigger might look:

```
CREATE OR REPLACE TRIGGER trig_compound
FOR INSERT ON audit_tab
COMPOUND TRIGGER
    g_max_val NUMBER;

    BEFORE STATEMENT IS
    BEGIN
        /* Some logic */
    END BEFORE STATEMENT;

    AFTER EACH ROW IS
    BEGIN
        /* Some logic */
    END AFTER EACH ROW;

    AFTER STATEMENT IS
    BEGIN
        /* Some logic */
    END AFTER STATEMENT;

END trig_compound;
/
```

Triggers can now be created in the disabled state and subsequently enabled. This prevents DML statements against the triggering table from failing in case the trigger has compile errors. To create a disabled trigger, you simply specify the DISABLE keyword.

Finally, DML triggers have been geared up to be 25% faster. Row-level triggers performing updates on tables other than the triggering table might benefit from this.

PL/SQL Intra-Unit Inlining (Efficiency)

Oracle 11g has incorporated intra-unit inlining of PL/SQL code, which allows for dynamically including subroutines whenever they are invoked. This means a subroutine call will be substituted by the actual code of the subroutine when the object code is generated. This is also true for locally declared subprograms. Oracle determines whether a particular subprogram can be inlined or not based on performance criteria. There is no coding change involved, but the PLSQL_OPTMIZE_LEVEL has to be set to 3 for automatic inlining. The value of 3 is new in Oracle 11g. Intra-unit inlining also works with PL/SQL_OPTIMIZE_LEVEL set to 2 (in fact, at least 2). However, in this case, a pragma has to be invoked programmatically just before the subprogram call to initiate the inlining process. Here's an example:

```
CREATE OR REPLACE PROCEDURE p_child
IS
BEGIN
    /* Some logic here */
END p_child;
/

CREATE OR REPLACE PROCEDURE p_parent
IS
BEGIN
    /* Some logic here */
    /* Conditionally call p_child here */
    IF (<condition>) THEN
        PRAGMA INLINE(p_child, 'yes');
        p_child;
    END IF;
END p_parent;
/
```

This code instructs the compiler that p_child is a potential candidate for inlining. Note the word *potential* in this context. This is because the compiler might reject the inlining for internal reasons. This is true even with automatic inlining. However, when both automatic inlining and the pragma are specified, the pragma takes precedence. Thus, when the second argument of the pragma has a value of 'no', the inlining is not done.

SQL AND PL/SQL RESULT CACHING (EFFICIENCY)

Using the RESULT_CACHE hint for SQL SELECT statements and RESULT_CACHE clause for functions, the repeated execution of these can be made many times faster in situations when the data is more or less static. The /*+result_cache*/ SQL hint lets the result data be cached in the data block buffers, and not in the intermediate data blocks, as in pre-Oracle 11g. This means that subsequent calls are super fast. In terms of PL/SQL functions using result caching, it is beneficial to result-cache functions that have data-intensive SELECTs inside them or that are called from SQL.

ENHANCED NATIVE COMPILATION

Now only one initialization parameter controls the native compilation—PLSQL_CODE_TYPE.

Pre-Oracle 11g, PL/SQL stored subprograms and anonymous PL/SQL blocks could be natively compiled to a DLL format and executed faster. However, this process involved several steps:

1. Translating the PL/SQL code to C-code.
2. Converting the C-code to a native DLL using an external C compiler that needs to be resident in the system.
3. Taking care of linking and loading.

Oracle 11g eliminates the need for the last two steps with direct generation of native DLL compatible with the system hardware and by internally performing the linking and loading functions. This in turn not eliminates only the third-party C compiler, but also the file system directories that needed to be maintained in earlier versions.

OTHER MISCELLANEOUS ENHANCEMENTS

Here's a list of some other miscellaneous enhancements to Oracle 11g that you might find helpful:

- PL/SQL data type simple_integer that has a native format, wraps instead of overflowing, and is faster than PLS_INTEGER.
- Fine Grained Access Control (FGAC) for UTL_SMTP, UTL_TCP, and UTL_HTTP that enables security to be defined on ports and URLs using Access Control Elements and Access Control Lists.
- Improved native Java and PL/SQL compilers.
- Support for "super." This is used with OO Oracle when instantiating a derivative type (overloading), to refer to the superclass from where the class was derived.
- Regular expression enhancements for SQL/PL/SQL.
- A "disabled" state for PL/SQL (in addition to "enabled" and "invalid" in dba_objects).
- Ability to perform PL/SQL assignments on sequence values, as in

```
v_new_val := seq_test.NEXTVAL:
```

- A CONTINUE statement. This statement allows you to eliminate extra loops when branching to an enclosing loop on a condition or an unstructured GOTO statement.
- Named and mixed notation when calling PL/SQL functions from SQL. You can now avoid the following error:

```
ORA- 00907: missing right parenthesis error.
```

New Features in Oracle 10g

Oracle version 10g introduced a number of great features available to the PL/SQL developer. The following sections highlight the top new features necessary for writing better and more efficient code.

An Enhanced DBMS_OUTPUT Package (Oracle 10gR2)

The DBMS_OUTPUT.PUT_LINE procedure is almost indispensable for any PL/SQL developer. In Oracle 10g Release 2, the line length has been increased to 32767 bytes; the same length as the maximum allowed for a PL/SQL VARCHAR2 variable. Also, the upper limit for the overall buffer size is now unlimited instead of 1,000,000. The corresponding DBMS_OUTPUT.ENABLE procedure also reflects this change by allowing a NULL value to be passed for the buffer size. This feature comes as a boon to the PL/SQL developer.

Tracking the Error Line Number

Oracle 10g PL/SQL offers an elegant way of knowing the actual line number where an exception was raised. Pre-Oracle 10g, it was possible to know only the error number, the error message text, and the error stack in a PL/SQL program. This was possible by calling the packaged function DBMS_UTILITY.FORMAT_ERROR_STACK.

In Oracle 10g PL/SQL, you can obtain the actual line number by calling the packaged function DBMS_UTILITY.FORMAT_ERROR_BACKTRACE. This is new in Oracle 10g and returns the error backtrace stack of the raised error, which includes the program owner, program name, and actual line number where the error occurred, but without the actual error number.

If this function is called in the block in which the error was raised, it gives the line number where the exception was first raised. In case the exception is re-raised, this function gives the line number where the last re-raise occurred.

The best way to utilize this feature is to call the FORMAT_ERROR_BACK-TRACE function as an argument to DBMS_OUTPUT.PUT_LINE procedure from a WHEN OTHERS exception handler. To get more elaborate information about the error, it pays to call the FORMAT_ERROR_STACK function as an argument to DBMS_OUTPUT.PUT_LINE in the same WHEN OTHERS handler.

This way, the subprogram owner, subprogram name, error number, error message text, actual line number, and error stack can be obtained for any PL/SQL error. In case of a package, the subprogram name returned is the name of the package and not that of the individual packaged subprogram. The code in Listing 3.2 illustrates this.

LISTING 3.2 USE OF DBMS_UTILITY.FORMAT_ERROR_BACKTRACE

```
CREATE OR REPLACE PROCEDURE p_insert(
    p_process_id IN NUMBER,
    p_job_id IN NUMBER,
    p_pj_flag IN VARCHAR2)
BEGIN
    INSERT INTO work_for_job VALUES(p_process_id,
      'Process '||TO_CHAR(p_process_id), p_pj_flag);
    COMMIT;
END;
/

CREATE OR REPLACE PROCEDURE p_delete
IS
BEGIN
    DELETE work_for_job WHERE process_id = 102;
    IF SQL%NOTFOUND THEN
        RAISE_APPLICATION_ERROR(-20001, 'Process '
        ||'is not in job queue. Cannot delete.');
    END IF;
    COMMIT;
END;
/

CREATE OR REPLACE PROCEDURE p_dml (
    p_flag IN VARCHAR2,
    p_process_id IN NUMBER,
    p_job_id IN NUMBER,
    p_pj_flag IN VARCHAR2)
```

```
IS
BEGIN
    IF (p_flag = 'I') THEN
        p_insert(p_process_id, p_job_id, p_pj_flag);
    ELSEIF (p_flag = 'D') THEN
        p_delete;
    END IF;
EXCEPTION WHEN OTHERS THEN
    dbms_output.put_line('Begin Error Stack');
    dbms_output.put_line(
        DBMS_UTILITY.FORMAT_ERROR_STACK);
    dbms_output.put_line('End Error Stack');
    dbms_output.put_line('Begin Error Backtrace');
    dbms_output.put_line(
        DBMS_UTILITY.FORMAT_ERROR_BACKTRACE);
    dbms_output.put_line('Begin Error Backtrace');
END p_dml;
/
```

The code in Listing 3.3 illustrates a call to p_dml and the corresponding output.

LISTING 3.3 SAMPLE OUTPUT OF DBMS_UTILITY.FORMAT_ERROR_BACKTRACE

```
SQL> begin
  2      p_dml('I',101,1,'PJ');
  3  end;
  4  /
Begin Error Stack
ORA-01722: invalid number

End Error Stack
Begin Error Backtrace
ORA-06512: at "PLSQL10G.P_INSERT", line 7
ORA-06512: at "PLSQL10G.P_DML", line
8

End Error Backtrace

PL/SQL procedure successfully completed.
```

Notice the error line number in the p_insert procedure. It indicates where the PL/SQL error occurred. The corresponding line number in p_dml indicates where p_insert was called.

COMPILE-TIME WARNINGS

These are warning messages that are thrown out at compile-time as a result of using improper or inefficient constructs. This feature enables code to be pre-tested in a development environment before deploying in production. Responding to the warnings given, the code can be improved before it runs live. These warnings start with the code PLW. You can enable and disable these warnings in three ways:

- At the database level by setting the plsql_warnings initialization parameter.
- At the session level using the ALTER SESSION SET plsql_warnings command.
- Using the DBMS_WARNING package.

The plsql_warnings parameter is to be set as follows:

```
[ENABLE | DISABLE | ERROR]:
[ALL|SEVERE|INFORMATIONAL|PERFORMANCE|warning_number]
```

As an example, the following command:

```
ALTER SESSION SET PLSQL_WARNINGS = 'enable:all'
```

sets all the three types of warnings to be enabled at the session level. To enable or disable a particular warning, use the five-digit warning number instead of all.

The messages ranging from PLW-5000 to 5999 are severe warnings, from 6000 to 6249 are informational warnings, and those ranging from 7000 to 7249 are performance-related warnings. The actual warning message can be obtained by issuing the command SHOW ERRORS in SQL*Plus or from the data dictionary view dba_errors.

The code in Listing 3.4 gives an example of a compile-time warning.

LISTING 3.4 COMPILE-TIME WARNINGS
_____

```
SQL> alter session set plsql_warnings='enable:all';

Session altered.

SQL> create or replace type t1 is table of varchar2(20);
  2  /

Type created.

SQL> create or replace procedure p1(iop1 in out t1)
  2  is
  3  begin
  4      dbms_output.put_line('This is a test.');
  5  end;
  6  /

SP2-0804: Procedure created with compilation warnings

SQL> show err
Errors for PROCEDURE P1:

LINE/COL ERROR
-------- ---------------------------------------------
1/14     PLW-07203: parameter 'IOP1' may benefit from
                    use of the NOCOPY compiler hint
```

PROGRAMMER-DEFINED QUOTE DELIMITER FOR STRING LITERALS

Pre-Oracle 10g, to include a quote as part of data in a SQL statement or a PL/SQL expression, you had to use two single quotes in succession. Oracle 10g allows for specifying a quote operator q, followed by a single quote and a single or multi-byte delimiter or the character pairs [], {}, (), and <>. This allows you to enclose quotes as part of the data, which gives more flexibility and readibility to the code. Listing 3.5 shows an example.

LISTING 3.5 PROGRAMMER-DEFINED QUOTE DELIMITER

```
SQL> set serverout on;
SQL> declare
  2      x varchar2(20);
  3      y varchar2(20);
  4  begin
  5      x := q'[It's sunny]';
  6      y := q'"It's raining"';
  7      dbms_output.put_line(x||' '||y);
  8  end;
  9  /

It's sunny It's raining
```

ENHANCED FORALL STATEMENT FOR HANDLING DML ARRAY PROCESSING WITH SPARSE COLLECTIONS

By default, the collection used in a FORALL statement cannot have missing elements. Oracle 10g allows you to use sparse collections (that is, collections with many intermediate missing elements) with the FORALL statement in two ways:

- Using the INDICES OF clause—Allows a collection with deleted intermediate elements to be a part of the FORALL statement. This is an efficient method to deal with sparse collections. Pre-Oracle 10g, too many intermediate deleted elements resulted in a performance overhead with the SAVE EXCEPTIONS clause.
- Using the VALUES OF clause—Allows you to create a secondary collection whose element values are the indices of the primary collection. This is a handy alternative to copying collections, as was the case with the traditional FORALL statement for handling deleted elements. Also, exception handling with INDICES OF and VALUES OF is possible.

INDICES OF in FORALL

If you have a sparse collection and want to take advantage of bulk operations, you can code a FORALL statement using the INDICES OF and SAVE EXCEPTIONS clauses. An example of this is shown in Listing 3.6.

LISTING 3.6 FORALL WITH INDICES OF CLAUSE

```
DECLARE
    TYPE region_id_tbl IS TABLE of NUMBER
    INDEX BY BINARY_INTEGER;
    TYPE region_name_tbl IS TABLE of VARCHAR2(20)
    INDEX BY BINARY_INTEGER;
    region_ids region_id_tbl;
    region_names region_name_tbl;
    ret_code NUMBER;
    ret_errmsg VARCHAR2(1000);
    -- This local procedure bulk populates
    -- the regions using two collections
    PROCEDURE load_regions_bulk_bind
        (region_ids IN region_id_tbl,
         region_names IN region_name_tbl,
         retcd OUT NUMBER,
         errmsg OUT VARCHAR2)
    IS
        bulk_bind_excep EXCEPTION;
        PRAGMA EXCEPTION_INIT(bulk_bind_excep, -24381);
    BEGIN
        -- clean up the region_tab table initially.
        DELETE FROM region_tab;
        -- Populate the region_tab table using array processing
        -- with input from the region_IDs collection.
        FORALL i IN INDICES OF region_ids SAVE EXCEPTIONS
            INSERT INTO region_tab
            values (region_ids(i), region_names(i));
        Retcd := 0;
    EXCEPTION WHEN bulk_bind_excep THEN
        -- This traps all errors resulting from the INSERT failure,
        -- e.g., for region_id 3 due to excessive length of value for
        -- region_name.
        -- If the INDICES OF clause were omitted, the second iteration
        -- of FORALL (for i= 2) would have failed due to the
        -- corresponding missing element.
        FOR i in 1..SQL%BULK_EXCEPTIONS.COUNT LOOP
            DBMS_OUTPUT.PUT_LINE('Iteration '||
            SQL%BULK_EXCEPTIONS(i).error_index||
            ' failed with error '||
            SQLERRM(-SQL%BULK_EXCEPTIONS(i).error_code));
        END LOOP;
```

```
                  COMMIT;
                  Retcd := SQLCODE;
                  Errmsg := 'Bulk DML error(s) ';
                  WHEN OTHERS THEN
                      Retcd := SQLCODE;
                      Errmsg := SQLERRM;
          END;
      BEGIN
          FOR i IN 1..5 LOOP
              Region_ids(i) := i;
              Region_names(i) := 'REGION'||i;
          END LOOP;
          Region_names(3) := 'REGION WITH NAME3';
          -- The second element is deleted from the
          -- region_ids and region_names arrays
          Region_ids.DELETE(2);
          Region_names.DELETE(2);
          Load_regions_bulk_bind(region_ids, region_names
                                  , ret_code, ret_errmsg);
      EXCEPTION WHEN OTHERS THEN
          RAISE_APPLICATION_ERROR(-20112, SQLERRM);
      END;
      /
```

VALUES OF in FORALL

Here, you create a secondary collection whose element values are the indices of the primary collection. Then, you use this value as the subscript in the original collection. This enables you to bulk process based on subsidiary collections that drive the DML being processed. This in turn eliminates the duplication or replication of the original collection elements to be included as part of the secondary collection, which is then used in the FORALL statement.

Listing 3.7 displays an example of this process.

LISTING 3.7 VALUES OF IN FORALL

```
DECLARE
    TYPE region_id_tbl IS TABLE of NUMBER
    INDEX BY BINARY_INTEGER;
    TYPE region_name_tbl IS TABLE of VARCHAR2(20)
    INDEX BY BINARY_INTEGER;
```

```
TYPE region_id_sub_tbl IS TABLE of PLS_INTEGER;
region_ids region_id_tbl;
region_ids_sub region_id_sub_tbl;
region_names region_name_tbl;
ret_code NUMBER;
ret_errmsg VARCHAR2(1000);
-- This local procedure bulk populates
-- the regions using two collections.
PROCEDURE load_regions_bulk_bind
          (region_ids IN region_id_tbl,
           region_names IN region_name_tbl,
           retcd OUT NUMBER,
           errmsg OUT VARCHAR2)
IS
    bulk_bind_excep EXCEPTION;
    PRAGMA EXCEPTION_INIT(bulk_bind_excep, -24381);
    excep_index BINARY_INTEGER;
    excep_error_code NUMBER;
BEGIN
    -- clean up the region_tab table initially.
    DELETE FROM region_tab;
    -- Populate the region_tab table using array processing
    -- with input from the region_ids collection.
    -- If the VALUES OF clause were omitted, the original
    -- iteration of FORALL would have to be worked around
    -- by replicating the corresponding subset elements
    -- from the original collection into a secondary collection,
    -- also establishing the link between the driving collection
    -- (subset) and the original collection: the tough part.
    -- Note that the subset collection is used in the FORALL
    -- statement, whereas the original collection is used
    -- in the actual DML statement associated with the FORALL.
    FORALL i IN VALUES OF region_ids_sub SAVE EXCEPTIONS
        INSERT INTO region_tab
        values (region_ids(i), region_names(i));
        Retcd := 0;
EXCEPTION WHEN bulk_bind_excep THEN
    -- This traps all errors resulting from the INSERT failure,
    -- such as for region_id 3 due to excessive length of the
    -- region_name.
    FOR i in 1..SQL%BULK_EXCEPTIONS.COUNT LOOP
        FOR j in region_ids_sub.FIRST..region_ids_sub.LAST
```

```
                LOOP
                    IF SQL%BULK_EXCEPTIONS(i).error_index = j THEN
                        excep_index := region_ids_sub(j);
                        excep_error_code :=
                        SQL%BULK_EXCEPTIONS(i).error_code;
                        DBMS_OUTPUT.PUT_LINE('Iteration '||
                        excep_index||' failed with error '||
                        SQLERRM(-excep_error_code));
                    END IF;
                END LOOP;
            END LOOP;
            COMMIT;
            Retcd := SQLCODE;
            Errmsg := 'Bulk DML error(s) ';
            WHEN OTHERS THEN
                Retcd := SQLCODE;
                Errmsg := SQLERRM;
        END;
    BEGIN
        FOR i IN 1..5 LOOP
            Region_ids(i) := i;
            Region_names(i) := 'REGION'||i;
        END LOOP;
        Region_names(3) := 'REGION WITH NAME3';
        -- Create a subcollection based on the original collection
        -- region_ids and populate it with a subset of elements from it.
        region_ids_sub := region_id_sub_tbl();
        Region_ids_sub.EXTEND;
        Region_ids_sub(1) := 2;
        Region_ids_sub.EXTEND;
        Region_ids_sub(2) := 3;
        Load_regions_bulk_bind(region_ids, region_names
                            , ret_code, ret_errmsg);
    EXCEPTION WHEN OTHERS THEN
        RAISE_APPLICATION_ERROR(-20112, SQLERRM);
    END;
    /
```

CONDITIONAL COMPILATION (ORACLE 10GR2)

Conditional compilation allows you to conditionally select or include PL/SQL source code to be compiled and thus executed, as for example, based on the version of the Oracle database. This is done by specifying certain conditions. The conditions are specified using preprocessor directives, inquiry directives, pre-defined compiler flags, PL/SQL expressions (with restrictions), initialization parameters, and pre-defined and user-defined package constants. One can draw an analogy of PL/SQL code incorporating conditional compilation with that of a UNIX shell script. A very good use of conditional compilation is to write code that is database multi-version specific and then compile and execute it on different database versions. This way it enables the same code to run on multiple versions of the database.

Also, activating debugging and tracing code conditionally is possible simply by recompiling.

The pre-processor directives are like UNIX shell environment variables starting with a $ sign followed by the identifier name. Examples are $IF, $ELSEIF, and $END. They are used as follows:

```
$IF condition1 $THEN
    action1
$ELSEIF condition2 $THEN
    action2
$END
```

Notice that they are similar to the PL/SQL IF statement, but not syntactically.

Inquiry directives start with $$ followed by a flag name and are mostly used to check the compilation environment. Here's an example:

```
$$warning_flag
```

It can be defined and its value set using the PLSQL_CCFLAGS initialization parameter as follows:

```
ALTER SESSION SET PLSQL_CCFLAGS = 'warning_flag:TRUE';
```

It can then be used as a condition in a pre-processor directive, as shown here:

```
$IF $$warning_flag $THEN
    action1
```

To check for the database version, the pre-defined package constants DBMS_DB_VERSION.VER_LE_10, DBMS_DB_VERSION.VER_10_1, DBMS_DB_VERSION_VER_LE_10_2, DBMS_DB_VERSION.VER_LE_9_2, DBMS_DB_VERSION.VER_LE_9_1, and DBMS_DB_VERSION.VER_LE_9 can be used. As an example:

```
$IF DBMS_DB_VERSION.VER_LE_10_1 $THEN

    ......

$ELSE

    ......

$END
```

A user-defined package specification with static constants can also be defined in place of pre-defined package constants. However, in this case, the package so defined should be exclusively used for conditional compilation.

Also, the post-processed source code resulting from conditional compilation can be obtained using the pre-defined packaged procedure DBMS_PREPROCESSOR.PRINT_POST_PROCESSED_SOURCE.

A complete example of conditional compilation is given in Listing 3.8.

LISTING 3.8 CONDITIONAL COMPILATION

```
CREATE OR REPLACE PROCEDURE cond_excep
IS
BEGIN
    $IF DBMS_DB_VERSION.VER_LE_10_2 AND
        NOT DBMS_DB_VERSION.VER_LE_10_1 $THEN
            DBMS_OUTPUT.PUT_LINE(
            DBMS_UTILITY.FORMAT_ERROR_BACKTRACE);
    $ELSE
        DBMS_OUTPUT.PUT_LINE(SQLERRM);
      $END
END;
/
```

This procedure displays the backtraced error stack that includes the error line number, if the database version is Oracle 10g Release 2. Otherwise, it just displays the error message returned by SQLERRM. As the line length of DBMS_OUTPUT.PUT_LINE is 32767 bytes in Oracle 10gR2, as opposed to 255 bytes in earlier versions, almost the entire backtraced error stack can be displayed.

NESTED TABLE ENHANCEMENTS

A set of conditions, operators, and functions that can be used with nested tables have been incorporated in PL/SQL. Table 3.1 details these. These enable you to compare nested tables for emptyness and equality, determine subset information, and perform set operations similar to union, intersect, and minus.

TABLE 3.1 LIST OF NEW CONDITIONS, OPERATORS, AND FUNCTIONS ON NESTED TABLES

Conditions	Operators	Functions
IN	MULTISET UNION	SET
SUBMULTISET OF	MULTISET UNION DISTINCT	CARDINALITY
NOT SUBMULTISET OF	MULTISET INTERSECT	
IS A SET	MULTISET INTERSECT DISTINCT	
IS NOT A SET	MULTISET EXCEPT	
IS EMPTY	MULTISET EXCEPT DISTINCT	
MEMBER OF		

REGULAR EXPRESSIONS

Oracle 10g introduced the ability to describe, query, and manipulate patterns of text in PL/SQL by means of regular expressions. UNIX-style based regular expressions for performing enhanced queries and string manipulations have been introduced in PL/SQL by means of pre-defined patterns and functions that are useable in SQL queries and PL/SQL assignment expressions. The patterns are bracket expressions, the escape character, alternation, subexpressions, back references, and more. The functions are REGEXP_LIKE, REGEXP_INSTR, REG_EXP_REPLACE, and REGEXP_SUBSTR. These are similar to the LIKE, INSTR, REPLACE, and SUBSTR functions pertaining to string manipulations For example, REGEXP_LIKE enables the matching to be performed beyond the realm of '_' and '%'.

Here's an example:

```
DECLARE
    v_src_str  VARCHAR2(200) := '998 999 7096';
    v_like_str VARCHAR2(10)  := '[0-9]{3} [0-9]{3} [0-9]{4}';
BEGIN
  IF NOT REGEXP_LIKE(v_src_str, v_like_str) THEN
    DBMS_OUTPUT.PUT_LINE('Invalid Phone Number');
  END IF;
END;
/
```

ENHANCED EMAIL FACILITY FROM PL/SQL

Oracle 10g has a new built-in package called UTL_MAIL that enables easy sending of emails from within PL/SQL. Pre-Oracle 10g, sending emails (especially with text and binary attachments) required the coding of SMTP details including MIME-Type, the content boundary, cc and bcc recipients, or SMTP-related details. The UTL_MAIL package makes this transparent by means of a single procedure. Even binary attachments can be sent in this manner. However, attachments have a maximum size of 32K when sent using UTL_MAIL. All sorts of data including text stored in a CLOB, raw binary data stored in a BLOB or BFILE, and file attachments can be used as attachments as long as the 32K size limit is not exceeded. Here's an example:

```
BEGIN
    UTL_MAIL.SEND_ATTACH_VARCHAR2(
        sender=>' "Lakshman Bulusu" lbulusu@coinfo.com',
        recipients=>' BL bl@coinfo.com',
        subject=>'From Lakshman Bulusu',
        message=>'This is a test from LB',
        att_mime_type=>'text/plain',
        attachment=>'Hi Hello......',
        att_inline=>FALSE,
        att_filename=>'c.txt');
END;
/
```

New PL/SQL API for Linear Matrix Math (Oracle 10gR2)

Oracle 10g PL/SQL Release 2 has introduced the new UTL_NLA package for performing matrix math operations by means of a matrix PL/SQL data type and wrapper procedures/functions similar to those of C APIs. Matrix operations via the UTL_NLA API have also been made efficient for faster performance. Applications in computational mathematics, numerical analysis, and algorithm design need faster matrix computations and using this efficient API simplifies the time and complexity of the algorithm involved. This package eliminates the need to code complex logic for implementing matrix operations as in pre-10g Release 2 PL/SQL programs.

And if that isn't enough, the mod_plsql module for handling HTTP requests has been directly integrated into the server in Oracle 10g Release 2. This eliminates the need to install an Apache listener separately for invoking PL/SQL Web-Toolkit based procedures over an HTTP connection by means of a URL.

Summary

This chapter described top new features introduced in Oracle 10g (R1 and R2) and Oracle 11g PL/SQL from an application development perspective. Starting with more robust debugging and error handling features, a description of other major improvements was presented. I hope you find these new features as useful as I have. The next chapter deals with techniques for data structure management in PL/SQL using records, associative arrays, nested tables, VARRAYS, multi-dimensional arrays, and objects.

Part II

Techniques for PL/SQL Programming

4 Data Structure Management in PL/SQL

In This Chapter

- Techniques for using records
- Techniques for using associative arrays
- Techniques for using nested tables
- Techniques for simulating multi-dimensional arrays
- Records versus objects

This chapter discusses the techniques for using PL/SQL data structures, namely records, collections (associative arrays, nested tables, and VARRAYS), and objects. Each of these is discussed in terms of performing data I/O using the particular data structure as well as other useful techniques pertaining to it. A section on simulating multi-dimensional arrays in PL/SQL is presented. The chapter ends with a comparative study of using record types versus object types in PL/SQL.

TECHNIQUES FOR USING RECORDS

Records or more specifically record types are most commonly used to represent composite data structures in PL/SQL. This section outlines the following:

- Data I/O using records
- Using functions to perform record comparison

DATA I/O USING RECORDS

Data I/O primarily refers to data input and output to and from a database. Such I/O essentially consists of inserting and retrieving the columns of a database table row. This section deals with how data I/O can be achieved using PL/SQL records.

A variable of a record type is a read-write variable and hence can be used for data performing I/O. The primary advantage of using a record for data I/O is simplification of code. This is especially true when passing composite-related data as a single unit. Data input to records takes place in the following ways:

- Using explicit assignment to each of the record's individual fields.
- Using an implicit SELECT...INTO in a record variable.
- Using an explicit FETCH...INTO in a record variable.

Data output from a record takes place in the following ways:

- Using a record as the return value of a function or an OUT parameter argument to a procedure, whether standalone or packaged.
- Reading the individual fields of a record after assignment. This obviously needs to be done for the record obtained by using an explicit assignment.

To implement data I/O to records, follow these steps:

1. Create a package specification containing the definition of the record type.
2. Use package level global variables or parameters of the record type.

I use an overloaded function to demonstrate explicit assignment and implicit SELECT...INTO and a procedure for explicit FETCH...INTO for data input. Data output is obvious from the calls to these functions and procedure.

Listing 4.1 shows the code that demonstrates the different methods of data input/output to records.

LISTING 4.1　VARIOUS METHODS OF DATA INPUT TO A RECORD

```
CREATE OR REPLACE PACKAGE pkg_records_data_io
IS
  TYPE rec IS RECORD (field1 VARCHAR2(20), field2 DATE,
        field3 NUMBER);

  FUNCTION f_data_input_to_record(ip_field1 VARCHAR2,
                          ip_field2 DATE,
                          ip_field3 NUMBER) RETURN rec;

  FUNCTION f_data_input_to_record RETURN rec;

  PROCEDURE p_data_input_to_record(op_rec OUT rec);

END pkg_records_data_io;
/
CREATE OR REPLACE PACKAGE BODY pkg_records_data_io
IS
  FUNCTION f_data_input_to_record(ip_field1 VARCHAR2,
                          ip_field2 DATE,
                          ip_field3 NUMBER) RETURN rec
  IS
      op_rec rec;
  BEGIN
      -- Explicit assignment
      op_rec.field1 := ip_field1;
      op_rec.field2 := ip_field2;
      op_rec.field3 := ip_field3;
      RETURN op_rec;
  END f_data_input_to_record;

  FUNCTION f_data_input_to_record RETURN rec
  IS
      op_rec rec;
  BEGIN
      -- Implicit SELECT…INTO
      SELECT rate_info, effective_date, rate
      INTO   op_rec
      FROM   rate_tab
      WHERE  rate_type = 'Monthly';
```

```
            RETURN op_rec;
    END f_data_input_to_record;

    PROCEDURE p_data_input_to_record(op_rec OUT rec)
    IS
        CURSOR csr_rate_info IS
            SELECT rate_info, effective_date, rate
            FROM   rate_tab
            WHERE  rate_type = 'Monthly';
    BEGIN

        -- Explicit FETCH…INTO
        OPEN csr_rate_info;
        FETCH csr_rate_info INTO op_rec;
        CLOSE csr_rate_info;

    END p_data_input_to_record;

END pkg_records_data_io;
/
```

USING FUNCTIONS TO PERFORM RECORD COMPARISON

By encapsulating functions in a package, an API can be built to perform record comparison for null and equality/inequality. This is necessary because record variable(s) cannot be directly tested using the IS NULL construct or the standard comparison operators like =, !=, <, and >.

Here, the technique for performing an equality comparison is highlighted using two PL/SQL packages. An implementation package pkg_records is defined that provides the API for doing the comparison. A second testing package pkg_test_records is used to define the actual record structures that need to be compared.

The steps involved in creating the implementation package are as follows:

1. Create a function that outputs the value of the record variable. The record variable is specified by passing in two parameters—the record name and field name. To make it more generic, this is done using native dynamic SQL. The f_getfieldvalue function does this job.
2. Create a second function that returns TRUE if the value of the record variable is null. Otherwise it returns FALSE. The f_isnull function is used to do this.

3. Create a third function that compares the values of a field of a source record with that of a target record for equality. Equality means either both the fields of the source and target records are equal or both are null. The f_equals function does this job.

An alternative approach is to pass the actual record variables to be compared as parameters to the packaged function. This makes it restrictive in the sense that this function works only for comparing records for one particular record type.

Listing 4.2 shows the code for the implementation package.

LISTING 4.2 RECORD COMPARISON

```
CREATE OR REPLACE PACKAGE pkg_records
IS
  FUNCTION f_isnull(ip_record_name VARCHAR2,
                 ip_field_name VARCHAR2) RETURN BOOLEAN;

  FUNCTION f_equals(ip_src_record_name VARCHAR2,
                 ip_src_field_name VARCHAR2,
                 ip_tgt_record_name VARCHAR2,
                 ip_tgt_field_name VARCHAR2) RETURN BOOLEAN;
END pkg_records;
/

CREATE OR REPLACE PACKAGE BODY pkg_records
IS
  -- Function to retrieve a given field value of a record
  FUNCTION f_getfieldvalue(ip_record_name VARCHAR2,
                      ip_field_name VARCHAR2)
  RETURN VARCHAR2
  IS
      dyn_str VARCHAR2(32767);
      v_var VARCHAR2(100);
      v_fieldvalue VARCHAR2(32767);

  BEGIN
      v_var := ip_record_name||'.'||ip_field_name;
      dyn_str := 'BEGIN :value := '||v_var|| '; END;';
      EXECUTE IMMEDIATE dyn_str USING OUT v_fieldvalue;
      RETURN (v_fieldvalue);
```

```
    EXCEPTION WHEN OTHERS THEN
        dbms_output.put_line('Function f_getfieldvalue
            failed with error '|| SQLERRM);
        RAISE;
    END;


    -- Function to check for nullity of a given record field
    FUNCTION f_isnull(ip_record_name VARCHAR2,
                        ip_field_name VARCHAR2) RETURN BOOLEAN
    IS
    BEGIN
      RETURN (f_getfieldvalue(ip_record_name,
                                ip_field_name) is NULL);
    END;


    -- Function to check for equality of two records
    -- based on a given field.
    FUNCTION f_equals(ip_src_record_name VARCHAR2,
                        ip_src_field_name VARCHAR2,
                        ip_tgt_record_name VARCHAR2,
                        ip_tgt_field_name VARCHAR2) RETURN BOOLEAN
    IS
        v_src_field_value VARCHAR2(1000);
        v_tgt_field_value VARCHAR2(1000);
    BEGIN
        v_src_field_value := f_getfieldvalue(ip_src_record_name,
                                        ip_src_field_name);
        v_tgt_field_value := f_getfieldvalue(ip_tgt_record_name,
                                        ip_tgt_field_name);
        RETURN (CASE WHEN v_src_field_value IS NULL AND
                        v_tgt_field_value IS NULL THEN TRUE
                    WHEN v_src_field_value IS NOT NULL AND
                        v_tgt_field_value IS NOT NULL AND
                          v_src_field_value = v_tgt_field_value
                    THEN TRUE
                    ELSE FALSE
                END);

    END;
END pkg_records;
/
```

Advantages to using the implementation package are as follows:

■ The code is more generic, as it uses dynamic SQL.
■ The code is record-definition independent. The programmer need not worry about a specific record structure. It accommodates any record structure with any number of fields. Only the testing package and associated code need to be changed.
■ The code can be generalized to determine in which fields the records differ.

Let's now consider how this package can be tested. First, you create a package for holding the record structures. Here's the code for the same:

```
CREATE OR REPLACE PACKAGE test_pkg_records
IS
    TYPE rec IS RECORD (field1 VARCHAR2(20),
                        field2 DATE, field3 NUMBER);
    src_rec rec;
    tgt_rec rec;
    empty_rec rec;
END test_pkg_records;
/
```

Then, you write the actual comparison code to test the different scenarios. Listing 4.3 shows the code for testing the equality of two records.

LISTING 4.3 TESTING THE EQUALITY OF TWO RECORDS

```
BEGIN
  test_pkg_records.src_rec.field1 := 'ABC';
  test_pkg_records.src_rec.field2 := TRUNC(SYSDATE);
  test_pkg_records.src_rec.field3 := 101;

  test_pkg_records.tgt_rec.field1 := 'ABC';
  test_pkg_records.tgt_rec.field2 := TRUNC(SYSDATE);
  test_pkg_records.tgt_rec.field3 := 101;

  IF (pkg_records.f_equals('test_pkg_records.src_rec','field1',
                           'test_pkg_records.tgt_rec','field1')
    AND
        pkg_records.f_equals('test_pkg_records.src_rec','field2',
                             'test_pkg_records.tgt_rec','field2')
```

```
    AND
        pkg_records.f_equals('test_pkg_records.src_rec','field3',
                            'test_pkg_records.tgt_rec','field3')
    )
    THEN
        DBMS_OUTPUT.PUT_LINE('Src and Tgt recs are same');
    ELSE
        DBMS_OUTPUT.PUT_LINE('Src and Tgt recs are different');
    END IF;
END;
/
```

Here's the output of the code in Listing 4.3:

```
Src and Tgt recs are same


PL/SQL procedure successfully completed.
```

This comparison code can be used for code centralization and reused whenever there is a need to compare records for equality.

The next four sections present techniques for using collections in PL/SQL in conjunction with SQL. Collections come as a boon to the PL/SQL developer and can be used in various situations, from performing data I/O to enabling the sharing of resultsets. As part of their usage for data I/O, collections provide the gateway to array processing in PL/SQL that in turn results in a performance gain.

TECHNIQUES FOR USING ASSOCIATIVE ARRAYS

Associative arrays are one-dimensional arrays of a particular data type that have the following specific characteristics:

- They are unbounded. This means there is no lower or upper limit on the number of elements the array can have.
- They can be sparse. This means that there can be (possibly many) intermediate missing elements; that is, the indexes of such an array can be non-consecutive.
- They are unordered.
- They are indexed by a numeric or VARCHAR2 value. (In fact, they can be indexed by different types of numeric values, including BINARY_INTEGER, PLS_INTEGER, or a subtype.)
- Array element allocation is dynamic.

Figure 4.1 depicts the structure of an associative array.

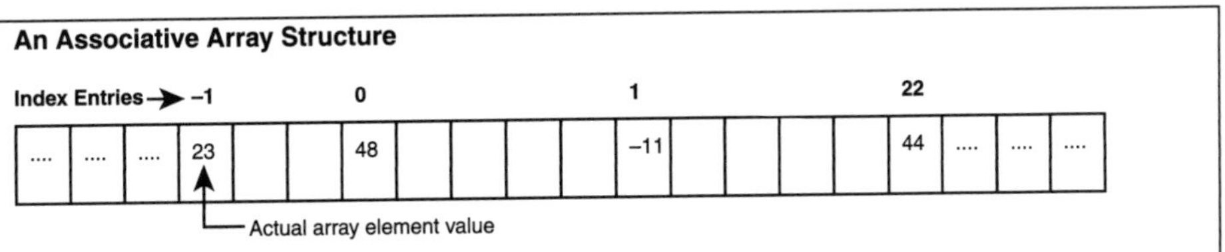

The bold integers on the top indicate array index values. The index values can be numeric or alphabetic.

The non-bold integers inside the cells indicate array element values.

Note that

i. The index values can be −ve, 0, or +ve numbers, without being consecutive.
ii. The array is unbounded on either side, that is, there is no lower or upper limit on the number of elements the array can have. So, the array can expand in either direction.
iii. The cells with no value represent missing elements, that is, they have no corresponding index entries.
iv. New elements can be added to fill these missing elements. Also, existing elements index can be deleted in any order.

FIGURE 4.1
The structure of an associative array in PL/SQL.

Associative arrays can be used to perform data I/O and when combined with records provide greater flexibility for the same. This section touches upon two techniques for using associative arrays—performing data I/O and caching lookup data.

Performing Data I/O

As mentioned, indexing an associative array by a BINARY_INTEGER allows a particular element to be read directly without looping through the entire array. However, this is possible only when the index value of the element being read is known beforehand. Otherwise, this method proves to be somewhat inefficient. This limitation is overcome by indexing the array by a VARCHAR2 value. This gives random (direct) access to an element without having to loop through. However, the ability to index provides an efficient way to access an element, as you'll see in the technique of using associative arrays for caching lookup data.

Writing to an associative array is possible in the following ways:

- By "creating" elements by directly assigning values or assigning values within a loop.
- By bulking up data into it from a database cursor, implicit or explicit.
- Data output from an associative array can be done:
  - By randomly assessing an element using a particular value.
  - By reading the elements one by one in a loop.

The implicit methods available on associative arrays enable the developer to manipulate the array. For example, the DELETE method enables you to remove one or more elements and the NEXT, PRIOR, FIRST, LAST methods enable you to navigate to the succeeding, previous, first, and last elements, respectively. The latter set of methods also enables you to read the elements one by one in a loop.

The implementation of data input and output is illustrated by means of a package that populates and reads an associative array indexed by both BINARY_INTEGER and VARCHAR2 values. The subtle differences in the use of both are noteworthy.

Here are the steps involved in implementing this package:

1. Define two associative array types, one indexed by BINARY_INTEGER and the other indexed by VARCHAR2. Both of these store the word and hash value equivalents, the former for the numeric value indexed by the number and the latter indexed by string value.

2. Define two overloaded procedures with name p_fill_array. The first one takes an IN parameter max_integer and an OUT parameter of the first array type and populates it with the word equivalent and hash values for numbers from 1 to max_integer, but indexed by the number itself. The second one has the same IN parameter but an OUT parameter of the second array type and populates it with the (word and hash) values for the string equivalents of numbers from 1 to max_integer, but indexed by the string value. These demonstrate data input to an associative array.

3. Define two additional overloaded procedures with name p_print_array, one that prints the first associative array and another that prints the second associative array. These demonstrate data output from an associative array by reading all of its elements.

4. Define three overloaded functions that return the hash representation of a particular number using each of the arrays. The first two return the hash value based on the numeric and word equivalent values using the numeric array and the third one returns the hash value based on the word equivalent value using the alphabetic array. This represents data output from an associative array by accessing a particular value.

Listing 4.4 shows the code for this process.

LISTING 4.4 PERFORMING DATA I/O USING AN ASSOCIATIVE ARRAY

```
CREATE OR REPLACE PACKAGE pkg_data_io_array IS

  c_max_integer CONSTANT NUMBER := 5373484;

  TYPE rec IS RECORD (string_equiv VARCHAR2(255),
                      hash_value   VARCHAR2(255));

  TYPE t_arr_numeric IS TABLE OF rec INDEX BY BINARY_INTEGER;

  TYPE t_arr_alphabetic IS TABLE OF rec INDEX BY VARCHAR2(255);

  PROCEDURE p_fill_array(ip_max_integer IN  NUMBER,
                         op_arr_numeric OUT arr_numeric);

  PROCEDURE p_fill_array(ip_max_integer IN  NUMBER,
                         op_arr_alphabetic OUT arr_alphabetic);

  PROCEDURE p_print_array(op_arr_numeric OUT arr_numeric);

  PROCEDURE p_print_array(op_arr_alphabetic OUT arr_alphabetic);

  FUNCTION f_get_hashval(ip_number NUMBER,
      op_arr_numeric arr_numeric)
  RETURN VARCHAR2;

  FUNCTION f_get_hashval(ip_varchar2 VARCHAR2,
      op_arr_numeric arr_numeric)
  RETURN VARCHAR2;

  FUNCTION f_get_hashval(ip_varchar2 NUMBER,
      op_arr_alphabetic arr_alphabetic) RETURN VARCHAR2;

END pkg_data_io_array;
/
CREATE OR REPLACE PACKAGE BODY pkg_data_io_array IS

  c_max_integer CONSTANT NUMBER := 5373484;

  -- Private function to compute hash value based on the
  -- input number and return the encoded value.
  FUNCTION compute_hashval(ip_number NUMBER) RETURN VARCHAR2
```

```
IS
    RETURN (utl_encode.text_encode(buf=>dbms_obfuscation_toolkit.md5
           (input_string => ip_number)));
END;


-- Private function to compute hash value for the input
-- string and return the encoded value.
FUNCTION compute_hashval(ip_varchar2 VARCHAR2) RETURN VARCHAR2
IS
BEGIN
    RETURN (utl_encode.text_encode(buf=>dbms_obfuscation_toolkit.md5
           (input_string => ip_varchar2)));
END;


-- Overloaded procedure to return an array based on arr_numeric,
-- consisting of the string equivalent and hash value corresponding
-- to the input numbers.
PROCEDURE p_fill_array(ip_max_integer IN  NUMBER,
     op_arr_numeric OUT arr_numeric)
IS
    hash_value varchar2(16);
BEGIN
    IF ip_max_integer > c_max_integer THEN
       RAISE_APPLICATION_ERROR(-20001, 'Input value too high');
    END IF;
    FOR i IN 1..ip_max_integer LOOP
       hash_value  := compute_hashval(i);
       op_arr_numeric(i).string_equiv :=
TO_CHAR(TO_DATE(i,'J'),'JSP');
       op_arr_numeric(i).hash_value := hash_value;
    END LOOP;
END;


-- Overloaded procedure to return an array based on arr_alphabetic,
-- consisting of the string equivalent and hash value corresponding
-- to the string equivalent based on the input numbers.
PROCEDURE p_fill_array(ip_max_integer IN  NUMBER,
     op_arr_alphabetic OUT arr_alphabetic)
IS
    hash_value VARCHAR2(16);
    string_equiv VARCHAR2(255);
```

```
BEGIN
   IF ip_max_integer > c_max_integer THEN
      RAISE_APPLICATION_ERROR(-20001, 'Input value too high');
   END IF;
   FOR i IN 1..ip_max_integer LOOP
      string_equiv := TO_CHAR(TO_DATE(i,'J'),'JSP')
      hash_value :=
      utl_encode.text_encode(buf=>dbms_obfuscation_toolkit.md5
                            (input_string => string_equiv));
      op_arr_alphabetic(string_equiv).string_equiv_value :=
      string_equiv;
      op_arr_alphabetic(string_equiv).hash_value := hash_value;
   END LOOP;
END;

-- Overloaded procedures to print numeric array populated above,
-- i.e., one based on arr_numeric
PROCEDURE p_print_array(op_arr_numeric OUT arr_numeric)
IS
   idx NUMBER;
BEGIN
   DBMS_OUTPUT.PUT_LINE('First method');
   FOR i IN 1..op_arr_numeric.COUNT LOOP
      DBMS_OUTPUT.PUT_LINE('The hash value of '||TO_CHAR(i)||
                           ' is '||op_arr_numeric(i).hash_value);
   END LOOP;
   DBMS_OUTPUT.PUT_LINE('Second method');
   idx := op_arr_numeric.FIRST;
   WHILE (idx IS NOT NULL) LOOP
      DBMS_OUTPUT.PUT_LINE('The hash value of '||TO_CHAR(idx)||
                           ' is '||op_arr_numeric(idx).hash_value);
      idx := op_arr_numeric.NEXT(idx);
   END LOOP;
END;

-- Overloaded procedures to print alphabetic array populated above,
-- i.e., one based on arr_alphabetic
PROCEDURE p_print_array(op_arr_alphabetic OUT arr_alphabetic)
IS
   idx VARCHAR2(255);
```

```
BEGIN
   idx := op_arr_alphabetic.FIRST;
   WHILE (idx IS NOT NULL) LOOP
      DBMS_OUTPUT.PUT_LINE('The hash value of '||idx||
                            ' is '||op_arr_alphabetic(idx));
      idx := op_arr_alphabetic.NEXT(idx);
   END LOOP;
END;




-- Overloaded function to return the hash value based on the
-- elements in the numeric array based on arr_numeric.
FUNCTION f_get_hashval(ip_number NUMBER,
   op_arr_numeric arr_numeric)
RETURN VARCHAR2
IS
BEGIN
   RETURN (op_arr_numeric(ip_number).hash_value;
END;

-- Overloaded function to return the hash value based on
-- the elements in the numeric array based on arr_numeric, but
-- corresponding to the string equivalent of the numeric element.
FUNCTION f_get_hashval(ip_varchar2 VARCHAR2,
   op_arr_numeric arr_numeric)
RETURN VARCHAR2
IS
   v_hash_value VARCHAR2(255);
BEGIN
   FOR i IN 1..op_arr_numeric.COUNT LOOP
      IF (op_arr_numeric(i).string_equiv = ip_varchar2) THEN
         v_hash_value := op_arr_numeric(i).hash_value;
         EXIT;
      END IF;
   END LOOP;
   RETURN (v_hash_value);
END;

-- Overloaded function to return the hash value based on the
-- elements in the alphabetic array based on arr_alphabetic.
```

```
FUNCTION f_get_hashval(ip_varchar2 VARCHAR2,
   op_arr_alphabetic arr_alphabetic) RETURN VARCHAR2
IS
BEGIN
   RETURN (op_arr_alphabetic(ip_varchar2).hash_value);
END;

END pkg_data_io_array;
/
```

CACHING LOOKUP DATA

Associative arrays can be used to cache lookup static data that needs to be accessed often. Most often this data is reference data that is created one time and used as lookup data for online applications and batch jobs. Hitting the database always has an overhead due to database calls, network roundtrips, and context switching. It is a good idea and a recommended practice to hold this data in memory and use it often rather than getting it from the database every time. Associative arrays are a good choice to perform this task because they provide random access to data based on a numeric or string index. Figure 4.2 depicts the use of an associative array in caching lookup data.

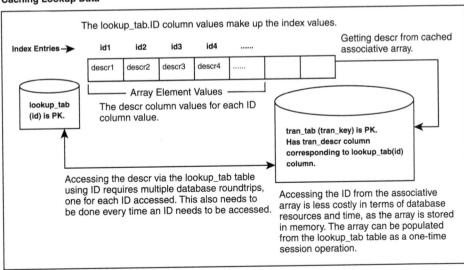

FIGURE 4.2
Using an associative array to cache lookup data.

The example of the previous section is extended to demonstrate caching. The implementation is by means of a package that consists of two procedures that populate a lookup table and an associative array, respectively, and two functions that return a record based on a lookup from a cached array and a database table, respectively.

Here are the steps involved for implementing this package:

1. Create a table that serves as a lookup table and stores a number, its word equivalent, and its hash value.
2. Define an associative array type, indexed by VARCHAR2. Each element of this array stores a record similar to the structure of the lookup table.
3. Define a procedure that populates this table.
4. Define a procedure that populates an associative array of the defined type.
5. Define two calling procedures that do some processing using the database lookup table and cached associative array, respectively.

Listing 4.5 shows the code to do this.

LISTING 4.5 CACHING LOOKUP DATA USING AN ASSOCIATIVE ARRAY

```
CREATE TABLE hash_ref_tab
(source_no    NUMBER NOT NULL PRIMARY KEY,
 string_equiv VARCHAR2(255) NOT NULL,
 hash_value   VARCHAR2(255) NOT NULL);

CREATE OR REPLACE PACKAGE pkg_cache_array IS

    c_max_integer NUMBER := 1000;

    TYPE rec IS RECORD (source_no NUMBER,
                        string_equiv VARCHAR2(255),
                        hash_value VARCHAR2(255));

    TYPE t_arr_numeric IS TABLE OF rec INDEX BY BINARY_INTEGER;

    PROCEDURE populate_hash_ref_tab(ip_max_integer NUMBER);

    PROCEDURE populate_hash_array;

    PROCEDURE p_process_using_cache(ip_max_integer NUMBER);

    PROCEDURE p_process_using_ref_tab(ip_max_integer NUMBER);
```

```
END pkg_cache_array;
/

CREATE OR REPLACE PACKAGE BODY pkg_cache_array
IS
    arr_numeric t_arr_numeric;
    arr_staging t_arr_numeric;

    -- Procedure to populate the database table hash_ref_tab,
    -- on a row by row basis
    PROCEDURE populate_hash_ref_tab(ip_max_integer NUMBER)
    IS
        hash_value VARCHAR2(16);
        string_equiv VARCHAR2(255);
        rec hash_ref_tab%ROWTYPE;
    BEGIN
        IF ip_max_integer > c_max_integer THEN
            RAISE_APPLICATION_ERROR(-20001, 'Input value too high');
        END IF;
        EXECUTE IMMEDIATE 'TRUNCATE TABLE hash_ref_tab REUSE STORAGE';

        FOR i IN 1..ip_max_integer LOOP
            string_equiv := TO_CHAR(TO_DATE(i,'J'),'JSP');
            hash_value :=
            utl_encode.text_encode(buf=>dbms_obfuscation_toolkit.md5
                                (input_string => string_equiv));
            rec.source_no := i;
            rec.string_equiv := string_equiv;
            rec.hash_value := hash_value;
            INSERT INTO hash_ref_tab VALUES rec;
        END LOOP;
        COMMIT;
    END;

    -- Procedure to populate the numeric array arr_numeric,
    -- from the table hash_ref_tab. The key point to be noted
    -- here is that index of this array is populated with the
    -- source_no column value, the PK of the hash_ref_tab table.
    PROCEDURE populate_hash_array
    IS
    BEGIN
        SELECT * BULK COLLECT INTO arr_staging FROM hash_ref_tab;
```

```
      IF arr_staging.COUNT > 0 THEN
         FOR idx IN arr_staging.FIRST..arr_staging.LAST LOOP
            arr_numeric(arr_staging(idx).source_no)
               := arr_staging(idx);
         END LOOP;
      END IF;
   END;


   -- Procedure to access the string equivalent and hash value
   -- for input source numbers from the cached array
   PROCEDURE p_process_using_cache(ip_max_integer NUMBER)
   IS
      v_ret_val VARCHAR2(512);
   BEGIN
      IF ip_max_integer > c_max_integer THEN
         RAISE_APPLICATION_ERROR(-20001, 'Input value too high');
      END IF;
      FOR i IN 1..ip_max_integer LOOP
         v_ret_val := arr_numeric(i).string_equiv||' '||
                         arr_numeric(i).hash_value;
      END LOOP;
   END;


   -- Procedure to access the string equivalent and hash value
   -- for input source numbers from the database table.
   PROCEDURE p_process_using_ref_tab(ip_max_integer NUMBER)
   IS
      v_string_equiv VARCHAR2(255);
      v_hash_value   VARCHAR2(255);
      v_ret_val VARCHAR2(512);
   BEGIN
      IF ip_max_integer > c_max_integer THEN
        RAISE_APPLICATION_ERROR(-20001, 'Input value too high');
      END IF;
      FOR i IN 1..ip_max_integer LOOP
         SELECT string_equiv, hash_value
         INTO   v_string_equiv, v_hash_value
         FROM   hash_ref_tab
         WHERE  source_no = i;
         v_ret_val := v_string_equiv||' '||
                         v_hash_value;
      END LOOP;
   END;
```

```
BEGIN
    populate_hash_array;
END pkg_cache_array;
/
```

Here's the code to test this package:

```
DECLARE
    begin_time NUMBER;
    end_time    NUMBER;
BEGIN
    pkg_cache_array.populate_hash_ref_tab(500);
    DBMS_OUTPUT.PUT_LINE('Start of p_process_using_cache');
    begin_time := DBMS_UTILITY.GET_TIME;
    pkg_cache_array.p_process_using_cache(500);
    end_time := DBMS_UTILITY.GET_TIME;
    DBMS_OUTPUT.PUT_LINE(
    'End of p_process_using_cache with processing time '||
    (end_time-begin_time));
    DBMS_OUTPUT.PUT_LINE('Start of p_process_using_ref_tab');
    begin_time := DBMS_UTILITY.GET_TIME;
    pkg_cache_array.p_process_using_ref_tab(500);
    end_time := DBMS_UTILITY.GET_TIME;
    DBMS_OUTPUT.PUT_LINE(
    'End of p_process_using_ref_tab with processing time '||
    (end_time-begin_time));
END;
/
```

Here's the output of this code:

```
Start of p_process_using_cache
End of p_process_using_cache with processing time 1
Start of p_process_using_ref_tab
End of p_process_using_ref_tab with processing time 8
```

This shows that accessing data using the cached array is significantly faster than using the database table.

TECHNIQUES FOR USING NESTED TABLES

Nested tables resemble an unordered list of a particular data type that have the following specific characteristics:

- They are unbounded and increase dynamically.
- They are unordered, but elements can be retrieved in the order created.
- They can be sparse in the sense that intermediate elements can be deleted.
- They are not indexed.
- The same nested table type can be shared with SQL and PL/SQL.
- They can be stored in the database as a table column (or object type attribute).
- They can take part in SQL operations such as a join operation with regular tables.

Like associative arrays, nested tables can be used to perform data I/O but are not efficient when a lookup needs to be done using a particular search value as they are not indexed and need to have their elements accessed in a loop. This section touches upon two techniques for using nested tables, namely, passing resultsets between PL/SQL programs and manipulating stored nested tables using SQL.

PASSING RESULTSETS BETWEEN PL/SQL PROGRAMS

Nested tables can be used efficiently to pass resultsets between PL/SQL programs. This way not only the structure but also the data is sharable across applications. A schema level type declared in the database or a PL/SQL type declared in a package specification can be used for this. The advantages of passing resultsets using collections are three-fold:

- Isolate calling applications from the physical schema dependencies.
- Process the resultset as if defined and accessed locally.
- Ideal for use by PL/SQL programs.

This section demonstrates the implementation by means of a package-level nested table of a table-based record type and shows how a packaged function can return this collection. This return value can be used by a second PL/SQL application to use the data returned for further processing.

Here are the steps needed to implement this package:

1. Define a package-level nested table type of a table-based record type.
2. Define a function that accepts an input parameter corresponding to a max value and returns a nested table of this type.
3. Define a procedure with a local variable accepting the return value as input.

Listing 4.6 shows the code.

LISTING 4.6 USING NESTED TABLES TO PASS RESULTSETS BETWEEN PL/SQL PROGRAMS

```
CREATE OR REPLACE PACKAGE pkg_share_resultset IS

    TYPE hash_ref_nt IS TABLE OF hash_ref_tab%ROWTYPE;

    FUNCTION f_get_resultset(ip_max_value NUMBER)
            RETURN hash_ref_nt;

END pkg_share_resultset;
/

CREATE OR REPLACE PACKAGE BODY pkg_share_resultset IS

    FUNCTION f_get_resultset(ip_max_value NUMBER)
            RETURN hash_ref_nt
    IS
        v_resultset hash_ref_nt;
    BEGIN
        SELECT *
        BULK COLLECT INTO v_resultset
        FROM hash_ref_tab
        WHERE source_no <= ip_max_value;

    /* Process this collection as per application-specific rules */

        RETURN v_resultset;
    END f_get_resultset;
END pkg_share_resultset;
/

CREATE OR REPLACE PROCEDURE
        p_use_shared_resultset(ip_max_value NUMBER)
IS
    v_resultset pkg_share_resultset.hash_ref_nt;
BEGIN
    v_resultset := pkg_share_resultset.
                    f_get_resultset(ip_max_value);

    /* Access the resultset locally */
```

```
END p_use_shared_resultset;
/
```

Here's the code to test this:

```
BEGIN
    p_use_shared_resultset(100);
END;
/
```

Special Cases of Passing Resultsets

The previously outlined method of using a collection to return a resultset is best suited when the calling application is PL/SQL based. However, client applications that are non-PL/SQL based often require a resultset to be cursor rather than a collection. Let's discuss that special case, as well as some others, next.

Transforming the Collection Resultset Into a Cursor

The TABLE operator can be used to transform a collection into a cursor without changing the code for the function. However, the collection needs to be of a global type such as a schema level type. This provides a relational view of the "nested" collection. A second advantage of using TABLE functions is their ability to participate in SQL operations such as joins and groupings.

In fact, table functions along with the TABLE operator can be used to translate data from nested to relational formats and vice-versa.

Here are the steps involved in carrying out the transformation from collection to REF CURSOR:

1. Convert the packaged nested table type to a schema-level nested table type. This schema-level type's elements should be instances of an object type that is also at the schema level.
2. Have the function return this nested table type.
3. Define a second function that uses the TABLE operator to transform the collection to a REF CURSOR query.

Listing 4.7 shows the code for this process.

LISTING 4.7 RETURNING RESULTSETS USING A TABLE FUNCTION

```
CREATE OR REPLACE TYPE hash_ref_obj_type AS OBJECT
(source_no    NUMBER,
 string_equiv VARCHAR2(255),
 hash_value   VARCHAR2(255));
/

CREATE OR REPLACE TYPE hash_ref_nt_type
            IS TABLE OF hash_ref_obj_type;
/

CREATE OR REPLACE PACKAGE pkg_share_resultset_obj IS

   FUNCTION f_get_resultset(ip_max_value NUMBER)
            RETURN hash_ref_nt_type;

END pkg_share_resultset_obj;
/

CREATE OR REPLACE PACKAGE BODY pkg_share_resultset_obj IS
   FUNCTION f_get_resultset(ip_max_value NUMBER)
            RETURN hash_ref_nt_type
   IS
        v_resultset hash_ref_nt_type;
   BEGIN
    SELECT hash_ref_obj_type(source_no, string_equiv, hash_value)
    BULK COLLECT INTO v_resultset
    FROM hash_ref_tab
    WHERE source_no <= ip_max_value;

    /* Process this collection as per application-specific rules */

    RETURN v_resultset;
  END f_get_resultset;
END pkg_share_resultset_obj;
/
```

Listing 4.8 shows the code for the transformation from nested table to cursor.

LISTING 4.8 ACCESSING THE TABLE FUNCTION VIA A REF CURSOR

```
CREATE OR REPLACE FUNCTION f_transform(ip_max_value NUMBER)
RETURN SYS_REFCURSOR
IS
  v_rc SYS_REFCURSOR;
BEGIN
  OPEN v_rc FOR
    SELECT *
    FROM
TABLE(pkg_share_resultset_obj.f_get_resultset(ip_max_value));
  RETURN(v_rc);
END;
/
```

Pipelined Table Functions

If the input source yields a large number of rows, a pipelined table function can be used to reduce memory consumption and enable faster execution. A pipelined table function returns rows as they are "available" instead of waiting for the function to complete execution.

Listing 4.9 shows the code rewritten to use a pipelined table function.

LISTING 4.9 RETURNING RESULTSETS USING A PIPELINED TABLE FUNCTION

```
CREATE OR REPLACE PACKAGE pkg_share_resultset_obj_p IS
  FUNCTION f_get_resultset(ip_max_value NUMBER)
  RETURN hash_ref_nt_type PIPELINED;

END pkg_share_resultset_obj_p;
/
CREATE OR REPLACE PACKAGE BODY pkg_share_resultset_obj_p IS
  FUNCTION f_get_resultset(ip_max_value NUMBER)
  RETURN hash_ref_nt_type
  PIPELINED
  IS
    v_resultset hash_ref_nt_type;
    v_row  hash_ref_obj_type;
```

```
BEGIN
  SELECT hash_ref_obj_type(source_no, string_equiv, hash_value)
  BULK COLLECT INTO v_resultset
  FROM hash_ref_tab
  WHERE source_no <= ip_max_value;

  /* Process this collection as per application-specific rules */
  FOR i IN 1..v_resultset.COUNT LOOP
      v_row := v_resultset(i);
      PIPE ROW(v_row);
  END LOOP;
  RETURN;
END f_get_resultset;
END pkg_share_resultset_obj_p;
/
```

Listing 4.10 shows the code for the transformation from nested table to cursor using the previous pipelined table function.

LISTING 4.10 ACCESSING THE PIPELINED TABLE FUNCTION VIA A REF CURSOR

```
CREATE OR REPLACE FUNCTION f_transform_p(ip_max_value NUMBER)
RETURN SYS_REFCURSOR
IS
    v_rc SYS_REFCURSOR;
BEGIN
    OPEN v_rc FOR
        SELECT *
        FROM
TABLE(pkg_share_resultset_obj_p.f_get_resultset(ip_max_value));
    RETURN(v_rc);
END;
/
```

MANIPULATING STORED NESTED TABLES USING SQL

The primary advantages of using nested tables over other collection types are twofold. First, they can be stored in the database and DML on their individual elements can be performed using SQL (and PL/SQL of course). The second advantage is specific only to nested tables and this makes them a popular choice for storing array-like structures as part of a database row.

This section demonstrates the manipulation of individual data elements of a nested table with SQL using a schema-level nested table of objects and a plain-vanilla database table having a column of this type. The API is presented using a PL/SQL package.

Here are the steps involved in manipulating a stored nested table using SQL:

1. Define a schema-level object type and a schema-level nested table type of this object type.
2. Create a table having a column with the same data type as the previously defined nested table type.
3. Populate this table with data using a packaged procedure.
4. Define three packaged procedures and one packaged function, one each for INSERT, UPDATE, DELETE, and SELECT operations respectively, based on a single element value to modify a row of the table. Each of these operations uses the TABLE operator to work on the nested table column.

Listing 4.11 shows the code for this process.

LISTING 4.11 CREATING STORED NESTED TABLES

```
CREATE OR REPLACE TYPE src_hash_type AS OBJECT
(source_no     NUMBER,
 string_equiv VARCHAR2(255),
 hash_value    VARCHAR2(255));
/

CREATE OR REPLACE TYPE src_hash_nt_type AS TABLE OF src_hash_type;
/

CREATE TABLE group_hash_tab
(group_code    VARCHAR2(10) PRIMARY KEY,
 src_hash_nt   src_hash_nt_type )
 NESTED TABLE src_hash_nt STORE AS src_hash_nt_tab;
```

To populate this table, use a packaged procedure p_populate_group_hash_tab, as shown in Listing 4.12.

LISTING 4.12 MANIPULATING STORED NESTED TABLES USING SQL

```
CREATE OR REPLACE PACKAGE pkg_dml_nt IS
  c_max_integer NUMBER := 100;

  PROCEDURE p_populate_group_hash_tab(ip_max_integer NUMBER);

  FUNCTION  f_select_nt_element(ip_group_code VARCHAR2,
                               ip_source_no NUMBER) RETURN VARCHAR2;

  PROCEDURE p_insert_nt_element(ip_group_code  VARCHAR2,
                               ip_element_new_value src_hash_type);
  PROCEDURE p_update_nt_element(ip_group_code VARCHAR2,
                               ip_source_no NUMBER,
                               ip_element_new_value src_hash_type);

  PROCEDURE p_delete_nt_element(ip_group_code VARCHAR2,
                               ip_source_no NUMBER);
END pkg_dml_nt;
/

CREATE OR REPLACE PACKAGE BODY pkg_dml_nt IS


  -- Procedure to populate the stored nested table
  -- group_hash_tab, on a row-by-row basis.
  PROCEDURE p_populate_group_hash_tab(ip_max_integer NUMBER)
  IS
    hash_value VARCHAR2(16);
    string_equiv VARCHAR2(255);
    rec group_hash_tab%ROWTYPE;
  BEGIN
    IF ip_max_integer > c_max_integer THEN
      RAISE_APPLICATION_ERROR(-20001, 'Input value too high');
    END IF;
    rec.group_code := 'GCD'||ip_max_integer;

    FOR i IN 1..ip_max_integer LOOP
        string_equiv := TO_CHAR(TO_DATE(i,'J'),'JSP');
        hash_value :=
          utl_encode.text_encode(buf=>dbms_obfuscation_toolkit.md5
                                (input_string => string_equiv));
```

```
          rec.src_hash_nt.EXTEND;
          rec.src_hash_nt(i) := src_hash_type(null, null, null);
          rec.src_hash_nt(i).source_no := i;
          rec.src_hash_nt(i).string_equiv := string_equiv;
          rec.src_hash_nt(i).hash_value := hash_value;
        END LOOP;
        INSERT INTO group_hash_tab VALUES rec;
        COMMIT;
      END;


      -- Function to return a row, dissected by individual element
      -- of the nested table column.
      FUNCTION  f_select_nt_element(ip_group_code VARCHAR2,
                                    ip_source_no NUMBER)
      RETURN VARCHAR2
      IS
        v_ret_val VARCHAR2(512);
      BEGIN
        SELECT b.string_equiv||' '||b.hash_value
        INTO   v_ret_val
          FROM   group_hash_tab a, TABLE(a.src_hash_nt) b
          WHERE  a.group_code = ip_group_code
             AND  b.source_no = ip_source_no;
          RETURN v_ret_val;
      EXCEPTION WHEN NO_DATA_FOUND THEN
          RETURN ('No info available for element '||ip_source_no);
      END f_select_nt_element;


      -- Procedure to insert a row, piecewise by individual element
      -- of the nested table column.
      PROCEDURE p_insert_nt_element(ip_group_code  VARCHAR2,
                              ip_element_new_value src_hash_type)
      IS
      BEGIN
        INSERT INTO TABLE(SELECT src_hash_nt FROM group_hash_tab
        WHERE group_code = ip_group_code) VALUES (ip_element_new_value);
        COMMIT;
      END p_insert_nt_element;


      -- Procedure to update a row, piecewise by individual element
      -- of the nested table column.
      PROCEDURE p_update_nt_element(ip_group_code VARCHAR2,
                              ip_source_no NUMBER,
                              ip_element_new_value src_hash_type)
```

```
IS
BEGIN
  UPDATE TABLE(SELECT src_hash_nt FROM group_hash_tab
      WHERE group_code = ip_group_code) a
      SET  a.source_no = ip_element_new_value.source_no,
           a.string_equiv = ip_element_new_value.string_equiv,
           a.hash_value = ip_element_new_value.hash_value
      WHERE a.source_no = ip_source_no;
      COMMIT;
END p_update_nt_element;

-- Procedure to delete a row, piecewise by individual element
-- of the nested table column.
PROCEDURE p_delete_nt_element(ip_group_code VARCHAR2,
                             ip_source_no NUMBER)
IS
BEGIN
   DELETE TABLE(SELECT src_hash_nt FROM group_hash_tab
   WHERE group_code = ip_group_code) a
   WHERE a.source_no = ip_source_no;
   COMMIT;
  END p_delete_nt_element;
END pkg_dml_nt;
/
```

Here's the code to test this package:

```
DECLARE
  v_group_code VARCHAR2(10) := 'GCD'||pkg_dml_nt.c_max_integer;
  string_equiv VARCHAR2(255);
  hash_value VARCHAR2(16);
  element_new_value src_hash_type := src_hash_type
                                  (null, null, null);
BEGIN

  EXECUTE IMMEDIATE 'TRUNCATE TABLE group_hash_tab REUSE STORAGE';

  pkg_dml_nt.p_populate_group_hash_tab(pkg_dml_nt.c_max_integer);

  string_equiv := TO_CHAR(TO_DATE(101,'J'),'JSP');
  hash_value := dbms_obfuscation_toolkit.md5
           (input_string => string_equiv);
  element_new_value := src_hash_type
           ('101', string_equiv, hash_value);
```

```
    pkg_dml_nt.p_insert_nt_element(v_group_code,element_new_value);

    DBMS_OUTPUT.PUT_LINE('Info for new element 101 is: '||
            pkg_dml_nt.f_select_nt_element(v_group_code, 101));

    string_equiv := TO_CHAR(TO_DATE(102,'J'),'JSP');
    hash_value := dbms_obfuscation_toolkit.md5
            (input_string => string_equiv);
    element_new_value := src_hash_type('102', string_equiv, hash_value);

    pkg_dml_nt.p_update_nt_element(v_group_code,
                    101, element_new_value);

    DBMS_OUTPUT.PUT_LINE('Info for element 101 is: '||
            pkg_dml_nt.f_select_nt_element(v_group_code, 101));
    DBMS_OUTPUT.PUT_LINE('Info for element 102 is: '||
            pkg_dml_nt.f_select_nt_element(v_group_code, 102));

    pkg_dml_nt.p_delete_nt_element(v_group_code, 102);

    DBMS_OUTPUT.PUT_LINE(pkg_dml_nt.f_select_nt_element
            ('Info for new element 101 is: '||v_group_code,
            102));

END;
/
```

Here's the output of this test script:

```
Info for new element 101 is: ONE HUNDRED ONE
Info for element 101 is: No info available for element 101
Info for element 102 is: ONE HUNDRED TWO
No info available for element 102

PL/SQL procedure successfully completed.
```

VARRAYS are ideal in the following situations:

- When the number of elements is pre-determined.
- When the order of elements is desirable.

Techniques for using VARRAYS are similar to those of using nested tables with the exception that the upper limit of VARRAYS should be kept in mind while populating them. However, as of Oracle 10g, the upper limit of VARRAYS can be increased dynamically. This gives you some flexibility in extending VARRAYS to an arbitrary size. Also, when you're deleting individual elements from a VARRAY, elements can be deleted only from the end—intermediate elements cannot be deleted.

SIMULATING MULTI-DIMENSIONAL ARRAYS

Pre-Oracle 9i, PL/SQL supported arrays in the form of PL/SQL tables (as they are initially termed) and then index-by tables. However, these tables were always single-dimensional based in a single BINARY_INTEGER index value. As of Oracle 9i, PL/SQL provided support for VARCHAR2 indexes as well. Non-index-based arrays were also supported in the form of nested tables and VARRAYS. A significant enhancement of this release was also the ability to define multilevel collections— also called collections of collections. Pre-Oracle 9i, the only way to simulate a multi-dimensional array was to take the indices of the source n-dimensional (n-D) array and apply a transformation on them to return a unique index in a linear array. This method then involves coding of write and read procedures to map the n-D array to the linear array and vice-versa.

A more elegant representation of an n-D array can be achieved by using a multilevel collection. In fact multilevel collections enable at least two typical operations on data:

- Modeling of n-dimensional arrays.
- Modeling of data hierarchies by factoring data by multiple levels.

The type of collection to be used is a factor of the ease of use in writing and reading the multi-dimensional array. Associative arrays greatly simplify this process and indexing the elements by VARCHAR2 further enhances its value by automatically grouping and ordering the data. This results in an obvious performance gain too.

Here's how a multilevel collection can be made to function as a multi-dimensional array:

1. The innermost collection elements store the value for each cell in the nth dimension of the array.
2. Each row in an outer collection represents a collection of the immediate inner dimension.
3. An element in the nth row and mth column is represented by the mth element in the nth dimension.

This method is pretty straightforward because you don't have to perform transformations on multiple indices, as was the case with Oracle 9i. Figure 4.3 depicts the structure of a multi-dimensional array organized as a multilevel collection.

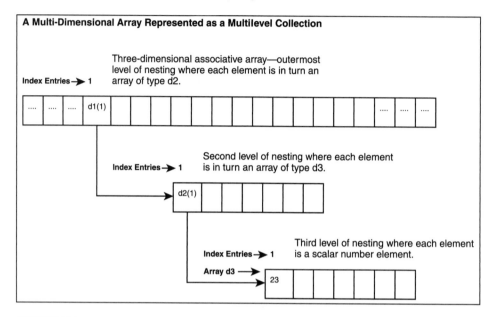

FIGURE 4.3
A multi-dimensional array represented as a multilevel collection.

The following example demonstrates a three-level nested associative array and its representation in a multilevel nested and flat (relational table-like)manner. The benefits of improved design and simpler code maintenance in using multi-dimensional arrays far outweigh that of using a flat database table.

Here are the steps involved:

1. Define a database table grpsrc_tab with the group code, the source number, the string equivalent, and its hash address as part of each row, as follows:

```
CREATE TABLE grpsrc_hash_tab
(group_code   VARCHAR2(10) NOT NULL,
 source_no    NUMBER NOT NULL,
 string_equiv VARCHAR2(255) NOT NULL,
 hash_value   VARCHAR2(255) NOT NULL);
```

2. Define a multi-dimensional associative array structure consisting of three arrays, one within the other to store the hash address as the innermost cell value and the source number, string equivalent, and group code as the other outer dimensions. Here's the code:

```
TYPE source_nos_type is TABLE OF VARCHAR2(255)
   INDEX BY grpsrc_hash_tab.source_no%TYPE;

TYPE string_equivs_type is TABLE OF source_nos_type
   INDEX BY grpsrc_hash_tab.string_equiv%TYPE;

TYPE group_codes_type is TABLE OF string_equiv_type
   INDEX BY grpsrc_hash_tab.group_code%TYPE;
```

3. Populate the final associative array with data from the grpsrc_hash_tab table, as follows:

```
TYPE source_nos_type is TABLE OF VARCHAR2(255)
  INDEX BY
grpsrc_hash_tab.source_no%TYPE;

source_nos source_nos_type;

TYPE string_equivs_type is TABLE OF source_nos_type
  INDEX BY
grpsrc_hash_tab.string_equiv%TYPE;

string_equivs string_equivs_type;

TYPE group_codes_type is TABLE OF
        string_equiv_type INDEX BY
grpsrc_hash_tab.group_code%TYPE;

group_codes group_codes_type;

TYPE hash_address_type is TABLE OF
        grpsrc_hash_tab%RWOTYPE INDEX BY
BINARY_INTEGER;

hash_addresses hash_address_type;

PROCEDURE p_load_multi_array IS
```

```
            CURSOR csr_hash IS
                SELECT * FROM grpsrc_hash_tab;

        BEGIN
            OPEN csr_hash;
            LOOP
                FETCH csr_hash BULK COLLECT INTO
                    hash_addresses LIMIT 1000;
                EXIT WHEN hash_addresses.COUNT = 0;

                FOR idx IN hash_addresses.FIRST..
                        hash_addresses.LAST LOOP
                    group_codes(hash_addresses(idx).group_code)
                    (hash_addresses(idx).string_equiv)
                    (hash_addresses(idx).source_no)
                            := hash_addresses(idx);
                END LOOP;
            END LOOP;
            CLOSE csr_hash;
        END p_load_multi_array;
```

4. Use the multi-dimensional array to read information. This requires procedures to read the multi-dimensional array and output the information desired. For example, to find out the string equivalents and their hash values for all the source numbers for a particular group code, you would define a procedure p_get_hash_info_by_group_code that takes as input a particular group code and displays the related information. Here's the code for this:

```
PROCEDURE p_get_hash_info_by_group_code(
    ip_group_code grpsrc_hash_tab.group_code%TYPE)
IS
  v_hash_row grpsrc_hash
BEGIN
  (group_codes(hash_addresses(idx).group_code)
  (hash_addresses(idx).string_equiv)
        (hash_addresses(idx).source_no);
END f_get_hash_info_by_group_code;
```

Listing 4.13 shows the code for the complete API.

LISTING 4.13 SIMULATING A MULTI-DIMENSIONAL ARRAY

```
CREATE OR REPLACE PACKAGE pkg_multi_array IS

  PROCEDURE p_load_multi_array;

END pkg_multi_array;
/

CREATE OR REPLACE PACKAGE BODY pkg_multi_array IS

  -- Define the structures for the multi-dimensional (3-D) array.
  TYPE source_nos_type is TABLE OF VARCHAR2(255) INDEX BY
  grpsrc_hash_tab.source_no%TYPE;

  source_nos source_nos_type;

  TYPE string_equivs_type is TABLE OF
       source_nos_type INDEX BY
  grpsrc_hash_tab.string_equiv%TYPE;

  string_equivs string_equivs_type;

  TYPE group_codes_type is TABLE OF string_equiv_type
       INDEX BY
  grpsrc_hash_tab.group_code%TYPE;

  group_codes group_codes_type;

  TYPE hash_address_type is TABLE OF grpsrc_hash_tab%ROWTYPE
       INDEX BY
  BINARY_INTEGER;

  hash_addresses hash_address_type;


  -- Procedure to populate the multi-dimensional array.
  PROCEDURE p_load_multi_array
  IS
     CURSOR csr_hash IS
       SELECT * FROM grpsrc_hash_tab;
  BEGIN
     OPEN csr_hash;
     LOOP
```

```
        FETCH csr_hash BULK COLLECT INTO hash_addresses
             LIMIT 1000;
        EXIT WHEN hash_addresses.COUNT = 0;

        FOR idx IN hash_addresses.FIRST..hash_addresses.LAST LOOP
           group_codes(hash_addresses(idx).group_code)
           (hash_addresses(idx).string_equiv)
           (hash_addresses(idx).source_no) := hash_addresses(idx);
        END LOOP;
     END LOOP;
     CLOSE csr_hash;
  END p_load_multi_array;

  -- Procedure to retrieve info based on one of the
  -- dimensions (i.e., group code).
  PROCEDURE p_get_hash_info_by_group_code(
             ip_group_code grpsrc_hash_tab.group_code%TYPE)
  IS
     v_hash_val VARCHAR2(255);
  BEGIN
     DBMS_OUTPUT.PUT_LINE('Info for Group Code '||ip_group_code);
     DBMS_OUTPUT.PUT_LINE('-----------------------------');

     FOR i IN string_equivs.FIRST..string_equivs.LAST LOOP
        FOR j IN source_nos.FIRST..source_nos.LAST LOOP
           v_hash_val := group_codes(ip_group_code)(i)(j);
           DBMS_OUTPUT.PUT_LINE(source_nos(j)||string_equivs(i)||
                               v_hash_val);
        END LOOP;
     END LOOP;
  END p_get_hash_info_by_group_code;
BEGIN
  p_load_multi_array;
END pkg_multi_array;
/
```

The performance benefit of using multi-dimensional arrays is quite significant as opposed to using queries to display the results, especially when they are used for reporting purposes multiple times. As an added benefit, the data in the multi-dimensional array remains up-to-date on a per-session basis.

RECORDS VERSUS OBJECTS

An object type can be perceived as a record type with methods. In addition to representing composite types, object types take the definition of the database to a higher level, relational to object-relational. Complex data relationships and representations can be accounted for in such a database design and thus object types make this happen at the database level. This is in contrast to record types, which enable this process (when used associatively with collections) at the programming level. The distinction between using record types versus object types is multi-fold and when to use one over the other is more a design issue than a programming guideline. Table 4.1 outlines the major differences between the two.

TABLE 4.1 DIFFERENCES BETWEEN RECORDS AND OBJECTS

Records	Objects
Cannot be stored in the database.	Can be stored as a database table column or as an entire row.
Complex data representation at the programming level.	Complex data representation and relationship at the database level.
Cannot be recursively referenced.	Can be recursively referenced using the SELF parameter.
Cannot have logic defined as part of their definition.	Can have logic defined as part of their definition using member methods.
Instances of a record type need not be initialized.	Instances of object types need to be initialized.
Do not provide code reusability.	Allow for code to be reused by means of inheritance.
Cannot be exposed directly at the top level.	Can be exposed directly at the top level—for example, by means of a view on top of collections. This way, object collections can be used to add a new layer between database and client. To achieve this with record types, virtual tables have to be used. This necessitates a pipelined table function along with PL/SQL collections defined in a package.

The primary factor in favor of record types is their ease of use and practically no overhead. They can and should be used in PL/SQL in a manner similar to pre-defined data types, but to represent composite types. Typical places to use PL/SQL record types are for array processing involving multi-column data I/O, record-based DML, and so on. Object types are good candidates when you need to store the composite type in the database.

SUMMARY

This chapter described techniques for use and management of PL/SQL data structures such as records, collections, and objects. Specifically, the techniques covered were performing data I/O and comparison using records. The next chapter deals with techniques for managing errors in PL/SQL.

5 Error Management in PL/SQL

In This Chapter

- Techniques for obtaining complete error information
- Techniques for customizing error information returned
- Techniques for halting further processing on error occurrence

Error handling constitutes a major piece of work in PL/SQL programming and applications, because running PL/SQL code mandates the proper trapping and output of error information to the calling environment. Errors in PL/SQL can be classified into two broad categories—compile-time errors and runtime errors. Compile-time errors occur while compiling a stored program unit. These mainly occur due to syntax or semantic discrepancies or, as of Oracle 10g, due to non-optimal or sub-optimal code and should be resolved before the code is ready for testing. Runtime errors are the real errors encountered during program execution and are critical to the productivity of an application. In addition to proper trapping and output of these errors, developers need to figure out why and at what point these errors occur and how to fix them.

The former (trapping and handling of runtime errors) falls into the category of error handling and the latter (why and where an error occurred) comes under the category of debugging. This chapter discusses the tricks of the trade for error handling in PL/SQL programs. For the purposes of this chapter, a stored program unit represents a PL/SQL stored procedure, function, package, database trigger, or object type method.

Basically, PL/SQL runtime errors can be classified into the following categories:

- Errors occurring due to failure of embedded SQL statements.
- Errors occurring due to failure of PL/SQL logic.
- Internal errors due to uncommon reasons, for example, a system or database crash.
- Application-specific validations resulting due to improper input from the end user or violation of business rules.

Furthermore, these errors may be cascading as a result of invocation of multiple PL/SQL programs. PL/SQL calls these errors exceptions and assigns an error code and a corresponding error message to each of them. The first three types of exceptions are implicitly raised and each is assigned a unique Oracle server error code and an error message. PL/SQL exception handling deals primarily with trapping and handling (and/or propagating) these errors. For the last type of errors that need to be explicitly raised, Oracle allows you to assign customized codes and messages. The default PL/SQL exception-handling capabilities provide ways to write code or exception handlers for obtaining the error information as completely as possible. This is the topic of the next section. To customize the error information returned as per application requirements, you need to code additional logic or even augment the default error-messaging capabilities (for example, extend the exception model). This is covered in the second section.

Another aspect of exception handling is how the calling application is affected when an error occurs. There are three basic options:

- Halt further execution when an exception occurs.
- Ignore the error and continue processing.
- Let the exception fall through and handle it elsewhere.

When to follow which option is application-specific. The first of these is very critical to the application and requires additional coding. The third and final section covers this issue and explains how and when to do this.

PL/SQL has built-in keywords, functions, procedures, pragmas, and packaged API as well as pre-defined exceptions to enable coding of these tasks. Before I delve into the specifics of these tasks, consider this list:

- Keywords: EXCEPTION, RAISE
- Functions: SQLCODE, SQLERRM
- Procedures: RAISE_APPLICATION_ERROR
- Pragmas: EXCEPTION_INIT
- Packaged APIs: DBMS_UTILITY.FORMAT_ERROR_STACK, DBMS_UTIL-ITY.FORMAT_ERROR_BACKTRACE, and DBMS_UTILITY.FORMAT_CALL_STACK

TECHNIQUES FOR OBTAINING COMPLETE ERROR INFORMATION

Complete error information for implicitly raised exceptions can be captured using an exception handler, the word *complete* meaning the following information can be tracked:

- Error code
- Error message text
- Error line number where the error first occurred
- Error execution stack
- Call execution stack

The call execution stack is more generic than the error execution stack and is primarily used to track the execution steps for debugging purposes. The error execution stack is enough to outline the sequence of program steps that lead to the error that originally occurred including the line number. Here the technique of obtaining complete error information is highlighted using two PL/SQL packages. An implementation package named pkg_error_info is defined that provides the API for getting the error information (all of the previous information listed, excluding the call execution stack). A second testing package, pkg_test_error_info, is used to define the actual subprograms that do the testing using the implementation package.

The steps involved in creating the implementation package are as follows:

1. Define an error_info record type having global scope that contains the error message text (error code is part of this), error line information, and the entire error execution stack. The error line information contains the

program owner, program name, and error line number for each line in the stack—here the program refers to the called subprograms in the top-level program of the stack hierarchy.

2. Define a function get_complete_error_info that processes the exception information, populates an instance of this record type, and returns the same. This function's input parameter is a flag that determines whether the entire error execution stack needs to be captured or just the line number where the error originally occurred.

3. Define a procedure print_complete_error_info that calls the get_complete_error_info function and displays the information to the user environment.

Listing 5.1 shows the code for the implementation of this package. The code in bold font suggests the particular API used to get the respective information.

LISTING 5.1 CAPTURING COMPLETE ERROR INFORMATION

```
CREATE OR REPLACE PACKAGE pkg_error_info IS

  TYPE error_info_rec IS RECORD
    (error_message_text    VARCHAR2(32767),
     error_line_info       VARCHAR2(1000),
     error_execution_stack CLOB);

  FUNCTION get_complete_error_info
        (ip_capture_full_stack BOOLEAN DEFAULT FALSE)
  RETURN error_info_rec;

  PROCEDURE print_complete_error_info
        (ip_print_full_stack BOOLEAN DEFAULT FALSE);

END pkg_error_info;
/
CREATE OR REPLACE PACKAGE BODY pkg_error_info IS

  -- Function to get complete error information including
  -- error execution stack.
  FUNCTION get_complete_error_info
        (ip_capture_full_stack BOOLEAN DEFAULT FALSE)
  RETURN error_info_rec
```

```
IS
    v_error_exec_stack CLOB;
    v_error_info  error_info_rec;
BEGIN
 -- The following line of code gives the full error execution
 -- stack, including the line number in the code where
 -- the error occurred.
 v_error_exec_stack := DBMS_UTILITY.FORMAT_ERROR_BACKTRACE;
 v_error_info.error_message_text := DBMS_UTILITY.FORMAT_ERROR_STACK;
 v_error_info.error_line_info := SUBSTR(v_error_exec_stack, 1,
                    INSTR(v_error_exec_stack, 'ORA', 1, 2)-1);
 IF ip_capture_full_stack THEN
  v_error_info.error_execution_stack := v_error_exec_stack;
 END IF;
 RETURN (v_error_info);
END get_complete_error_info;


 -- Procedure to print complete error information including
 -- error execution stack.
 PROCEDURE print_complete_error_info
     (ip_print_full_stack BOOLEAN DEFAULT FALSE)
 IS
   v_error_info error_info_rec;
 BEGIN
   v_error_info := get_complete_error_info;
   DBMS_OUTPUT.PUT_LINE('Error message text:');
   DBMS_OUTPUT.PUT_LINE(v_error_info.error_message_text);
   DBMS_OUTPUT.PUT_LINE('Error line info:');
   DBMS_OUTPUT.PUT_LINE(v_error_info.error_line_info);
   IF ip_print_full_stack THEN
       DBMS_OUTPUT.PUT_LINE('Error execution stack:');
       DBMS_OUTPUT.PUT_LINE(v_error_info.error_execution_stack);
   END IF;
 END print_complete_error_info;

END pkg_error_info;
/
```

The following points are worth noting:

■ As defined previously, the get_complete_error_info function can be used in-dependently of the print_complete_error_info procedure to facilitate error logging or otherwise use the error information returned for customization.

■ The get_complete_error_info function isolates the application programs from the actual error information trapping API.

Listing 5.2 shows the code for the testing package.

LISTING 5.2   TESTING THE COMPLETE ERROR INFORMATION PACKAGE

```
CREATE OR REPLACE PACKAGE pkg_test_error_info
IS

  PROCEDURE proc1;
  PROCEDURE proc2;
  PROCEDURE proc3;

END pkg_test_error_info;
/

CREATE OR REPLACE PACKAGE BODY pkg_test_error_info
IS

  PROCEDURE proc3
     IS
  BEGIN
     RAISE NO_DATA_FOUND;
  END;

  PROCEDURE proc2
     IS
  BEGIN
     proc3;
  END;

  PROCEDURE proc1
     IS
  BEGIN
     proc2;
  EXCEPTION WHEN OTHERS THEN
     pkg_error_info.print_complete_error_info(TRUE);
  END;

END pkg_test_error_info;
/
```

Here's the code to test the output:

```
BEGIN
  pkg_test_error_info.proc1;
END;
/
```

Here's the output of this code:

```
SQL> BEGIN
  2   pkg_test_error_info.proc1;
  3   END;
  4   /
Error message text:
ORA-01403: no data found

Error line info:
ORA-06512: at "PLSQL10G.PKG_TEST_ERROR_INFO", line 7

Error execution stack:
ORA-06512: at "PLSQL10G.PKG_TEST_ERROR_INFO", line 7
ORA-06512: at "PLSQL10G.PKG_TEST_ERROR_INFO", line 13
ORA-06512: at "PLSQL10G.PKG_TEST_ERROR_INFO", line 19


PL/SQL procedure successfully completed.
```

Although the individual procedures in the package are pkg_test_error_info are not listed for the program names, the line numbers are a clear indication where the actual error occurred in the subprogram stack.

The function for getting complete error information is to be used in all PL/SQL-based applications, whether the error is logged or presented to the user interface. This helps in trapping all possible server errors as well as when debugging.

In the custom package pkg_error_info code, two PL/SQL packaged functions were highlighted—DBMS_UTILITY.FORMAT_ERROR_BACKTRACE and DBMS_ UTILITY.FORMAT_ERROR_STACK. The second function returns the complete error message without trimming it to 512 characters, as in SQLERRM. The word STACK in this function is a misnomer and it doesn't return the error stack. Of special mention is the first function, DBMS_UTILITY.FORMAT_ERROR_BACKTRACE, new to Oracle 10g. Before you learn some techniques for customizing error information obtained, let's consider this function briefly in the next section.

TRACKING THE ERROR LINE NUMBER

Oracle 10g PL/SQL offers an elegant way of knowing the actual line number where an exception was raised. Pre-Oracle 10g, it was possible to know only the error number, error message text, and execution call stack in a PL/SQL program. This was possible by calling the packaged function DBMS_UTILITY.FORMAT_CALL_STACK.

In Oracle 10g PL/SQL, the actual line number can be obtained by calling the packaged function DBMS_UTILITY.FORMAT_ERROR_BACKTRACE. This is new in Oracle 10g and returns the error backtrace stack of the raised error, which includes the program owner, the program name, and the actual line number where the error originally occurred, but without the actual error number. If this function is called in the block in which the error was raised, it gives the line number where the exception was first raised. In case the exception is re-raised, this function gives the line number where the last re-raise occurred.

The best way to utilize this feature is to call the FORMAT_ERROR_BACK-TRACE function as an argument to the DBMS_OUTPUT.PUT_LINE procedure from a WHEN OTHERS exception handler. To get more elaborate information about the error, it pays to call the FORMAT_ERROR_STACK function also as an argument to DBMS_OUTPUT.PUT_LINE in the same WHEN OTHERS handler.

This way, the subprogram owner, subprogram name, error number, error message text, actual line number, and error stack can be obtained for any PL/SQL error. With a package, the subprogram name returned is the name of the package and not that of the individual packaged subprogram.

The code in the package pkg_test_error_info illustrates the use of DBMS_UTILITY.FORMAT_ERROR_BACKTRACE. As can be seen from the code, the proc3 procedure raises a NO_DATA_FOUND exception that is propagated to proc2 and proc1. The exception handler in the final proc1 procedure calls the FORMAT_ERROR_BACKTRACE function. The test output displayed shows the line number where the exception was first raised (that is, in proc3).

The next example, in Listing 5.3, illustrates behavior of this function when the exception is re-raised multiple times.

LISTING 5.3 USE OF DBMS_UTILITY.FORMAT_ERROR_BACKTRACE WHEN A RE-RAISE OCCURS

```
CREATE OR REPLACE PACKAGE pkg_test_error_info2
IS

    PROCEDURE proc1;
    PROCEDURE proc2;
```

```
     PROCEDURE proc3;

END pkg_test_error_info2;
/


CREATE OR REPLACE PACKAGE BODY pkg_test_error_info2
IS

     PROCEDURE proc3
         IS
     BEGIN
         RAISE NO_DATA_FOUND;
     END;

     PROCEDURE proc2
         IS
     BEGIN
         proc3;
     EXCEPTION WHEN OTHERS THEN
         RAISE;
     END;

     PROCEDURE proc1
         IS
     BEGIN
         proc2;
     EXCEPTION WHEN OTHERS THEN
         pkg_error_info.print_complete_error_info(TRUE);
     END;

END pkg_test_error_info2;
/
```

Here's the code to test this:

```
BEGIN
     pkg_test_error_info2.proc1;
END;
/
```

Here's the output of this code:

```
SQL> begin
  2        pkg_test_error_info2.proc1;
  3   end;
  4   /
Error message text:
ORA-01403: no data found

Error line info:
ORA-06512: at "PLSQL10G.PKG_TEST_ERROR_INFO2", line 15

Error execution stack:
ORA-06512: at "PLSQL10G.PKG_TEST_ERROR_INFO2", line 15
ORA-06512: at
"PLSQL10G.PKG_TEST_ERROR_INFO2", line 21


PL/SQL procedure successfully completed.
```

Notice the error line number changed to 15 from 7. This represents the line number in the package body (in proc2) where the original exception was re-raised with the RAISE statement (that is, where the last re-raise occurred).

TECHNIQUES FOR CUSTOMIZING THE ERROR INFO RETURNED

The key information returned about an error is the error code, error message text, and error execution stack. The error message text begins with the error code prefixed by ORA. You can customize the error information returned in the following ways:

- Extracting only the error message text from the output returned by SQLERRM or DBMS_UTILITY.FORMAT_ERROR_STACK. You can do this by performing string operations on each of these functions.
- Parsing the error execution stack returned by DBMS_UTILITY.FORMAT_ERROR_BACKTRACE. This can be used to obtain the original line number from the entire error stack along with the program name in which the error occurred. The pkg_error_info.get_complete_error_info function (discussed in the previous section) demonstrates an example of this. The parsed information can be stored in a database table or file for logging purposes or otherwise in a PL/SQL table for processing purposes.

■ Mapping the Oracle server error message with a more meaningful error message. This can be done based on the error code by assigning a customized error message from a lookup table cached in the PGA. The Oracle error code can be replaced by a more distinct error ID that can correspond to a particular instance of the SQLCODE that is application-specific. This can be done by assigning a unique ID to each SQLCODE instance that is most likely to be returned, from a lookup cache similar to a customized error message. Note that the same SQLCODE can map to multiple instance IDs in this scenario.

■ Throwing, trapping, and handling customized error messages based on application-specific requirements. This also includes associating programmer-defined exceptions with these customized error messages that correspond to logical errors. This is discussed in the next section.

TECHNIQUES FOR HALTING FURTHER PROCESSING ON ERROR OCCURRENCES

An important aspect of exception handling is what to do when an error occurs. As mentioned in the introduction to this chapter, this raises three issues:

■ Halt further execution when an exception occurs.
■ Ignore the error and continue processing.
■ Let the exception fall through and handle it elsewhere.

The first issue is discussed in this section. This type of action is important for critical errors that are application-specific—for example, errors resulting out of high-severity validations and business rules. The second issue, of ignoring the error and continuing processing, is a good option for errors that can be done away with and that do not affect the flow of the application from one logical point to another. A typical example is the NO_DATA_FOUND exception raised in the middle of application code while retrieving a description for a non-key code value. The third option, of letting the exception fall through, should be employed when the exception occurring is handled at a later point of time but not let loose until the outermost calling program. This is done by re-raising the exception in each of the enclosing blocks. This means if there is a sequence of subprograms, one calling another resulting in a call stack, the exception that first occurred should be re-raised in each of the subprograms and handled by either raising it in the outermost calling program or handling it otherwise.

The example package pkg_test_error_info2 detailed earlier presents a good example of this type. The NO_DATA_FOUND exception raised in proc1 is re-raised in proc2, which then lets it fall through to proc3 where it is handled. If the exception handler in proc2 was omitted, the control does not flow to any executable statements if present in proc2.

The technique of halting further processing on error occurrence is highlighted by means of a package pkg_test_error_info3, which is a modified version of the earlier pkg_test_error_info package.

PL/SQL provides a packaged procedure called DBMS_STANDARD.RAISE_APPLICATION_ERROR that halts further execution from the point this procedure is called.

Here are the steps involved in creating the implementation package:

1. Define a procedure proc3 with a call to RAISE_APPLICATION_ERROR procedure.
2. Define a procedure proc2 that returns a VARCHAR2 string.
3. Define a procedure proc1 that calls proc3 followed by proc2 and displays the character string returned by proc2.

Listing 5.4 shows the code for this process.

LISTING 5.4   HALTING FURTHER PROCESSING UPON ERROR OCCURRENCE

```
CREATE OR REPLACE PACKAGE pkg_test_error_info3
IS

    PROCEDURE proc1;
    PROCEDURE proc2(op_value OUT VARCHAR2);
    PROCEDURE proc3;

END pkg_test_error_info3;
/



CREATE OR REPLACE PACKAGE BODY pkg_test_error_info3
IS

    PROCEDURE proc3
        IS
    BEGIN
        RAISE_APPLICATION_ERROR
            (-20001, 'STOP! No further processing');
    END;
```

```
    PROCEDURE proc2(op_value OUT VARCHAR2)
        IS
    BEGIN
        op_value := 'Further away';

    END;

    PROCEDURE proc1
        IS
        v_value VARCHAR2(20);
    BEGIN
        proc3;
        proc2(v_value);
        DBMS_OUTPUT.PUT_LINE(v_value);
    END;

END pkg_test_error_info3;
/
```

Here's the code to test this and its output:

```
SQL> BEGIN
  2        pkg_test_error_info3.proc1;
  3  END;
  4  /
BEGIN
*
ERROR at line 1:
ORA-20001: STOP! No further processing
ORA-06512: at "PLSQL10G.PKG_TEST_ERROR_INFO3", line 7
ORA-06512: at "PLSQL10G.PKG_TEST_ERROR_INFO3", line 21
ORA-06512: at line 2
```

The following points are worth noting:

- The procedure RAISE_APPLICATION_ERROR causes the termination of program execution at the point it is called in a manner *similar to an un-handled exception*. This means the entire error execution stack is displayed similar to the output of DBMS_UTILITY.UTILITY.FORMAT_ERROR_BACKTRACE.
- This procedure also allows you to assign a customized error message and a pre-assigned error number that doesn't represent an Oracle server error number. In fact, Oracle has reserved the range of numbers −20999 to −20000 for use

as the first argument to this procedure. These are the only numbers that can be used when calling this procedure.

RAISE_APPLICATION_ERROR should be used in the following situations:

- When an application needs to raise an error with a customized error message and stop execution at that point.
- When a customized error needs to be thrown, trapped, and handled in a manner commensurate with the application/user requirements.

The second use mentioned here is a special case of using RAISE_APPLICATION_ERROR and is described in the subsection that follows.

THROWING, TRAPPING, AND HANDLING CUSTOMIZED ERRORS

This technique is implemented using the package called pkg_customized_error_info, which is a modified version of pkg_test_error_info3. Here are the steps involved:

1. Define procedures proc3 and proc2, as in pkg_test_error_info3.
2. Define a procedure proc1 that calls proc3 followed by proc2 and displays the character string returned by proc2. Additionally, this procedure has an exception handler that calls the pkg_error_info.get_complete_error_info function.

Listing 5.5 shows the code for this process.

LISTING 5.5   CUSTOMIZING ERROR INFORMATION

```
CREATE OR REPLACE PACKAGE pkg_customized_error_info
IS

    PROCEDURE proc1;
    PROCEDURE proc2(op_value OUT VARCHAR2);
    PROCEDURE proc3;

END pkg_customized_error_info;
/

CREATE OR REPLACE PACKAGE BODY pkg_customized_error_info
IS
```

```
    PROCEDURE proc3
        IS
    BEGIN
        RAISE_APPLICATION_ERROR
            (-20001, 'STOP! No further processing');
    END;

    PROCEDURE proc2(op_value OUT VARCHAR2)
        IS
    BEGIN
        op_value := 'Further away';

    END;

    PROCEDURE proc1
        IS
        v_value VARCHAR2(20);
    BEGIN
        proc3;
        proc2(v_value);
        DBMS_OUTPUT.PUT_LINE(v_value);
    EXCEPTION WHEN OTHERS THEN
        -- Reset package variables pertaining to error state
        -- Rollback any DML statements executed previously
        pkg_error_info.print_complete_error_info(TRUE);
    END;

END pkg_customized_error_info;
/
```

Here's the code to test this technique and its output:

```
SQL> BEGIN
  2       pkg_customized_error_info.proc1;
  3  END;
  4  /
Error message text:
ORA-20001: STOP! No further processing

Error line info:
ORA-06512: at "PLSQL10G.PKG_CUSTOMIZED_ERROR_INFO", line 7

Error execution stack:
ORA-06512: at "PLSQL10G.PKG_CUSTOMIZED_ERROR_INFO", line 7
```

```
ORA-06512: at
"PLSQL10G.PKG_CUSTOMIZED_ERROR_INFO", line 21
```

The following points are worth noting:

- The customized error message is thrown using the built-in RAISE_ APPLICA-TION_ERROR.
- This error message is trapped by the EXCEPTION WHEN OTHERS exception handler in proc1 procedure and is also handled customarily. As an example handler, it simply outputs the complete error message text, the actual error line number, and the error execution stack, bottom up.
- The exception handler could have been coded in proc3 itself instead of in proc1. Notice how the SQLCODE and SQLERRM (or DBMS_UTILITY.FOR-MAT_ERROR_STACK) are set to the customized error number and error message text (−20001 and STOP! No further processing, in this case), respectively. Also notice how the number −20001 is preceded by ORA just like a pre-defined Oracle error.
- The customized error number can also be associated with a programmer-defined exception by using the EXCEPTION_INIT pragma. This provides greater flexibility to the developer and enhances code readability and comprehension with the customized error being tracked and handled by means of an exception, just like a pre-defined exception.

Listing 5.6 shows the code for the pkg_customized_error_info package with this change in place followed by the test results.

LISTING 5.6 SECOND IMPLEMENTATION OF THE PACKAGE FOR CUSTOMIZING ERROR INFORMATION, USING PROGRAMMER-DEFINED EXCEPTIONS

```
CREATE OR REPLACE PACKAGE BODY pkg_customized_error_info2
IS

    PROCEDURE proc3
       IS
    BEGIN
       RAISE_APPLICATION_ERROR
           (-20001, 'STOP! No further processing');
    END;
```

```
    PROCEDURE proc2(op_value OUT VARCHAR2)
        IS
    BEGIN
        op_value := 'Further away';

    END;

    PROCEDURE proc1
        IS
        v_value VARCHAR2(20);
    BEGIN
        proc3;
        proc2(v_value);
        DBMS_OUTPUT.PUT_LINE(v_value);
    EXCEPTION WHEN critical_error THEN
        -- Reset package variables pertaining to error state
        -- Roll back any DML statements executed previously
        pkg_error_info.print_complete_error_info(TRUE);
    END;

END pkg_customized_error_info2;
/

SQL> BEGIN
  2      pkg_customized_error_info2.proc1;
  3  END;
  4  /
Error message text:
ORA-20001: STOP! No further processing

Error line info:
ORA-06512: at "PLSQL10G.PKG_CUSTOMIZED_ERROR_INFO2", line 7

Error execution stack:
ORA-06512: at "PLSQL10G.PKG_CUSTOMIZED_ERROR_INFO2", line 7
ORA-06512: at
"PLSQL10G.PKG_CUSTOMIZED_ERROR_INFO2", line 21


PL/SQL procedure successfully completed.
```

The output is the same as that of the pkg_customized_error_info package.

SUMMARY

This chapter described error-management techniques in PL/SQL. It touched upon how to get the complete error information that includes the complete error message text, the actual line number where the error first occurred, and the complete error execution stack. Subsequent sections dealt with techniques for customizing the error information obtained and halting execution at the point an error occurs. The next chapter deals with techniques for data management in PL/SQL, including data retrieval and manipulation, dynamic SQL and PL/SQL, array processing using static and dynamic SQL in PL/SQL, and using DDL in PL/SQL.

6

Data Management in PL/SQL

In This Chapter

- Data retrieval techniques
- Data manipulation techniques
- Array processing using static SQL
- Array processing using dynamic SQL

The primary purpose of a database is conglomeration and dissemination of data. The major challenge of any database then is how data is managed for both internal storage and external use. This issue involves a lot of aspects, starting from database structure to data type. This chapter focuses on the "data" part of the management in that it concentrates on how to input and output the data into and out of the database and how to change the existing data to facilitate its use by various entities such as end users (ranging from corporate personnel to data entry operators), inter-related and integrated applications, and applications external to the database (such as third-party systems not linked to the Oracle database). Integrated applications include OLTP, OLAP, DW (data warehousing), BI (business intelligence), and data mining.

From an application development perspective and a PL/SQL standpoint, data management primarily constitutes data retrieval and manipulation. These functions mandate the use of SQL and/or PL/SQL techniques that need to be both database- and application-centric. All of these techniques apply when using static and/or dynamic SQL and PL/SQL. Using a mix and match of these techniques can result in optimal data retrieval and manipulation. The sections that follow detail several of these techniques.

DATA-RETRIEVAL TECHNIQUES

Data retrieval from an Oracle database can be performed in two major ways:

- Data retrieval using SQL
- Data retrieval using PL/SQL

Using either of these ways, PL/SQL applications can use the data retrieved for further processing. The primary element for data retrieval in both cases is the SELECT statement. SQL data retrieval employs SELECT statements (along with its SQL-only variations) that are directly embedded in PL/SQL code that pull data from Oracle tables into PL/SQL memory structures. This method can be used to retrieve a single row or multiple rows. PL/SQL data retrieval involves using the SELECT statement with its PL/SQL variations to retrieve multiple rows at a time. In fact, this method is a superset of the former, as the SELECT statement (along with its SQL-only variations) is used along with the PL/SQL variations.

When to use pure embedded SQL and when to use the PL/SQL approach depends on several factors, including:

- The number of rows to be retrieved
- The time taken to retrieve all the required rows
- How the retrieved data should be used

Using the SELECT statement along with its SQL-only variations is usually the most optimal way when the following conditions exist:

- Only one row needs to be retrieved.
- The SQL involved is not resource intensive.
- The rows retrieved do not involve further intermediate processing on a row-by-row or set-by-set basis.

- The rows to be retrieved are to be fed directly into a DML statement such as INSERT, UPDATE, DELETE, or MERGE.
- The data retrieved does not need to be part of complex application logic.

Using the PL/SQL method can result in a performance benefit when the following conditions exist:

- Multiple rows need to be retrieved that require additional processing on a row-by-row or set-by-set basis.
- The number of records is large, ranging from hundreds of thousands to millions—for example, when loading/querying a data warehouse.
- The SQL method is not optimal.

Here's a list of some variations that can be used with the SELECT statement for data retrieval:

- Using aggregation (for example, at single or multiple levels with ROLLUP, CUBE, and so on)
- Using analytic functions (for example, for combining summary and detail information in the same query)
- Using SQL MODEL clause (for example, to perform inter-row and inter-referencing calculations that can be used for time-series and other types of statistical reporting)
- Using cursor sub-queries (for example, to eliminate multiple/complex joins)
- Using the WITH clause for sub-query factoring

Here's the list of techniques for data retrieval using PL/SQL:

- Using cursors
- Using cursor expressions
- Using array processing

The techniques for using the SQL-only variations are standard methods that augment the use of the SELECT statement. This section discusses the more predominant PL/SQL way in terms of the techniques for data retrieval.

The first technique—using cursors—pertains to the standard cursor usage in PL/SQL. The second technique—using cursor expressions—is an extension of the first and describes the use of cursor expressions in PL/SQL, a feature introduced from Oracle 9iR2 onward. The details pertaining to these two topics do not mandate any special techniques to be used except some important tips that need to be kept in mind when using them. This chapter concentrates on specifying these tips and proceeds to techniques for array processing, which is discussed in detail in the sections entitled "Array Processing Using Static SQL" and "Array Processing Using Dynamic SQL."

Here's a list of the tips pertaining to using cursors and cursor expressions:

- Use static implicit cursors to retrieve only one row. It's more efficient than the corresponding explicit cursor version, when using both INTERPRETED and NATIVE (compilation) modes.
- Use static cursor FOR loops to retrieve a smaller set of rows, such as from 100 to 250 rows, and for (mostly) unconditional processing of ALL of these rows.
- Use cursor expressions in PL/SQL so you don't have to use complex joins (that might require additional cost of processing, especially when linking two independent multi-valued relationships in a single query) without worrying about other overheads. Such use is tightly integrated into the SQL and database engines. Secondly, using cursor expressions opens the door for optimal table function input. Thirdly, cursor expressions offer the flexibility of easy and elegant coding style.

DATA-MANIPULATION TECHNIQUES

Data manipulation from an Oracle database can be performed in two major ways:

- Data manipulation using SQL
- Data manipulation using PL/SQL

Using either of these ways, PL/SQL applications can perform DML operations. The primary operations for data manipulation in both cases are INSERT, UPDATE, DELETE, and MERGE.

The SQL method employs these DML statements (along with its SQL-only variations) that are directly used in scripts for batch processing or embedded in 3GL and/or other development environments requiring database connectivity. The PL/SQL method involves using these DML statements with their PL/SQL variations embedded in PL/SQL application logic that are stored inside the database. In fact, this method is a superset of the former, because the DML statement (along with its SQL-only variations) is used along with the PL/SQL variations.

When to use which method depends on the requirement as well as the performance achieved by the DML statement.

Using the SQL-only method is useful when any of the following conditions are met:

- The application is not PL/SQL-centric.
- The application requires processing in a batch that in turn requires database updates.
- The DML statement execution impacts performance in terms of execution time and resources consumed.
- The processing logic is too complex to be packed into a single DML statement.

Using the PL/SQL way is beneficial when any of the following conditions are met:

- The application is PL/SQL-centric.
- The DML statement needs to use PL/SQL variations along with the SQL.
- Row-wise exceptions need to be taken care of while performing the DML in case multiple rows are affected by the DML. This is in addition to the SQL way of doing the same using the LOG ERRORS clause (introduced in Oracle 10g).
- When the SQL way is not optimal.

Here's a list of techniques for data manipulation using PL/SQL:

- Using array processing for the DML to be performed.
- Using table functions that can be called from SQL SELECT that in turn act as source for the DML.
- Using autonomous transaction processing for the DML involved.

The first technique pertains to using bulk DML and is discussed in detail in the sections "Array Processing Using Static SQL" and "Array Processing Using Dynamic SQL." The second and third techniques are discussed in Chapters 7 and 8.

ARRAY PROCESSING IN PL/SQL

Array processing involves the execution of multiple DML statements in a single context switch by binding together an entire set of values in a single database operation. This can involve either static or dynamic SQL and is implemented in PL/SQL using native bulk binds. The corresponding operations are known as bulk DML, bulk query, and bulk dynamic SQL. The process involves an entire collection of values as input or output for the DML operation involved and passes this entire collection between the PL/SQL and the SQL engines in a single context switch.

The sections that follow explore the capabilities of array processing in PL/SQL in the area of improving performance with respect to static SQL and dynamic SQL. Specifically, the following techniques are discussed:

- Bulk DML
- Selective bulk DML supporting sparse table/collections
- Bulk querying
- Bulk dynamic SQL

Oracle bulk binding has been further enhanced in Oracle 9i by the addition of the following features:

- Bulk binding using record types for bulk DML and bulk query. This can be used with FORALL and FORALL…RETURNING…BULK COLLECT INTO… statements and FETCH BULK COLLECT INTO for bulk fetching into a collection of records. However, this cannot be done when using bulk dynamic SQL. Use of record types for bulk binding is permitted as of Oracle 9i, Release 2.
- The SAVE EXCEPTIONS clause in the FORALL statement enables processing to continue in case of row-wise exceptions.
- Direct support for bulk dynamic SQL. Prior to Oracle 9i, native dynamic SQL supported bulk SQL indirectly if the bulk SQL statement was enclosed with a BEGIN…END statement.
- Returning multiple rows with the RETURNING BULK COLLECT INTO clause for updates and deletes using native dynamic SQL.

Oracle 10g went a step ahead and introduced the capability of processing the FORALL statement involving collections with nonconsecutive indices using the INDICES OF and VALUES OF clauses. This is also a performance gain over the FORALL statement in pre-Oracle 10g, when the number of deleted elements in the sparse collection is large.

ARRAY PROCESSING USING STATIC SQL

Array processing using static SQL involves using bulk DML and bulk query with SQL statements parsed at compile-time. This section details the method of implementing array processing with static SQL.

Why Use Array Processing

One area that's important when you're executing SQL within PL/SQL (and more specifically, when you're executing SQL within loops) is that of optimization. Because your code contains a mixture of PL/SQL and SQL, two parsing processes are involved.

The PL/SQL engine, which is usually located on the server side, executes the PL/SQL. Remember, though, that client-side programs can also have their own PL/SQL engine. Any SQL DML statements are forwarded to the SQL engine for execution. The resulting data or DML after execution results is passed back to the PL/SQL engine. This can lead to a performance overhead, particularly when you're working with looping constructs.

This process of passing statements to different engines is known as *context switching* and can result in less than optimal execution of your code. But so what? As long as execution takes place and the results are correct, who cares? Well, your users will care for one thing. You should always be working toward optimal performance. The context switching results in to-and-fro traffic from PL/SQL to SQL and vice-versa. Every roundtrip involves overhead. And too many roundtrips can hinder performance. Now the question is, why are so many roundtrips required? One of the causes of such roundtripping between engines is iterative execution, as many roundtrips may be involved.

One solution to this performance problem is provided via the use of array processing. Array processing is a feature introduced in Oracle 8i and is implemented using bulk binding. Bulk binding initially improves overall PL/SQL performance in at least two ways:

- It performs array processing that processes rows set-at-a-time rather than row-by-row. This process reduces the number of roundtrips from SQL to PL/SQL and vice-versa and hence reduces the number of context switches between the PL/SQL and SQL engines. The overhead involved in each roundtrip is minimized, thus resulting in optimal execution of code.
- Using bulk binding with native dynamic SQL combines the performance benefit of using bulk binds to reduce context switching with the ability to execute faster, thus providing increased performance.

However, both of these advantages come at the cost of in-memory caching involved for temporary storage of rows retrieved set-at-a-time. This is not a major concern if the array size is set optimally and the set of rows cached is not held (that is, is released quickly).

When to Use Array Processing

Array processing is a viable option in the following scenarios:

- When the number of records processed is huge, ranging from many thousands to hundreds of thousands to millions. The point to be kept in mind is that array processing is effective when the bulk operation is done a large number of times.
- When performing ETL operations in a data warehousing environment to either extract data into staging tables or load the transformed data into target tables.
- When performing business intelligence/data mining operations to enable intra-ETL and inter-ETL development between the base database and the aggregate, derived, and/or ROLAP/OLAP/data mining layers.

Table 6.1 summarizes the various PL/SQL statements used in array processing with static SQL.

TABLE 6.1 VARIOUS PL/SQL STATEMENTS USED IN
ARRAY PROCESSING WITH STATIC SQL

Operation	PL/SQL Statement	Usage	Comments
Bulk DML	FORALL…	FORALL index IN lower_bound.. upper_bound [SAVE EXCEPTIONS] dml_statement;	DML statement can be one of INSERT, UPDATE, or DELETE. SAVE EXCEPTIONS is new in Oracle 9i.
	FORALL… RETURNING… BULK COLLECT INTO…	FORALL index IN lower_bound.. upper_bound [SAVE EXCEPTIONS] dml_statement RETURNING column_name BULK COLLECT INTO collection_name;	The collection name can be a NESTED TABLE, a VARRAY, or an index-by table.
	FORALL… INDICES OF…	FORALL index IN INDICES OF sparse_collection	This is new in Oracle 10g.

Continued

	FORALL... VALUES OF...	[BETWEEN lower_bound AND upper_bound] [SAVE EXCEPTIONS] dml_statement	This is new in Oracle 10g.
		FORALL index IN VALUES OF sparse_collection [SAVE EXCEPTIONS] dml_statement	
Bulk query	SELECT... BULK COLLECT INTO...	SELECT column_name BULK COLLECT INTO collection_name;	The collection_ name can be a NESTED TABLE, a VARRAY, or an index-by table.
	FETCH... BULK COLLECT INTO...	FETCH cursor_name BULK COLLECT INTO collection_name;	

TECHNIQUES FOR BULK DML

Bulk DML consists of executing INSERT, UPDATE, or DELETE statements in bulk using associative arrays or collections as the input for the DML statement. Bulk DML is performed using the FORALL statement. This section highlights the following techniques for bulk DML:

- Using bulk DML
- Getting number of rows processed and failed in bulk DML

TIP

The FORALL statement is an implementation of an iteration algorithm and not a FOR loop. You can't use the FORALL statement as a cursor FOR loop.

The normal FOR loop is an iterative loop construct, whereas the FORALL statement is an implementation of an iteration algorithm. Table 6.2 summarizes the essential differences.

TABLE 6.2 DIFFERENCES BETWEEN **FORALL** AND A **FOR** LOOP

FORALL	FOR Loop
Is not a loop construct; only an implementation of an iteration algorithm.	Is a loop construct.
Associated only with INSERT, UPDATE, DELETE, or MERGE.	Can be associated with SELECT and can also invoke stored subprograms.
Opens an implicit cursor.	Can be used as an explicit CURSOR FOR loop.
Can be used with native dynamic SQL.	Cannot be used with native dynamic SQL.

To use FORALL, follow these steps:

1. Define a collection to hold the driving data values of the UPDATE or DELETE statement. In case of an INSERT statement, define one collection corresponding to the entire record to be inserted, or a separate collection, one each for each column to be inserted.
2. Populate the newly defined collection with consecutive index values. Non-existing intermediate elements raise the following exception:

```
ORA-22160: element at index[i] does not exist
```

3. Use the FORALL statement to perform the desired DML operation.
4. Perform a COMMIT after the FORALL.

Listing 6.1 shows an example.

LISTING 6.1 USING **FORALL**

```
DECLARE
  Type region_id_tbl IS TABLE of NUMBER INDEX BY BINARY_INTEGER;
  Type region_name_tbl IS TABLE of VARCHAR2(20)
                      INDEX BY BINARY_INTEGER;
  region_ids region_id_tbl;
  region_names region_name_tbl;
  ret_code NUMBER;
  ret_errmsg VARCHAR2(1000);
```

```
Procedure load_regions_bulk_bind
        (region_ids IN region_id_tbl,
         region_names IN region_name_tbl,
         retcd OUT NUMBER,
         errmsg OUT VARCHAR2)
IS
BEGIN
  -- clean up the region_tab table initially.
  DELETE FROM region_tab;
  FORALL i IN region_ids.FIRST..region_ids.LAST
    INSERT INTO region_tab values (region_ids(i),
               region_names(i));
  Retcd := 0;
EXCEPTION WHEN OTHERS THEN
  COMMIT;
  Retcd := SQLCODE;
  Errmsg := SQLERRM;
END;
BEGIN
  FOR i IN 1..5 LOOP
    Region_ids(i) := i;
    Region_names(i) := 'REGION'||i;
  END LOOP;
  Load_regions_bulk_bind(region_ids, region_names,
                     ret_code, ret_errmsg);
EXCEPTION WHEN OTHERS THEN
  RAISE_APPLICATION_ERROR(-20112, SQLERRM);
END;
/
```

This program declares two associative arrays named region_ids and region_names of the NUMBER and VARCHAR2 types, respectively. It also declares a local procedure named load_regions_bulk_bind that takes as input two index-by tables of type region_id_tbl and region_name_tbl and does the following:

■ Cleans up the region_tab table initially.
■ INSERTS into the region_tab table using the bulk DML FORALL statement, taking the input for region_id from the region_ids index-by table and the input for region_name from the region_names index-by table. This single statement inserts five rows into the region_tab table in a single database call.
■ COMMITS the inserted rows.

- Outputs a return code of 0 on success in the form of an OUT parameter named retcd. On error, it outputs the corresponding SQLCODE and SQLERRM in the form of two OUT parameters, retcd and errmsg.

Finally, the body of the PL/SQL block populates the two index-by tables, region_ids and region_names, with five region IDs and five region names. Then it invokes the load_regions_bulk_bind procedure that performs the bulk bind.

When to Use FORALL

FORALL can be used to perform a massive INSERT, UPDATE, DELETE, or MERGE operation from a source table or view to a target table. It can also be used to perform a set-at-a-time INSERT, UPDATE, DELETE, or MERGE operation from a source table or view to a target table by performing intermediate processing of each row retrieved from the source. This means it takes as input the row set retrieved by bulk query. This in turn mandates the use of FORALL in an enclosing loop.

Performance Benefit of FORALL

To verify the performance of bulk binds, you can do a massive INSERT once with a normal FOR loop and a second time using a FORALL statement. A reduced timing difference in the case of the FORALL statement illustrates the performance improvement. Listing 6.2 shows a sample program that shows this process.

LISTING 6.2 THE PERFORMANCE BENEFIT OF USING FORALL

```
DECLARE
   Type region_id_tbl IS TABLE of NUMBER INDEX BY BINARY_INTEGER;
   Type region_name_tbl IS TABLE of VARCHAR2(20)
      INDEX BY BINARY_INTEGER;
   region_ids region_id_tbl;
   region_names region_name_tbl;
   Ret_code NUMBER;
   Ret_errmsg VARCHAR2(1000);
   time1 number;
   time2 number;
   time3 number;
Procedure load_regions
         (region_ids IN region_id_tbl,
          region_names IN region_name_tbl,
          retcd OUT NUMBER,
          errmsg OUT VARCHAR2)
```

```
IS
BEGIN
 FOR i in 1..10000 LOOP
    INSERT INTO region_tab_temp
    values (region_ids(i), region_names(i));
 END LOOP;
COMMIT;
EXCEPTION WHEN OTHERS THEN
  Retcd := SQLCODE;
  Errmsg := SQLERRM;
END;
Procedure load_regions_bulk_bind
          (region_ids IN region_id_tbl,
           region_names IN region_name_tbl,
           retcd OUT NUMBER,
           errmsg OUT VARCHAR2)
 IS
BEGIN
  FORALL i IN 1..10000
     INSERT INTO region_tab_temp values
         (region_ids(i), region_names(i));
  Retcd := 0;
EXCEPTION WHEN OTHERS THEN
  COMMIT;
  Retcd := SQLCODE;
  Errmsg := SQLERRM;
END;
BEGIN
  DELETE region_tab_temp;
  FOR i IN 1..10000 LOOP
    Region_ids(i) := i;
    Region_names(i) := 'REGION'||i;
  END LOOP;
  time1 := dbms_utility.get_time;
  Load_regions(region_ids, region_names,
      ret_code, ret_errmsg);
  time2 := dbms_utility.get_time;
  Load_regions_bulk_bind(region_ids, region_names,
      ret_code, ret_errmsg);
  time3 := dbms_utility.get_time;
  dbms_output.put_line('Time without bulk bind is
       '||to_char(time2-time1)|| ' secs');
  dbms_output.put_line('Time with bulk bind is
       '||to_char(time3-time2)||' secs');
```

```
EXCEPTION WHEN OTHERS THEN
  RAISE_APPLICATION_ERROR(-20111,SQLERRM);
END;
/
```

Here's the output of this program:

```
Time without bulk bind is 339 secs
Time with bulk bind is 19 secs

PL/SQL procedure successfully completed.
```

As you can see, the FORALL statement is significantly faster than not using the bulk bind.

With FORALL, multiple INSERT, UPDATE, DELETE, or MERGE statements are processed in a single call to the database. This improves execution time. Only a single INSERT, UPDATE, DELETE, or MERGE statement that references collection elements can be executed by FORALL. The SQL statement is executed once for each index of the specified range. The DML statement must reference collection elements indexed by index in the FORALL statement. The collection can either be an associative array, a nested table, a VARRAY, or a host array. Only subscripted collections are bulk bound. The index has to be referenced only within the FORALL statement and only as a collection subscript. Also, the collection subscript cannot be an expression and the subscripted index cannot be an expression. The bounds must specify a valid range of consecutive index numbers. However, the upper and lower bounds need not have to span the entire range of the collection. The SQL statement can reference more than one collection. You can use FORALL while performing native dynamic SQL.

TIP

TIP

As of Oracle 9i, Release 2, %ROWTYPE associative arrays can be bulk bound for DML. This means record types can be used for bulk DML using static SQL. However, this is not supported when using native dynamic SQL with bulk DML (Refer to the section "Array Processing with Dynamic SQL" for more information.) However, you cannot reference individual record fields in FORALL, but you can use the entire record as a whole. This is particularly useful when bulk binding the DML statement involved in the USING clause. Here, using the entire record as an in-bind can incur the added cost of additional redo being generated by using the entire record, especially when the DML statement is an UPDATE. This will cause all the columns to be updated to their same values even if only a part of the columns have to be updated.

What Cannot Be Done with FORALL

Although FORALL enables bulk execution of INSERT, UPDATE, DELETE, and MERGE, it has the following limitations:

- An error occurs if the collection involved in the FORALL has missing elements.
- The processing stops if a row-wise failure occurs.

The methods to overcome these limitations are discussed in the sections that follow.

What Happens on SQL Error?

On SQL error, the immediate SQL operation is terminated by means of an automatic rollback. Then the execution stops.

If the exception is unhandled, all rows affected by the DML statement until the point the error occurred are rolled back. If the exception is handled, only the immediate SQL statement is rolled back. The preceding SQL statements once succeeded are not rolled back. A COMMIT as follows saves the successful SQL statements that preceded the failed one:

```
EXCEPTION WHEN OTHERS THEN
   COMMIT;
```

So all the rows that are meant to be processed by the bulk DML statement are not processed and it seems there is no way to continue after a row-wise exception. However, this was the case with PL/SQL prior to Oracle 9i. There is an enhancement introduced in Oracle 9i to bulk DML with the capability to handle the error and continue processing after the failed row. This is discussed in the next section.

How Do You Continue Past Row-Wise Exceptions?

There is an enhancement to bulk DML that allows it to handle the error in the case of a row-wise exception and continue processing after the failed row. This is done with the SAVE EXCEPTIONS clause of the FORALL statement.

The SAVE EXCEPTIONS clause was first introduced in Oracle 9i, and it saves the error rows in an implicit cursor attribute named SQL%BULK_EXCEPTIONS and allows the FORALL statement to continue processing the remaining rows. Along with this comes a new exception with error code 224381. Here's a description of this error:

```
ORA-24381: error(s) in array DML
```

This error can be associated with a user-defined exception using the pragma EXCEPTION_INIT.

The implicit cursor attribute SQL%BULK_EXCEPTIONS works as follows:

- It resembles an associative array of records containing the error_index and error_code as the record fields.
- The number of rows in this array is obtained by using the SQL%BULK_EXCEPTIONS.COUNT function.
- Information of any rows rejected from the processing of the DML statement is also recorded in this array and the corresponding error_index and error_code are also populated. The retrieval of the error details has to be done in a FOR loop with a lower bound of 1 and an upper bound equal to the total number of errors in the SQL%BULK_EXCEPTIONS associative array. The error_index gives the iteration index or the row number of the failed row in the FORALL statement and is referenced by SQL%BULK_EXCEPTIONS(index).error_index. The error_code gives the SQLCODE corresponding to the failed row in the FORALL statement and is referenced by SQL%BULK_EXCEPTIONS(index).error_code.

The corresponding error message is obtained by using SQLERRM as follows:

```
SQLERRM(-SQL%BULK_EXCEPTIONS(index).error_code);
```

Here's the code to illustrate this:

```
FOR i in 1..SQL%BULK_EXCEPTIONS.COUNT LOOP
   DBMS_OUTPUT.PUT_LINE(''Iteration ''||
            SQL%BULK_EXCEPTIONS(i).
                error_index||'' failed with error ''||
            SQLERRM(-SQL%BULK_EXCEPTIONS(i).error_code));
END LOOP;
```

TIP

SQL%BULK_EXCEPTIONS can be used to trap errors in a FORALL statement irrespective of using the SAVE EXCEPTIONS clause. In this case it gives the error details of only the last iteration that resulted in an error.

Here are the steps involved in using SAVE EXCEPTIONS:

1. Code a FORALL statement with the SAVE EXCEPTIONS clause.
2. Define a pragma EXCEPTION_INIT directive and associate the Oracle error 224381 with a user-defined exception.
3. Define an exception-handling block to handle the declared exception with the following logic in it:
    A. Initialize the SQL%BULK_EXCEPTIONS.COUNT to a numeric variable.
    B. In a FOR loop iterating from 1 to the above count, trap the error iteration index using

    ```
    SQL%BULK_EXCEPTIONS(i).error_index;
    ```

    and trap the error message using

    ```
    SQLERRM(-SQL%BULK_EXCEPTIONS(i).error_code);
    ```

Listing 6.3 shows a complete example of using the FORALL statement with the SAVE EXCEPTIONS clause.

LISTING 6.3 USE OF **FORALL** WITH **SAVE EXCEPTIONS**

```
DECLARE
   Type region_id_tbl IS TABLE of NUMBER INDEX BY BINARY_INTEGER;
   Type region_name_tbl IS TABLE of VARCHAR2(20)
                          INDEX BY BINARY_INTEGER;
   region_ids region_id_tbl;
   region_names region_name_tbl;
   ret_code NUMBER;
   ret_errmsg VARCHAR2(1000);
Procedure load_regions_bulk_bind
         (region_ids IN region_id_tbl,
          region_names IN region_name_tbl,
          retcd OUT NUMBER,
          errmsg OUT VARCHAR2)
  IS
   bulk_bind_excep EXCEPTION;
   PRAGMA EXCEPTION_INIT(bulk_bind_excep, -24381);
BEGIN
   -- clean up the region_tab table initially.
   DELETE FROM region_tab;
```

```
      FORALL i IN region_ids.FIRST..region_ids.LAST SAVE EXCEPTIONS
        INSERT INTO region_tab values (region_ids(i),
                                           region_names(i));
    Retcd := 0;
  EXCEPTION WHEN bulk_bind_excep THEN
      FOR i in 1..SQL%BULK_EXCEPTIONS.COUNT LOOP
          DBMS_OUTPUT.PUT_LINE('Iteration '||
                SQL%BULK_EXCEPTIONS(i).error_index||
                           ' failed with error '||
                SQLERRM(-SQL%BULK_EXCEPTIONS(i).error_code));
      END LOOP;
      COMMIT;
      Retcd := SQLCODE;
      Errmsg := 'Bulk DML error(s) ';
    WHEN OTHERS THEN
      Retcd := SQLCODE;
      Errmsg := SQLERRM;
  END;
  BEGIN
    FOR i IN 1..5 LOOP
      Region_ids(i) := i;
      Region_names(i) := 'REGION'||i;
    END LOOP;
    Region_names(3) := 'REGION WITH NAME3';
    Load_regions_bulk_bind(region_ids, region_names,
                             ret_code, ret_errmsg);
  EXCEPTION WHEN OTHERS THEN
    RAISE_APPLICATION_ERROR(-20112, SQLERRM);
  END;
  /
```

Here's the output of the preceding code:

```
Iteration 3 failed with error ORA-01401:
      inserted value too large for column

PL/SQL procedure successfully completed.

SQL> select * from region_tab;

 REGION_ID REGION_NAM
---------- ----------
         1 REGION1
         2 REGION2
```

```
      4 REGION4
      5 REGION5
```

Note that region 3 is not inserted. To restore the row for region 3, you do the following INSERT followed by a COMMIT:

```
BEGIN
   insert into region_tab values (3, 'REGION3');
   commit;
END;
/
```

TIP

TIP

The SAVE EXCEPTIONS clause not only enables continued processing if a particular iteration fails but also enables FORALL to execute in case of missing elements in the driving collection. If the SAVE EXCEPTIONS clause is not used, the behavior of FORALL resembles that of pre-Oracle 9i; it will stop execution when an exception occurs.

The SAVE EXCEPTIONS clause is also supported in native dynamic SQL using FORALL.

When Do You Use SAVE EXCEPTIONS?

SAVE EXCEPTIONS should be used in the following situations:

■ When there are missing elements in the collection involved in the FORALL. However, if the number of deleted elements is large, there is a performance bottleneck. Refer to the section "Bulk DML with Sparse Collections" to learn how to overcome this situation.
■ To continue FORALL processing when a particular iteration fails.
■ To trap row-wise errors occurring in the execution of FORALL.

When the SAVE EXCEPTIONS is not used, only the error of the last executed DML statement is trapped. This involves the following steps:

■ Code a FORALL statement without the SAVE EXCEPTIONS clause.
■ Define an EXCEPTION WHEN OTHERS exception handler with the following logic in it:
   A. Initialize the SQL%BULK_EXCEPTIONS.COUNT to a numeric variable, say num_errors.

B. Trap the error code using

```
SQL%BULK_EXCEPTIONS(num_errors).error_code;
```

and trap the error message using

```
SQLERRM(-SQL%BULK_EXCEPTIONS(num_errors).error_code);
```

Listing 6.4 shows code to illustrate this process.

**LISTING 6.4 USE OF FORALL WITHOUT SAVE EXCEPTIONS
TO TRAP THE ERROR OF THE LAST EXECUTED DML STATEMENT**

```
DECLARE
   Type region_id_tbl IS TABLE of NUMBER INDEX BY BINARY_INTEGER;
   Type region_name_tbl IS TABLE of VARCHAR2(20)
                        INDEX BY BINARY_INTEGER;
   region_ids region_id_tbl;
   region_names region_name_tbl;
   ret_code NUMBER;
   ret_errmsg VARCHAR2(1000);
Procedure load_regions_bulk_bind
        (region_ids IN region_id_tbl,
         region_names IN region_name_tbl,
         retcd OUT NUMBER,
         errmsg OUT VARCHAR2)
IS
 num_errors NUMBER;
BEGIN
  -- clean up the region_tab table initially.
  DELETE FROM region_tab;
  FORALL i IN region_ids.FIRST..region_ids.LAST
     INSERT INTO region_tab values (region_ids(i), region_names(i));
  Retcd := 0;
EXCEPTION WHEN OTHERS THEN
   num_errors := SQL%BULK_EXCEPTIONS.COUNT;
      DBMS_OUTPUT.PUT_LINE('Error while inserting Region Id '||
            regions_ids(SQL%BULK_EXCEPTIONS(num_errors).error_index)
                                      ||' is '||
          SQLERRM(-SQL%BULK_EXCEPTIONS(num_errors).error_code));
   COMMIT;
END;
```

```
BEGIN
  FOR i IN 1..5 LOOP
    Region_ids(i) := i;
    Region_names(i) := 'REGION'||i;
  END LOOP;
  Region_names(3) := 'REGION WITH NAME3';
  Load_regions_bulk_bind(region_ids, region_names, ret_code,
                         ret_errmsg);
EXCEPTION WHEN OTHERS THEN
  RAISE_APPLICATION_ERROR(-20112, SQLERRM);
END;
/
```

Here's the output of the preceding code:

```
Error while inserting Region Id 3 is ORA-01401:
     inserted value too large for column
```

How Do You Use FORALL Statement Attributes SQL%BULK_ROWCOUNT and SQL%ROWCOUNT?

Similar to the implicit cursor attributes, the bulk bind operation has the scalar attributes %FOUND, %NOTFOUND, and %ROWCOUNT associated with it. %ROWCOUNT functions on ALL executions of the SQL statement involving the bulk bind. However, %FOUND and %NOTFOUND refer to the last execution of the SQL statement.

In addition, the implicit cursor (opened by Oracle when the FORALL executes an INSERT, UPDATE, DELETE, or MERGE statement and identified by the keyword SQL) has one more composite attribute, %BULK_ROWCOUNT, which has the semantics of an associative array. Its ith element stores the number of rows processed by the ith execution of a SQL statement. If the ith execution affects no rows, %BULK_ROWCOUNT(i) returns 0.

Using the composite attribute SQL%BULK_ROWCOUNT along with SQL%ROWCOUNT involves the following steps:

1. Define a collection to hold the driving data values of the UPDATE or DELETE statement.
2. Populate the collection.
3. Use the FORALL statement to perform the desired UPDATE or DELETE operation.
4. Perform a COMMIT after the FORALL.

5. Define a loop using the same collection as the driving collection of the FORALL with starting index as 1 and upper bound as the COUNT of the elements in the driving collection. Inside the loop, obtain the number of records affected by the ith iteration of the FORALL using SQL%BULK_ROWCOUNT(i). Note that the subscripts of the FORALL and SQL%BULK_ROWCOUNT should be the same.

6. Outside this loop, obtain the overall count of all iterations of the FORALL using SQL%ROWCOUNT.

The first example involves bulk binds that can be rewritten to use both SQL%BULK_ROWCOUNT and SQL%ROWCOUNT. In Listing 6.5, all the executions in which the SQL statement affected zero rows are tracked. Overall, if no rows are affected, SQL%ROWCOUNT returns 0.

LISTING 6.5 THE DIFFERENCE BETWEEN SQL%BULK_ROWCOUNT AND SQL%ROWCOUNT

```
DECLARE
   Type region_id_tbl IS TABLE of NUMBER INDEX BY BINARY_INTEGER;
   Type region_name_tbl IS TABLE of VARCHAR2(20)
                      INDEX BY BINARY_INTEGER;
   region_ids region_id_tbl;
   region_names region_name_tbl;
   ret_code NUMBER;
   ret_errmsg VARCHAR2(1000);
   Procedure load_regions_bulk_bind
               (region_ids IN region_id_tbl,
                region_names IN region_name_tbl,
                retcd OUT NUMBER,
              errmsg OUT VARCHAR2)
   IS
   BEGIN
     FORALL i IN region_ids.FIRST..region_ids.LAST
       INSERT INTO region_tab values (region_ids(i),
                                  region_names(i));
     FOR i in 1..region_ids.COUNT LOOP
       IF SQL%BULK_ROWCOUNT(i) > 0 THEN
         -- <track this particular execution>
         dbms_output.put_line(to_char(sql%bulk_rowcount(i)));
         NULL;
       END IF;
```

```
      END LOOP;
         IF SQL%ROWCOUNT = 0 THEN
            DBMS_OUTPUT.PUT_LINE('No Rows inserted overall');
         ELSE
            COMMIT;
         END IF;
EXCEPTION WHEN OTHERS THEN
   COMMIT;
   Retcd := SQLCODE;
   Errmsg := SQLERRM;
END;
BEGIN
   region_ids(1) := 6;
   region_names(1) := 'region6';
   load_regions_bulk_bind(region_ids, region_names,
                          ret_code, ret_errmsg);
END;
/
```

TIP

%BULK_ROWCOUNT and the FORALL statement use the same subscripts. %BULK_ROWCOUNT cannot be used as an input value in an assignment statement involving another collection. %BULK_ROWCOUNT cannot be passed as a parameter to subprograms.

Referencing a row in SQL%BULK_ROWCOUNT that is outside the defined subscripts returns a NULL value and will not raise the NO_DATA_FOUND exception. This illustrates the deviation of %BULK_ROWCOUNT from an associative array, although it is similar in semantics to an associative array. Thus, the methods for associative array cannot be applied to %BULK_ROWCOUNT.

When Do You Use SQL%BULK_ROWCOUNT?

The SQL%BULK_ROWCOUNT attribute is useful in the following situations:

- When the DML statement in the FORALL is mostly an UPDATE or a DELETE. In case of an INSERT INTO…VALUES statement, the count is always 1 for each iteration of the FORALL.
- For logging the number of rows affected by each iteration of the FORALL statement.

This section discussed the method of performing bulk DML in PL/SQL. Starting with a discussion of what array processing is, it covered bulk DML using FORALL. It then discussed the exception handling mechanism involved in bulk DML followed by FORALL statement attributes. The next section presents a discussion of bulk DML features involving sparse collections, which is a new feature introduced in Oracle 10g.

BULK DML WITH SPARSE COLLECTIONS

By default, the collection used in a FORALL statement cannot have missing elements. Oracle 10g allows you to use sparse collections with the FORALL statement in two ways:

- By using the INDICES OF clause—Allows a collection with deleted intermediate elements to be a part of FORALL.
- By using the VALUES OF clause—Allows you to create a secondary collection whose element values are the indices of the primary collection.

Using INDICES OF in FORALL

This is an enhancement in Oracle 10g that enables bulk DML using FORALL involving a sparse collection with missing intermediate elements. This is a performance improvement over using SAVE EXCEPTIONS when the driving collection has many missing elements.

To use FORALL with INDICES OF, follow these steps:

1. Define a main collection having missing intermediate elements. This collection is referenced in the FORALL index as well as the DML statement.
2. Code a FORALL statement using the INDICES OF and SAVE EXCEPTIONS clauses with the associated DML statement and the defined collection as the driving collection (that is, both the FORALL index and this DML statement reference the previous collection).
3. Define a pragma EXCEPTION_INIT directive and associate the Oracle error 224381 with a user-defined exception.
4. Code an exception-handling block to handle the declared exception. Within the block, use a FOR loop to iterate from 1 to the value initialized in SQL%BULK_EXCEPTIONS.COUNT and trap the error iteration index using the SQL%BULK_EXCEPTIONS(i).error_index and the error message using SQLERRM(-SQL%BULK_EXCEPTIONS(i).error_code).

To get the element corresponding to the iteration that caused the exception, loop through the elements of the collection to obtain the one corresponding to the SQL%BULK_EXCEPTIONS(i).error_index. Listing 6.6 shows an example.

LISTING 6.6 USE OF FORALL WITH THE INDICES OF CLAUSE

```
DECLARE
  Type region_id_tbl IS TABLE of NUMBER
  INDEX BY BINARY_INTEGER;
  Type region_name_tbl IS TABLE of VARCHAR2(20)
  INDEX BY BINARY_INTEGER;
  region_ids region_id_tbl;
  region_names region_name_tbl;
  ret_code NUMBER;
  ret_errmsg VARCHAR2(1000);
Procedure load_regions_bulk_bind
          (region_ids IN region_id_tbl,
           region_names IN region_name_tbl,
           retcd OUT NUMBER,
           errmsg OUT VARCHAR2)
  IS
  bulk_bind_excep EXCEPTION;
  PRAGMA EXCEPTION_INIT(bulk_bind_excep, -24381);
BEGIN
  -- clean up the region_tab table initially.
  DELETE FROM region_tab;
  FORALL i IN INDICES OF region_ids SAVE EXCEPTIONS
     INSERT INTO region_tab
     values (region_ids(i), region_names(i));
  Retcd := 0;
EXCEPTION WHEN bulk_bind_excep THEN
    FOR i in 1..SQL%BULK_EXCEPTIONS.COUNT LOOP
       DBMS_OUTPUT.PUT_LINE('Iteration '||
          SQL%BULK_EXCEPTIONS(i).error_index||
          ' failed with error '||
          SQLERRM(-SQL%BULK_EXCEPTIONS(i).error_code));
    END LOOP;
    COMMIT;
    Retcd := SQLCODE;
    Errmsg := 'Bulk DML error(s) ';
  WHEN OTHERS THEN
    Retcd := SQLCODE;
```

```
      Errmsg := SQLERRM;
  END;
  BEGIN
    FOR i IN 1..5 LOOP
      Region_ids(i) := i;
      Region_names(i) := 'REGION'||i;
    END LOOP;
    Region_names(3) := 'REGION WITH NAME3';
    Region_ids.DELETE(2);
    Region_names.DELETE(2);
    Load_regions_bulk_bind(region_ids, region_names
                          , ret_code, ret_errmsg);
  EXCEPTION WHEN OTHERS THEN
    RAISE_APPLICATION_ERROR(-20112, SQLERRM);
  END;
  /
```

TIP

A secondary collection can also be used as the driving collection provided its indices match those of the rows in the main collection that has missing elements.

Using VALUES OF in FORALL

The VALUES OF clause is used to process rows in the main collection whose indices match the element values in a secondary collection. This is useful only if a portion of rows in the main collection is needed for the FORALL DML processing. The advantage is that there is no need to copy the required rows and hence the entire record in the main collection into a secondary collection. This saves processing time and memory.

To use FORALL with VALUES OF, follow these steps:

1. Define a secondary collection with the element values as the indices of the required subset of rows of the main collection. This collection becomes the driving collection of the FORALL.
2. Code a FORALL statement using the VALUES OF and SAVE EXCEP-TIONS clauses with the FORALL index referencing this driving collection. The main collection is referenced in the DML statement of the FORALL.
3. Define a pragma EXCEPTION_INIT directive and associate the Oracle error 224381 with a user-defined exception.

4. Code an exception-handling block to handle the declared exception. Within the block, use a FOR loop to iterate from 1 to the value initialized in SQL%BULK_EXCEPTIONS.COUNT and trap the error iteration index using SQL%BULK_EXCEPTIONS(i).error_index and the error message using SQLERRM(-SQL%BULK_EXCEPTIONS(i).error_code).
5. While inside the FOR loop, to get the iteration where the exception occurred, use an inner loop inside this loop and get the value of the element in the secondary collection whose subscript matches SQL%BULK_EXCEPTIONS(i).error_index. Then use this value as the subscript in the original collection.

The error message is still obtained using the following code but should be specified in the inner loop:

```
SQLERRM(-SQL%BULK_EXCEPTIONS(i).error_code)
```

Listing 6.7 shows the code for this process.

LISTING 6.7 USE OF **FORALL** WITH **VALUES OF** CLAUSE

```
DECLARE
  Type region_id_tbl IS TABLE of NUMBER
  INDEX BY BINARY_INTEGER;
  Type region_name_tbl IS TABLE of VARCHAR2(20)
  INDEX BY BINARY_INTEGER;
  Type region_id_sub_tbl IS TABLE of PLS_INTEGER;
  region_ids region_id_tbl;
  region_ids_sub region_id_sub_tbl;
  region_names region_name_tbl;
  ret_code NUMBER;
  ret_errmsg VARCHAR2(1000);
Procedure load_regions_bulk_bind
        (region_ids IN region_id_tbl,
         region_names IN region_name_tbl,
         retcd OUT NUMBER,
         errmsg OUT VARCHAR2)
IS
  bulk_bind_excep EXCEPTION;
  PRAGMA EXCEPTION_INIT(bulk_bind_excep, -24381);
  excep_index BINARY_INTEGER;
  excep_error_code NUMBER;
```

```
BEGIN
  -- clean up the region_tab table initially.
  DELETE FROM region_tab;
  FORALL i IN VALUES OF region_ids_sub SAVE EXCEPTIONS
    INSERT INTO region_tab
    values (region_ids(i), region_names(i));
  Retcd := 0;
EXCEPTION WHEN bulk_bind_excep THEN
  FOR i in 1..SQL%BULK_EXCEPTIONS.COUNT LOOP
   FOR j in region_ids_sub.FIRST..region_ids_sub.LAST
   LOOP
     IF SQL%BULK_EXCEPTIONS(i).error_index = j THEN
       excep_index := region_ids_sub(j);
       excep_error_code :=
          SQL%BULK_EXCEPTIONS(i).error_code;
       DBMS_OUTPUT.PUT_LINE('Iteration '||
          excep_index||' failed with error '||
       SQLERRM(-excep_error_code));
     END IF;
    END LOOP;
   END LOOP;
   COMMIT;
   Retcd := SQLCODE;
   Errmsg := 'Bulk DML error(s) ';
  WHEN OTHERS THEN
   Retcd := SQLCODE;
   Errmsg := SQLERRM;
END;
BEGIN
  FOR i IN 1..5 LOOP
    Region_ids(i) := i;
    Region_names(i) := 'REGION'||i;
  END LOOP;
  Region_names(3) := 'REGION WITH NAME3';
  region_ids_sub := region_id_sub_tbl();
  Region_ids_sub.EXTEND;
  Region_ids_sub(1) := 2;
  Region_ids_sub.EXTEND;
  Region_ids_sub(2) := 3;
  Load_regions_bulk_bind(region_ids, region_names
                   , ret_code, ret_errmsg);
EXCEPTION WHEN OTHERS THEN
  RAISE_APPLICATION_ERROR(-20112, SQLERRM);
END;
/
```

SAVE EXCEPTIONS still needs to be used to continue past row-wise exceptions resulting from the failure of the DML statement, in the cases of both INDICES OF and VALUES OF.

The next section discusses the techniques for bulk querying.

TECHNIQUES FOR BULK QUERYING

Bulk querying refers to the retrieval of rows (usually a large number of rows) into a PL/SQL collection to be used for further processing. This is possible by the uses of both implicit and explicit cursors.

Using an implicit SELECT...INTO when bulk querying involves using the BULK COLLECT clause with the INTO clause.

Here's an example:

```
DECLARE
    t_outtab_type IS TABLE OF input_table%ROWTYPE;
    v_outtab t_outtab_type;
BEGIN
    SELECT *
    BULK COLLECT INTO v_outtab
    FROM    input_table
    WHERE key_col = '<val1>';

    FOR i IN 1..v_outtab.COUNT LOOP
        -- Process the rows one by one according to required logic.
    END LOOP;
END;
/
```

The explicit cursor version of this code involves using the BULK COLLECT clause in the FETCH statement. Here's the code:

```
DECLARE
    t_outtab_type IS TABLE OF input_table%ROWTYPE;
    v_outtab t_outtab_type;
    CURSOR c_in IS
        SELECT *
        FROM    input_table
        WHERE key_col = '<val1>';

BEGIN
    OPEN c_in;
```

```
    FETCH c_in BULK COLLECT INTO v_outtab;

    FOR i IN 1..v_outtab.COUNT LOOP
          -- Process the rows one by one according to required logic.
    END LOOP;

    CLOSE c_in;
END;
/
```

The primary advantages of doing a bulk query are performance, reduced elapsed time, and less amount of latching. However, this comes at an expense of memory if the number of rows fetched is huge (that is, in the hundreds of thousands). The memory limitation can be overcome if the number of rows fetched is limited to a certain value each time they are fetched. This way the entire set of rows can be fetched in multiple sets of this limit value, thus eliminating the need to cache all the rows. This technique is discussed with its pros and cons in the subsection that follows.

Set-at-a-Time Row Retrieval with Bulk Querying

In the context of bulk querying, set-at-a-time row retrieval means fetching the required rows in sets instead of fetching all rows at once. This amounts to limiting the number of rows fetched at a time—that is, in a single fetch—instead of fetching all the rows in a single fetch. This may result in more context switches than when all the rows are fetched in a single fetch but is optimal when the limiting value is correctly specified. An accurate limiting value results in both performance and memory benefits. Here's how this can be achieved:

- Using an explicit cursor and specifying the LIMIT clause in the FETCH...BULK COLLECT statement.
- Using an implicit cursor and specifying the SAMPLE or SAMPLE BLOCK clauses in the INTO clause.

The most accurate way of retrieving all the rows using set-at-a-time processing with bulk query is by using the first method mentioned previously, iteratively in a loop. The second method gives an approximate chunk of rows and relies heavily on the total number and distribution of rows (in the data blocks) of the source table(s). Here are the steps involved in using an explicit cursor with LIMIT:

1. Define a collection corresponding to the output row structure.
2. Define an explicit cursor to select from the source table(s).
3. Define a FETCH...BULK COLLECT INTO...LIMIT statement in a loop to retrieve the rows in sets of the limit value.

Listing 6.8 shows the code for the explicit cursor version of bulk querying presented earlier using the LIMIT clause.

LISTING 6.8 BULK QUERYING WITH THE LIMIT CLAUSE

```
DECLARE
    t_outtab_type IS TABLE OF input_table%ROWTYPE;
    v_outtab t_outtab_type;
    CURSOR c_in IS
        SELECT *
        FROM    input_table
        WHERE key_col = '<val1>';

BEGIN
    OPEN c_in;

    LOOP

        FETCH c_in BULK COLLECT INTO v_outtab LIMIT 100;


        FOR i IN 1..v_outtab.COUNT LOOP
         -- Process the rows one by one according to required logic.
            NULL;
        END LOOP;

        EXIT WHEN c_in%NOTFOUND;

    END LOOP;
    CLOSE c_in;
END;
/
```

The following points are worth noting:

- The limit value affects the performance of the bulk querying. A larger limit value may not always result in the best performance. This is discussed in the subsection that follows.
- The exit condition for the outer cursor loop is specified after the returned rows are processed. This differs from normal explicit cursor loop where the exit condition is coded immediately following the FETCH statement. This is because the %NOTFOUND cursor attribute returns TRUE if the number of rows actually retrieved is less than the limit value. This will result in the remainder of rows in the last chunk not being processed if the EXIT is coded immediately following the FETCH. An alternative way to avoid this is to code the exit condition in the following manner:

```
EXIT WHEN v_outtab.COUNT = 0;
```

This way, it can immediately follow the FETCH.

Choosing the LIMIT Value

The correct value for LIMIT depends on two factors: the number of users involved and the session PGA memory available. A very high limit value increases the session PGA memory significantly, more so, if the number of users is large. An increase in the LIMIT value from 100 to 1000 can increase the memory consumption 4 to 5 times for a single user. A value of 10000 in the same scenario can result in an additional 2 to 3 fold increase from that of a 1000 value. In both cases, the performance indicator in terms of time elapsed is almost same. Choosing the right LIMIT value involves a trade-off between the memory available and scalability in terms of number of users. The following guidelines can help:

- Keep the LIMIT value to a reasonable value, like 100 or 1000. This will still result in optimal performance even when the result set to be retrieved is huge.
- If a higher limit value like 10000 (or for that matter, any value greater than 1000) is desired, check whether the set of rows retrieved in batches is being held for a long time during processing before the next batch is retrieved. If the set of rows is being released very quickly, a value of 10000 *might* work provided scalability is not an issue. Note the phrase *might work*.

The previous guidelines are only an approximation based on test cases. The actual value to be used is best determined using the application environment and resources available.

ARRAY PROCESSING USING DYNAMIC SQL

Array processing using dynamic SQL is best utilized for PL/SQL-centric applications that make use of native dynamic SQL but need to perform bulk DML (bulk binding) or bulk querying operations. This gives the added benefits of using native dynamic SQL in addition to reduced elapsed time, reduced context switching (obtained from bulk DML), and reduced context switching and latching (obtained from bulk querying). Latching is in reference to the physical read operation and ensures that the database block (matching the required data and obtained from the disk) is present in the block buffer cache and that this particular database block containing the data needed is not modified or removed from the buffer cache. Reduction in latching will increase scalability across a large number of users.

There are four methods in which array processing can be implemented with dynamic SQL:

- Using implicit cursors with native dynamic SQL with EXECUTE IMMEDIATE and BULK COLLECT INTO in case of bulk querying.
- Using explicit cursors with native dynamic SQL with FETCH...BULK COLLECT INTO in case of bulk querying.
- Using bulk DML with native dynamic SQL with FORALL. In this case, bulk bound collections can be used in both the USING and RETURNING INTO clauses.
- Using bulk binding and bulk query with DBMS_SQL (and their interoperability with native dynamic SQL), as of Oracle 11g.

Each of these methods is straightforward and does not require any special treatment in regard to coding.

Here's a checklist of points to be kept in mind when using array processing with dynamic SQL:

- Entire records cannot be for bulk binding (bulk DML) in the USING clause when using native dynamic SQL (up to Oracle 10gR2). However, they can be used for bulk querying when using the BULK COLLECT clause.
- Array processing in PL/SQL should be employed with dynamic SQL only when required. Keep in mind the disadvantages of using dynamic SQL, such as greater cost involved and loss of compile-time errors and dependency checking.

SUMMARY

This chapter discussed the various techniques for data management in PL/SQL. Starting with data retrieval, it explored the techniques involved in data manipulation and array processing. The more complex techniques of using array processing in PL/SQL were covered in detail with special reference to static and dynamic SQL. The specific techniques covered include techniques for bulk DML with dense and sparse collections, techniques for bulk querying, and set-at-a-time row retrieval with bulk querying. The next chapter discusses the various techniques involved in application management in PL/SQL.

7
Application Management in PL/SQL

In This Chapter

- Procedures versus functions
- User-defined operators versus functions
- Coding packages to globalize data and code
- Packages versus contexts
- Coding packages to localize data and privatize code
- Coding packages to break dependency chains
- Reading and writing package variables dynamically
- Coding packages to pass data between applications
- Packages versus objects as application structures
- Supplementing data integrity using triggers

Application management deals primarily with segmentation of code into modules stored in the database in the form of procedures, functions, packages, and triggers. This segmentation is based on functional grouping as well as grouping based on design and code relating to better performance and scalability.

Procedures versus Functions

Given the fact that what can be achieved by functions can also be achieved by using procedures with OUT parameters, the reasons for using functions and, for that matter, the reasons for having two separate CREATE PROCEDURE and CREATE FUNCTION "subprogram entities" boil down to the following:

- A coding standards violation that prevents the use of a procedure for returning only one value. A second implication of this is to use procedures only for returning multiple values using OUT parameters, because using OUT parameters with functions again violates such standards. However, this is more concerned with code ethics than code technicality.
- The most invaluable use of a function comes in calling it from SQL. This is where procedures cannot be used and the complexity of logic involved makes it otherwise impossible or impractical to conglomerate such logic into a single query. This mandates the encapsulation of such logic into a function callable from SQL.
- A second use of functions instead of procedures is when using function-based indexes. Using function-based indexes on complex expressions on the left side of WHERE conditions in queries enables the query to use the so-created index, resulting in optimal execution. This is required in data warehousing and business intelligence environments. Another use of function-based indexes relates to the previous point mentioned here.
- A third use of functions over procedures is for simulating datasets using pipelined table functions. Procedures cannot be used for this purpose. A primary use of such datasets is, again, while performing ETL operations in data warehousing and business intelligence applications. This use is discussed in detail in Chapter 11.

The following examples illustrate when a function can be used and a procedure equivalent of the same cannot.

Calling a Function from SQL

First, you create a function as follows:

```
CREATE OR REPLACE FUNCTION f_complex_logic
            (ip_parm1 IN VARCHAR2, ip_parm2 IN NUMBER)
RETURN VARCHAR2
IS
    v_ret_val VARCHAR2(32767);
```

```
BEGIN
    /* Some complex processing logic here */
    RETURN (v_ret_val);
EXCEPTION WHEN OTHERS THEN
    -- Handle exception here and return a null value.
    RETURN (NULL);
END f_complex_logic;
/
```

This function is callable from SQL, for example, from a SELECT statement as follows:

```
SELECT a.*, f_complex_logic(a.dim_cd, a.id) computed_string
FROM   olap_src_tab a;
```

CREATING A FUNCTION-BASED INDEX

The function created in the last section can be used as part of an index to speed up queries involving the function in the LHS of WHERE clauses (by using the index) or to speed up the query calling the function in SQL (by not executing the function again when the calling query is run). Here's the code for creating a function-based index.

First, you recreate the function with the DETERMINISTIC keyword specified. This guarantees that for a particular combination of actual parameter values, the function always returns the same result and is needed for a function to be part of an index.

```
CREATE OR REPLACE FUNCTION f_complex_logic
          (ip_parm1 IN VARCHAR2, ip_parm2 IN NUMBER)
RETURN VARCHAR2 DETERMINISTIC
IS
    v_ret_val VARCHAR2(32767);
BEGIN
    /* Some complex processing logic here */
    RETURN (v_ret_val);
EXCEPTION WHEN OTHERS THEN
    -- Handle exception here and return a null value.
    RETURN (NULL);
END f_complex_logic;
/
```

This function can be used to create a function-based index as follows:

```
CREATE INDEX olap_tab_fb_idx_ON
olap_tab (f_complex_logic(a.dim_cd, a.id));
```

CREATING A TABLE FUNCTION

Here's an example of such a use:

```
SELECT *
FROM   TABLE(f_complex_logic_tbl(CURSOR
            (SELECT * FROM olap_tab)));
```

A detailed explanation of what this is and how it can be used can be found in Chapter 11 in the section "Simulating a Dataset Stage Using Pipelined Table Functions."

USING USER-DEFINED OPERATORS AND FUNCTIONS

User-defined operators are domain-specific operators that can be used as native SQL built-in operators and integrated into the Oracle server. They are another way of defining function-like functionality, especially when the functional logic is complex.

However, there are a few subtle differences between function bindings in operators and user-defined functions:

- The signatures of the bindings of a user-defined operator cannot have OUT or INOUT parameters. A function can have OUT or INOUT parameters in addition to a return value.
- The binding functions of a user-defined operator cannot perform INSERT, UPDATE, or DELETE operations whereas these operations are allowed in regular functions.
- The return value of a user-defined operator or the parameters of the corresponding function cannot be PL/SQL-specific types or a REF type, whereas regular functions can have their return values or their parameters based on these types.
- An operator (and hence the associated binding function) can be used in SQL within PL/SQL only and not in PL/SQL-only code.

When to use user-defined operators is more of a project-specific issue than a technical issue.

- To simulate a complex function (for example, involving bitwise arithmetic) in a way similar to a built-in operator, you can define a user-defined operator. However, for implementing simple functional logic, using an operator would involve an administrative overhead.
- When you're creating pluggable reusable components.

This gives you a way to expose PL/SQL "declaratively" by extending it using operators.

If you want to create a reusable component whose status as either an Oracle built-in or a custom built-in is transparent and seamless to the developer (for example, as part of a template library), you can build your function, place it in a package, and place an operator wrapper around it. Used in this way, the limitations of operators (only IN parameters) actually strengthen the case for their utilization. This operator can then be called from SQL (either standalone SQL or SQL within PL/SQL).

For large projects, you should consider using operators as part of template construction. They can effectively be used to provide developer access to functions that can be safely used within SQL. Although not providing any additional functionality in comparison with functions, operators can assist with the organization of a code library.

Both of these points benefit from the so-achieved tight integration and greater security of operators over functions.

So you might wonder when you should use a function as compared to an operator. An operator is simply a way of calling a function. There is no place where you can use an operator where you couldn't use a function just as well. But the vice-versa is not true, especially taking into account the fourth difference mentioned previously. These differences place a restriction on the use of operators for creating "custom built-ins" and this is where functions have to be used for the purpose. Although not as transparent in their use compared to operators, these are the only choice in this case.

CODING PACKAGES TO GLOBALIZE DATA AND CODE

The definition of a PL/SQL package involves defining two separate components: the package specification that houses the declarations like variables, PL/SQL types, and subprogram headers and the package body that provides the actual implementation details of these subprograms. Packages are subdivided into two components—the package specification and the package body—for a very specialized reason. This reason is to use packages for globalization of data and code. Any data structures and subprograms placed in a package specification are accessible to external programs, that is, code that resides outside of the particular package body. In particular, all variables so declared act as "public" or "global" variables that can be accessed by all other applications having execute privilege on this package. However, the scope of "global" is limited to (at most) the current session only. This means the data held in each of these globals is per session. This can be relaxed to remain persistent only for the duration of the call by making the package serially reusable.

Now what about the subprogram headers defined in the package specification? The session limitation of data doesn't apply to these. However, the phrase "globalize code" is restrictive to the accessibility of these subprograms by code outside of the current package. This is different from the centralization of code provided by invoker rights programs. In fact these are two different scenarios. In the case of the former, the reference is to the accessibility and thus related to semantic checking. In the latter case, one copy of code resides in the database that can be invoked by multiple user-schemas. This code can still be part of a package. The difference is how the code is executed and where the output of the code is created.

This globalization of code comes with two primary advantages:

- Referencing application programs need not be recompiled only when the package body is recompiled.
- This breaks the dependency chain by eliminating cascading invalidations by placing dependent subprograms in a package instead of creating them as standalone. The technique of using packages to provide this advantage is discussed in a subsequent section.

There are two caveats to be mentioned in regard to this globalization:

- The public variables defined in the package specification are persistent only for the duration of the session. However, they can be made to last for the duration of the database call by declaring the package as serially reusable.
- They form the "runtime state" of the package.

A level of information hiding is thus provided as follows:

- The code has been made "public" only in terms of its ability to call the packaged subprograms hiding their implementation details from referencing application programs and hence from other application developers other than its definer.
- If the package source code is kept unavailable by wrapping (or obfuscating) it into a PL/SQL binary, both these public data structures and subprograms are unavailable to other programmers.

PACKAGES VERSUS CONTEXTS AND GLOBALIZING DATA

The difference between packages and application contexts is best demonstrated when using global variables (or global constants). Application contexts as referred to here pertain to session-specific application contexts. In this case, both a package specification and a database context can be used to set and get the values of the globals. When to use what is largely a trade-off between the usage/maintenance of the globals and the performance achieved. The former is an issue when there are numerous programs that reference these globals and there is a frequent need to add/modify/delete them. This in turn requires the package specification to be changed that results in the dependency issue of cascading invalidations. The latter is a concern when the globals are being referenced in PL/SQL-only statements. Here's a list of guidelines to follow when choosing between the two:

- Use SYS_CONTEXT for writing and reading global variables over packages if the number of subprograms referencing such globals are large and there is no need for frequent maintenance operations on these. This facilitates addition and update of globals as contexts insulate the application from dependency issues that arise when using packages. The package spec has to be changed if a new global is added or the value of an existing global is changed, thus necessitating recompilation of both the global package spec and all its dependent application programs.
- Use SYS_CONTEXT if the global variables need to be used from within SQL in PL/SQL. This statement holds true even if a single global is being referenced multiple times from multiple programs.

This is because the use of contexts comes with a performance cost when not used in pure SQL due to increased executions. Each call to SYS_CONTEXT performs a SELECT...FROM SYS.DUAL. This results in a recursive query to the database if it is called from PL/SQL, resulting in multiple re-executions to get the value of the same global each time the global is referenced. So do not use SYS_CONTEXT for accessing global variables (that are frequently needed) from within pure PL/SQL. If SQL is the only place where these globals are to be used, an application control table is a good place to store them. By this, I mean that this SQL is not called within PL/SQL.

Using contexts over packages is advantageous in terms of intersession sharing of these globals by means of global contexts created as follows:

```
CREATE OR REPLACE CONTEXT appl_cxt USING pkg_appl_cxt
        ACCESSED GLOBALLY;
```

Packages enable intra-session sharing of global data only. Note that, although packaged global variables or constants can be referenced by many sessions, the data held by these globals is scoped for a particular session only.

CODING PACKAGES TO LOCALIZE DATA AND PRIVATIZE CODE

This comes as a complement to using packages for globalization of data and code. In an earlier section, you saw how data structures and subprograms defined as part of package specification are "global" in nature and also saw how and in what way they were global. Additionally, a package can also be used to localize data and privatize code. Any data structures and subprograms defined only in the package body are "local" to that package and cannot be referenced by external programs, that is, other than code in this package. In this way, data is localized by means of variables defined in the packaged body. The code is privatized because it's defined in and accessible only to code in this package body and hence "known" only to the definer of this package.

This provides a more granular level of information hiding in two ways:

- The code has been made "private" in a way by hiding its definition as well as its implementation from referencing application programs.
- If the package source code is kept unavailable by wrapping (or obfuscating) it into a PL/SQL binary, these "private" data structures and subprograms are unavailable to other programmers without proper access.

There are two caveats to be mentioned in regard to this localization:

- The private variables defined only in the package body are still persistent for the duration of the session.
- They do contribute to the runtime state of the package.

CODING PACKAGES TO BREAK THE DEPENDENCY CHAIN

Using packages to break the dependency chain is foremost of the advantages of the real use of packages. As of Oracle 10g Release 2, changes to a standalone procedure or function that necessitated its recompilation mandated the recompilation of all other subprogram units that were dependent on them. This is disadvantageous for two reasons:

- Applications consisting of hundreds of dependent subprograms became invalid due to the recompilation of the particular procedure or function on which they all were dependent. This needed all of these subprograms to be recompiled manually, or automatically when the individual subprograms were called. The latter case is mainly a type of "on-demand" recompilation that occurred only when the dependent subprogram was invoked the next time. However, this recompiled that particular subprogram only (and its dependents down the chain). All others were still left invalid.

- This reason comes as a direct consequence of the previous point. Recompilation is resource-intensive in terms of parsing, redo allocation, CPU usage, and execution time.

This dependency of cascading invalidations is true even when a package specification is changed and multiple application subprograms reference this package. The invalidated objects all along the dependency chain can be recompiled programmatically by using the API in the UTL_RECOMP package (as of Oracle 10g).

Excessive recompilations could be reduced in Oracle 11g with fine-grained dependency tracking where only the subprogram being recompiled and its immediate dependent subprogram in the whole chain were rendered invalid. However, even though it reduced excessive recompilations to a large extent, still the presence of this problem is conspicuous when even a single subprogram that needs to be recompiled due to changes in this body is being referenced by multiple (and a large number of) independent subprograms. This resulted in excessive recompilation (even though the amount of excessiveness was less than in Oracle 10g).

The use of packages eliminates this dependency overhead if each of the stand-alone procedures or functions is placed in a package, either individually one-to-one or all of them collectively in a single package, *as long as the package specification is not changed.* The primary reason for packages to be able to break the dependency chain is that a package is exposed to the calling environment by means of its specification only (one of the reasons for having a package specification and body separately). As long as the specification remains unchanged, any number of changes to the logic of the individual procedures/functions doesn't impact any of the referencing application programs. This in turns prevents cascading invalidations in the dependency chain.

To start with, you create two procedures, p_A and p_B, and a function, f_C. p_B calls p_A and f_C calls both p_A and p_B.

Listing 7.1 shows the code for this.

LISTING 7.1   STANDALONE PROCEDURES CANNOT BREAK THE DEPENDENCY CHAIN:
PROCEDURE CREATION AND OBJECT STATUS VERIFICATION

```
CREATE OR REPLACE PROCEDURE p_A(ip_A IN OUT NUMBER)
IS
BEGIN
    ip_A := ip_A*2;
END;
/

CREATE OR REPLACE PROCEDURE p_B(ip_B  IN OUT VARCHAR2)
IS
    v_A NUMBER := 10;
BEGIN
    p_A(v_A);
    ip_B := 'This is just A: '||TO_CHAR(v_A);
END p_B;
/

CREATE OR REPLACE FUNCTION f_C RETURN VARCHAR2
IS
    v_A NUMBER;
    v_B VARCHAR2(30);
BEGIN
    p_A(v_A);
    P_b(v_B);
    RETURN (v_A||' '||v_B);
END f_C;
/
```

Here's the SQL to verify this process:

```
SQL> WITH
  2  oqry AS
  3  (SELECT object_type, object_name , status
  4   FROM   user_objects
  5   WHERE  object_name in ('P_A', 'P_B', 'F_C'))
  6  SELECT b.name, (SELECT object_type
  7                  FROM   oqry
  8                  WHERE  object_name = b.name) type,
  9                 (SELECT status
 10                  FROM   oqry
 11                  WHERE  object_name = b.name) status,
 12          b.referenced_name
```

```
13  FROM    user_dependencies b
14  WHERE   name IN ('P_A', 'P_B', 'F_C')
15  ORDER BY DECODE(b.name, 'P_A', b.name, NULL),
16           DECODE(b.name, 'P_B', b.name, NULL),
17           DECODE(b.name, 'F_C',  b.name, NULL)
18  /
```

```
NAME               TYPE               STATUS  REFERENCED_NAME
-----------  ----  ----------------   -----   -----------
P_A                PROCEDURE          VALID   STANDARD
P_B                PROCEDURE          VALID   P_A
P_B                PROCEDURE          VALID   STANDARD
F_C                FUNCTION           VALID   P_A
F_C                FUNCTION           VALID   P_B
F_C                FUNCTION           VALID   STANDARD

6 rows selected.
```

Next, let's change the body of procedure p_A. Here's the code for this change:

```
CREATE OR REPLACE PROCEDURE p_A(ip_A IN OUT NUMBER)
IS
BEGIN
    ip_A := ip_A*2*3;
END;
/
```

Now check the status of each of the procedures/functions. Here's the code for this:

```
SQL> WITH
  2  oqry AS
  3  (SELECT object_type, object_name , status
  4   FROM   user_objects
  5   WHERE  object_name in ('P_A', 'P_B', 'F_C'))
  6  SELECT b.name, (SELECT object_type
  7                   FROM   oqry
  8                   WHERE  object_name = b.name) type,
  9                  (SELECT status
 10                   FROM   oqry
 11                   WHERE  object_name = b.name) status,
 12           b.referenced_name
 13  FROM   user_dependencies b
 14  WHERE  name IN ('P_A', 'P_B', 'F_C')
 15  ORDER BY DECODE(b.name, 'P_A', b.name, NULL),
```

```
16              DECODE(b.name, 'P_B', b.name, NULL),
17              DECODE(b.name, 'F_C',  b.name, NULL)
18  /

NAME            TYPE             STATUS    REFERENCED_NAME
-----------  ---- ---------------- -----   -----------
P_A             PROCEDURE        VALID     STANDARD
P_B             PROCEDURE        INVALID   P_A
P_B             PROCEDURE        INVALID   STANDARD
F_C             FUNCTION         INVALID   P_A
F_C             FUNCTION         INVALID   P_B
F_C             FUNCTION         INVALID   STANDARD


6 rows selected.
```

As is evident, a small change to p_A resulted in (cascading) invalidations of p_B and f_C. This type of behavior comes at a huge cost when the code is running in a production environment consisting of a significantly large dependency chain. To overcome the problem, you can encapsulate the procedure in a package and test the same scenario.

Listing 7.2 shows the code for this encapsulation.

LISTING 7.2   STANDALONE PROCEDURES CANNOT BREAK THE DEPENDENCY CHAIN: PACKAGED-PROCEDURE CREATION, ALTERATION, AND RECOMPILATION; AND OBJECT STATUS VERIFICATION

```
ALTER PROCEDURE p_B COMPILE;
ALTER FUNCTION  f_C COMPILE;
CREATE OR REPLACE PACKAGE pkg_cd_tracking IS

    PROCEDURE p_A(ip_A IN OUT NUMBER);

END pkg_cd_tracking;
/

CREATE OR REPLACE PACKAGE BODY pkg_cd_tracking IS

    PROCEDURE p_A(ip_A IN OUT NUMBER)
    IS
    BEGIN
        ip_A := ip_A*2;
    END p_A;
```

```
END pkg_cd_tracking;
/

SQL> WITH
  2   oqry AS
  3   (SELECT object_type, object_name , status
  4    FROM   user_objects
  5    WHERE  object_name in ('PKG_CD_TRACKING', 'P_B', 'F_C'))
  6   SELECT b.name, (SELECT object_type
  7                   FROM   oqry
  8                   WHERE  object_name = b.name
  9                   AND    object_type = b.type) type,
 10                  (SELECT status
 11                   FROM   oqry
 12                   WHERE  object_name = b.name
 13                   AND    object_type = b.type) status,
 14          b.referenced_name, b.referenced_type
 15   FROM   user_dependencies b
 16   WHERE  name IN ('PKG_CD_TRACKING', 'P_B', 'F_C')
 17   ORDER BY DECODE(b.name, 'PKG_CD_TRACKING', b.name, NULL),
 18           DECODE(b.name, 'P_B', b.name, NULL),
 19           DECODE(b.name, 'F_C',  b.name, NULL)
 20   /
```

NAME	TYPE	STATUS	REFERENCED_NAME	REFERENCED_TYPE
PKG_CD_TRACKING	PACKAGE BODY	VALID	STANDARD	PACKAGE
PKG_CD_TRACKING	PACKAGE	VALID	STANDARD	PACKAGE
PKG_CD_TRACKING	PACKAGE BODY	VALID	PKG_CD_TRACKING	PACKAGE
P_B	PROCEDURE	VALID	STANDARD	PACKAGE
P_B	PROCEDURE	VALID	P_A	PROCEDURE
F_C	FUNCTION	VALID	P_B	PROCEDURE
F_C	FUNCTION	VALID	P_A	PROCEDURE
F_C	FUNCTION	VALID	STANDARD	PACKAGE

```
8 rows selected.

CREATE OR REPLACE PACKAGE BODY pkg_cd_tracking IS

    PROCEDURE p_A(ip_A IN OUT NUMBER)
    IS
    BEGIN
        ip_A := ip_A*2*3;
```

```
      END p_A;

END pkg_cd_tracking;
/
SQL> WITH
  2  oqry AS
  3  (SELECT object_type, object_name , status
  4   FROM    user_objects
  5   WHERE   object_name in ('PKG_CD_TRACKING', 'P_B', 'F_C'))
  6  SELECT b.name, (SELECT object_type
  7                    FROM    oqry
  8                    WHERE   object_name = b.name
  9                    AND     object_type = b.type) type,
 10                 (SELECT status
 11                    FROM    oqry
 12                    WHERE   object_name = b.name
 13                    AND     object_type = b.type) status,
 14            b.referenced_name, b.referenced_type
 15  FROM    user_dependencies b
 16  WHERE   name IN ('PKG_CD_TRACKING', 'P_B', 'F_C')
 17  ORDER BY DECODE(b.name, 'PKG_CD_TRACKING', b.name, NULL),
 18           DECODE(b.name, 'P_B', b.name, NULL),
 19           DECODE(b.name, 'F_C',  b.name, NULL)
 20  /
```

NAME	TYPE	STATUS	REFERENCED_NAME	REFERENCED_TYPE
PKG_CD_TRACKING	PACKAGE BODY	VALID	STANDARD	PACKAGE
PKG_CD_TRACKING	PACKAGE	VALID	STANDARD	PACKAGE
PKG_CD_TRACKING	PACKAGE BODY	VALID	PKG_CD_TRACKING	PACKAGE
P_B	PROCEDURE	VALID	STANDARD	PACKAGE
P_B	PROCEDURE	VALID	P_A	PROCEDURE
F_C	FUNCTION	VALID	P_B	PROCEDURE
F_C	FUNCTION	VALID	P_A	PROCEDURE
F_C	FUNCTION	VALID	STANDARD	PACKAGE

```
8 rows selected.
```

What a magnificent result! Just moving the standalone procedure p_A to a packaged procedure did the job (and saved a lot of time and cost to the development/DBA team as well as a lot of screaming from the users!).

TIP

Using a single package or separate packages makes no difference as long as the application requirement is not affected, because it is always important that the package specification not be changed frequently.

Breaking the dependency chain of packages is useful as long as the function is re-executed in the calling environment. This is most often the case in a production-environment scenario for an OLTP system. However, in certain cases, the function return value may be stored after the first execution as when the function involved is being called in the SELECT of a view that in turn is the input for a materialized view (MV) query with fast refresh or when using function-based indexes. If the function involved is placed in a package and the function logic is changed, these dependent objects are not invalidated or made unusable. Unless the MV is refreshed or the index is re-built, the final queries may be incorrect in the data they return.

READING AND WRITING PACKAGE VARIABLES DYNAMICALLY

The need to write and read global variables dynamically arises when these variables have to be created dynamically, meaning the number of global variables to be created is not known at programming time. This means the names of the global variables are generated dynamically. The final step is to place all of these dynamically generated globals in a package specification. Once this has been done, referencing application programs have to set (write) and get (read) these globals. That is why these globals have been generated in the first place. This so-called dynamic read and write when the name of the global variable is unknown at compile-time can be achieved by using native dynamic SQL. The implementation is by means of a package with a procedure to write the value of the dynamic global and a function to read (return) the value of the same.

Here are the steps involved for writing and reading global variables dynamically:

■ Create a packaged procedure that takes two VARCHAR2 input parameters, the former representing the *name* of the dynamic global variable and the latter containing the actual value to be written to this variable. A dynamic PL/SQL block executed using native dynamic SQL sets the value to the dynamic global.

■ Create a packaged function that takes a VARCHAR2 input parameter holding the *name* of the dynamic global whole value that is to be read. A dynamic PL/SQL block executed, using a bind variable, returns the value of the dynamic global.

Listing 7.3 shows the code for this process.

LISTING 7.3 PACKAGE THAT WRITES AND READS GLOBAL VARIABLES DYNAMICALLY

```
CREATE OR REPLACE PACKAGE pkg_dyn_global
    AUTHID CURRENT_USER
IS
    PROCEDURE p_write (ip_var_name IN VARCHAR2,
                       ip_write_val IN VARCHAR2);
    FUNCTION f_read (ip_var_name IN VARCHAR2) RETURN VARCHAR2;
END pkg_dyn_global;
/

CREATE OR REPLACE PACKAGE BODY pkg_dyn_global
IS

    PROCEDURE p_write (ip_var_name IN VARCHAR2,
                       ip_write_val IN VARCHAR2)
    IS
        dyn_plsql_string VARCHAR2(32767);
    BEGIN
        dyn_plsql_string :=
        'BEGIN ' ||ip_var_name|| ' := '''||ip_write_val||'''; END;';
        EXECUTE IMMEDIATE dyn_plsql_string;
    EXCEPTION WHEN OTHERS THEN
        DBMS_OUTPUT.PUT_LINE('Writing to variable
            '||ip_var_name||' failed with error '||SQLERRM);
        RAISE;
    END p_write;

    FUNCTION f_read (ip_var_name IN VARCHAR2) RETURN VARCHAR2
    IS
        v_dyn_plsql_string VARCHAR2(32767);
        v_ret_val VARCHAR2(32767);
    BEGIN
        v_dyn_plsql_string :=
        'BEGIN :1 := ' ||ip_var_name || '; END;';
        EXECUTE IMMEDIATE v_dyn_plsql_string USING OUT v_ret_val;
        RETURN (v_ret_val);
    EXCEPTION WHEN OTHERS THEN
        DBMS_OUTPUT.PUT_LINE('Reading variable '||ip_var_name||'
                             failed with error '||SQLERRM);
```

```
        RAISE;
    END f_read;


END pkg_dyn_global;
/
```

Listing 7.4 shows the code for testing the previous package.

LISTING 7.4 PACKAGE FOR WRITING AND READING GLOBAL VARIABLES DYNAMICALLY

```
CREATE OR REPLACE PACKAGE pkg_test_dyn_global
IS
    global_var1 VARCHAR2(1000);
    global_var2 DATE;
    global_var3 NUMBER;
END pkg_test_dyn_global;
/

DECLARE
    x vARCHAR2(1000);
    y DATE;
    z NUMBER;
BEGIN
    pkg_test_dyn_global.global_var1 := 'ABC1';
    pkg_test_dyn_global.global_var2 := '23-JUL-67';
    pkg_test_dyn_global.global_var3 := 15;
    x := pkg_dyn_global.f_read('pkg_test_dyn_global.global_var1');
    y := pkg_dyn_global.f_read('pkg_test_dyn_global.global_var2');
    z := pkg_dyn_global.f_read('pkg_test_dyn_global.global_var3');
    DBMS_OUTPUT.PUT_LINE(x||' '||TO_CHAR(y)||' '||TO_CHAR(z));

    x := 'pkg_test_dyn_global.global_var1';
    pkg_dyn_global.p_write('pkg_test_dyn_global.global_var1', 'ABC1');
    DBMS_OUTPUT.PUT_LINE(pkg_test_dyn_global.global_var1);

    pkg_dyn_global.p_write(x, 'ABC2');
    DBMS_OUTPUT.PUT_LINE(pkg_test_dyn_global.global_var1);

EXCEPTION WHEN OTHERS THEN
    DBMS_OUTPUT.PUT_LINE(SQLERRM);
END;
/
```

```
ABC1 23-JUL-67 15
ABC1
ABC2

PL/SQL procedure successfully completed.
```

The following points are worth noting:

- A direct literal value or a variable holding a direct literal value cannot be used as an argument for the ip_var_name parameter. This is because the dynamic PL/SQL block being executed within each of the p_write and f_read subprograms expects either a variable whole value as the *name* of the dynamic global or the actual *name* of the dynamic global enclosed in single quotes.
- The previous package kind of deals with data about data, that is, the value of a variable whose *name* is contained in another variable.

CODING PACKAGES TO PASS DATA BETWEEN APPLICATIONS

Often there is a requirement to pass data between applications that are composed of integrated modules with data from one module as input to another module. Retrieval of the same data each time it is required (by different modules) is a time- and memory-consuming process that impacts the performance of the application. If this data were re-used, either by passing or sharing, the downtime is reduced further down the line. PL/SQL has the following ways of passing data between applications:

- Using cursor variables
- Using collections

Both collections as well as cursor variables can be used for passing data between PL/SQL programs and between PL/SQL and client programs. The most obvious implementation is to use packaged procedures and/or functions.

The method of using each of these ways has been well described in the Oracle PL/SQL documentation as well as in my previous book (see Chapters 5 and 11 of my earlier book, *Oracle 9i PL/SQL: A Developer's Guide*, ISBN: 978-1-59059-049-2). Here, this is discussed from the perspective of application management with special reference to the optimality of the use of the same.

USING CURSOR VARIABLES

Cursor variables are variables in PL/SQL of type REF CURSOR or SYS_REFCUR-SOR (as of Oracle 9i). Essentially, a cursor variable is a pointer to a cursor result-set. The pointer, but not the SELECT query associated with it, is static. However, whether the resultset is static or not depends on how the cursor variable is used. Cursor variables introduce some amount of dynamism in query execution in the sense that they allow multiple queries to be associated with a single cursor variable and allow multiple programs to reference the same query resultset associated with a single cursor variable. Cursor variables can be used to pass data between applications in the following ways:

■ As procedure OUT parameters or function return values
■ As table-function input parameters (in default IN mode)

The following sections discuss using each method.

Using Cursor Variables as OUT Parameters or Function Return Values

When used this way, cursor variables are declared as of SYS_REFCURSOR data type or of TYPE REF CURSOR, opened for a SELECT query, and returned as function return value. Note that a pointer to a resultset, not the actual data (that is, rows) in the resultset, is passed.

Using Cursor Variables as Table-Function IN Parameters

When used this way, cursor variables are passed as arguments to IN parameters of type SYS_REFCURSOR. This provides flexibility in the implementation of table functions. This is described in the subsection that follows.

USING COLLECTIONS

Collections have been a boon to database developers since their inception and their use has solved many intricate problems that were otherwise complicated to code. Examples include array processing (in both SQL and PL/SQL), inducing some kind of dynamism in handling variable lists (in SQL), and of course, passing data between applications.

Collections in PL/SQL are typically in-memory structures that enable storage of data in the form of (multi-dimensional) arrays. However, this use comes at a cost of memory usage that is architecture-dependent. This is in addition to processing cost. Collections can typically be used in the following ways to pass data between applications:

- As a function or procedure OUT or (IN OUT) parameter.
- As an intermediate pool of data (in-memory) while streaming data between inter-related processes and finally delivered to a target location. This involves using table functions, in which case they are used as a function return value.

The following sections include the details of using each method.

Using Collections as OUT or IN OUT Parameters

When used this way, collections are passed using a call-by value that impacts performance if the collection is large. Using the NOCOPY hint provides a workaround for this, when the parameter is passed by reference, but has the disadvantage of indeterminate parameter values in case of exceptions.

Using Collections as Part of Table Functions

This is a viable option when the incoming data needs to be transformed and streamed to a target location. This involves a function that takes the incoming data as a REF CURSOR parameter, applies processing logic to each record, and outputs the transformed record(s) as a collection via the function return value. Mostly, the streaming is done on a record-by-record basis, by applying a technique called *pipelining*, wherein the input dataset is processed record by record. This means the retrieve-transform-deliver processing chain is done incrementally without having the entire function to complete execution and also without having to materialize the entire output dataset. However, the retrieval process can be optimized by employing bulk set-at-a-time array processing. This implementation of combining bulk array processing with pipelining provides optimal performance in terms of both execution time and memory consumption. Note that the incoming data is "streamed" row-by-row and not "loaded" in its entirety using this technique.

The outputted collection can be queried as an inline view in a SELECT…FROM clause that can directly be used to perform DML to the target location. This integration with SQL gives it added flexibility for its use in PL/SQL. Also, the table function can be parallel-enabled to further enhance its performance.

Sharing Data Using Collections versus Sharing Data Using REF CURSORS

When to use collections and when to use cursor variables for sharing data is dependent on the application architecture, the amount of data returned, and how the data needs to be shared. Here's a brief checklist of when to use each technique:

- Use collections when passing data between PL/SQL programs, especially when done frequently. Use the OUT parameter approach if the dataset is small or of reasonably medium size.

- Use cursor variables when passing huge datasets. Also, use this approach when passing data between PL/SQL and non-Oracle applications like Java applications, in a .Net environment, or for the presentation layer employing GUI tools. In the latter case, collections can be used, but this involves a large overhead in terms of type checking, data structure mappings, data translations, and call overhead.
- Use cursor variables to take advantage of the dynamism provided by them. This allows for passing multi-type data using a cursor variable. For example, the same cursor variable can pass numeric data from one module and character data to another depending on certain criteria. This cannot be done using collections and also reduces the number of such variables needed, thus reducing the overhead involving cursor processing such as extra parsing and memory.
- Use pipelined table functions when there is a need not to load data in its entirety, but instead when data needs to be streamed on a row-by-row basis. This approach can also be used to pass huge datasets between PL/SQL programs (when combined with bulk array processing). A good example of streaming is eliminating intermediate tables in ETL processing.
- A second use of table functions is when there is a requirement to funnel multiple output rows from a single input row. In this case, using table functions is an optimal choice.
- A third use of table functions is when there is a need to return the first n rows from an input dataset involving complex transformations that otherwise cannot use direct SQL. This makes it somewhat similar to getting the FIRST n ROWS in a SQL SELECT statement.
- Use collections when passing data between applications accessing remote databases. In such a case, cursor variables cannot be used.

The optimal use of collections and cursor variables is also dependent on at least two other factors:

- What other PL/SQL features are being used in combination with them, such as dynamic SQL, array processing and dynamic array processing, definer and invoker rights, and parallel processing. An example of one such combination is when using collections and cursor variables with bulk querying, as has been stated earlier.
- Whether the stored subprogram used in passing data is being called from SQL or not.

Each of these factors contribute to the impact of such use in terms of performance and scalability. In fact, data sharing and code sharing is one side of the equation. The other side of the equation is how the SQL used to access the data is shared. This adds a performance benefit to the application. Again, each of these two points relate directly or indirectly to decide this SQL sharing.

PACKAGES VERSUS OBJECTS AS APPLICATION STRUCTURES

The use of packages versus objects as application structures is based on the design as well as on the technical functionality of each of them. Here's a list of caveats that can help you decide when to use what:

■ Packages are purely application structures that are stored inside the database as "active" code. They cannot be part of any DDL. Objects, on the other hand, are based on object types that are essentially data structures that combine together methods that operate on those data. In this way an object type can be part of a DDL for a database table or collection. This brings a declarative and seamless integration of data and code into the database in the case of object types. Thus, using objects over packages involves an extra overhead—administrative, programmatic, and processing—in terms of accessing its members and methods.

■ Individual subprograms in a single package can be referenced in any order as long as its dependents are available. This is not always true in the case of object methods that mandate order in certain cases when they are defined as per the OPP paradigm.

■ Although the advantages of globalization and localization of data and code are also provided by object types, the one advantage of breaking the dependency chain is particular to packages only. This is a primary factor in choosing between the two.

■ There are certain rules and restrictions as to how data variables defined in one object type can be accessed in another.

■ As a rule of thumb, use packages for coding applications that are purely code-based and database-definition independent. This way, the package can be used as a template or to simulate a code library. Use object types as data structures combining code that can be used for OO design and coding. Although they offer some flexibility over packages in terms of code reuse, the cons of using them as mentioned in the previous list is a negative factor in using them primarily for providing "public" and "private" use.

SUPPLEMENTING DATA INTEGRITY USING TRIGGERS

Data integrity that cannot be controlled declaratively is most often implemented using database triggers. Examples include row-wise validations, access-control mechanisms, and preserving data across parent-child relationships. Special cases of maintaining consistent data parent-child tables are those of DELETE CASCADE and UPDATE CASCADE. DELETE CASCADE refers to automatic deletion of child rows when a parent row is deleted and can be specified declaratively using foreign keys. UPDATE CASCADE functionality refers to the automatic update of the primary key in a child table when the corresponding primary key in a parent table is updated. Pre-Oracle 8i, this posed a challenge to PL/SQL developers with the mutating table effect preventing the child row from being updated after updating the parent row in case the parent and child rows were linked by a foreign key (that is most often the case).

As the mutating table error due to constraining table effect no longer occurs as of Oracle 8i, an AFTER UPDATE row-level trigger can be defined on the parent table to implement update cascade functionality. This section highlights the implementation of an UPDATE CASCADE functionality to preserve data integrity between parent and child tables. This eliminates the need to delegate the same task to the front-end application or to have to control it otherwise.

Listing 7.5 shows the code for implementing UPDATE CASCADE functionality.

LISTING 7.5   IMPLEMENTING UPDATE CASCADE FUNCTIONALITY

```
CREATE TABLE parent (id NUMBER PRIMARY KEY,
                     descr VARCHAR2(20) NOT NULL);

CREATE TABLE child (id NUMBER PRIMARY KEY,
                    descr VARCHAR2(20) NOT NULL,
                    parent_id NUMBER NOT NULL REFERENCES parent(id));

INSERT INTO parent VALUES (10, 'Parent 10');

INSERT INTO child VALUES (101, 'Child 101', 10);
INSERT INTO child VALUES (102, 'Child 102', 10);
INSERT INTO child VALUES (103, 'Child 103', 10);

CREATE OR REPLACE TRIGGER trg_update_cascade
AFTER UPDATE ON parent
FOR EACH ROW
```

```
BEGIN
  UPDATE child SET parent_id = :NEW.id WHERE parent_id = :OLD.id;
END;
/
```

Now issuing an UPDATE statement on the parent statement to update the id column cascades the new value of id to the child table parent_id column. Here's the code to demonstrate this process:

```
SQL> SELECT * FROM parent;

        ID DESCR
---------- -----------------
        10 Parent 10

SQL> SELECT * FROM child;

        ID DESCR                 PARENT_ID
---------- -------------------- ----------
       101 Child 101                    10
       102 Child 102                    10
       103 Child 103                    10

SQL> UPDATE parent SET id = 1001 WHERE id = 10;

1 row updated.

SQL> SELECT * FROM parent;

        ID DESCR
---------- --------------------
      1001 Parent 10

SQL> SELECT * FROM child;

        ID DESCR                 PARENT_ID
---------- -------------------- ----------
       101 Child 101                  1001
       102 Child 102                  1001
       103 Child 103                  1001
```

Pre-Oracle 8i, the update statement would have caused a mutating table error as follows:

```
ORA-04091: table NEWUSER.PARENT is mutating,
           trigger/function may not see it
```

SUMMARY

This chapter described application management techniques in PL/SQL. Starting with the notion of the so-appearing redundancy issue of both procedure and function existence and why functions have a special role to play, it touched upon the use of user-defined operators versus functions and the indispensable role of packages in application coding. The chapter covered the multi-faceted uses for packages such as globalizing data and code, localizing data and privatizing code, and breaking the dependency chain. Finally, a brief comparison between packages and objects as application structures was presented. The next chapter deals with techniques for transaction management in PL/SQL that covers asynchronous COMMIT and techniques for using autonomous transactions and auditing queries and using DDL in PL/SQL.

8

Transaction Management in PL/SQL

Transaction management deals primarily with the commit and rollback of DML. Related to this process is the locking issue involved while performing DML. This chapter highlights the techniques involved in transaction management in detail.

Asynchronous **COMMIT**

A normal COMMIT of a transaction (involving single or multiple DML statements) consists of two primary steps:

1. Writing the changed data back to the database table. This is also called posting.
2. Making the data posted persistent or permanent until a subsequent change (on the same data). This second step essentially involves writing a redo-log entry of the changes to the redo-log buffer (residing in memory) and the subsequent transfer of the changes from the buffer onto the actual redo-log files (residing on disk).

The process of COMMIT-ing in this manner is synchronous in the sense that control is transferred back to the calling environment only *after* both of the steps have been completed. So far, so good. However, this takes some extra time due to the second step. The time delay is acceptable in most transactional applications, given the fact that the success signal for the COMMIT operation is provided only when the whole COMMIT operation is successful. However, the redo-log entry process is needed only if the database is recovery-based. For applications that can do away with recovery, the second step is not required. This gives rise to the notion of the *asynchronous COMMIT*.

Asynchronous COMMIT relaxes the time delay by releasing the control of the COMMIT operation to the calling environment after posting the changed data. The changes are still written to a redo-log, but control is released after the completion of the first step and the outcome of the COMMIT is signaled back.

In order to use asynchronous COMMIT, you simply specify the COMMIT followed by WRITE IMMEDIATE NOWAIT, as follows:

```
BEGIN
    INSERT......;
    UPDATE......;
    DELETE........;
    COMMIT WRITE IMMEDIATE NOWAIT;
END;
/
```

Asynchronous COMMITs are best used in the following situations:

- Use asynchronous COMMIT in systems that are not recovery-oriented, for example, data warehousing or business intelligence applications. For such systems, the incremental loads can be committed asynchronously. This saves a lot of time, especially when these loads are scheduled frequently (hourly and so on).
- Asynchronous COMMIT can also be used in OLTP systems that require high transactional throughput but are not prone (or not sensitive) to unexpected failures like database, system, or network crashes.

The following caveats reveal some details to be kept in mind when coding COMMIT asynchronously:

- A failure of a DML statement during posting has the same effect as committing synchronously because the COMMIT operation has not yet reached the second step of making the change permanent.
- A failure after the first step has completed, but before the redo-logs have been written, impacts the outcome of the whole COMMIT operation. Because the mode of operation is asynchronous, a success signal might have been sent after the first step is done but the second step failed. This incorrect signaling, in turn, might impact the overall application. There is also a chance of losing the redo-log entries written to the redo-log buffer if such a failure occurs before the redo-log buffer is flushed to disk. That is why non-recovery dependent systems benefit most from this type of COMMIT.

AUTONOMOUS TRANSACTION TECHNIQUES

Normal transaction processing in PL/SQL is bound by the following rules:

- All DML statements executed from within a single PL/SQL block are treated as one transaction and all are committed or all are rolled back.
- Implicit rollback is performed only when there's an unhandled exception in a PL/SQL block. Such a rollback undoes only the DML present within that PL/SQL block. This follows as direct consequence of the previous rule. This means that transactions that made changes to the database before the execution of the PL/SQL are not undone and an explicit COMMIT is needed to make them permanent.
- Explicit COMMITs or ROLLBACKs cause all uncommitted transactions to be committed or rolled back. This is true whether the COMMIT or ROLLBACK statement is coded inside the PL/SQL block or outside of it in the calling environment.

Autonomous transactions break these rules by limiting the scope of the COMMIT or ROLLBACK to just one transaction that is spawned off independently of the active transaction existing at that point. This is achieved by coding the following line before executing any DML statements:

```
PRAGMA AUTONOMOUS_TRANSACTION;
```

Any DML statements specified after this line are treated as part of the newly spawned transaction and are committed and/or rolled back independently of the DML that precedes this PRAGMA and hence is part of a separate transaction. The need for such a scenario arises in the following situations:

- When only some of the DML statements that are part of a single transaction need to be committed. A good example is with error logging. In this case, the original DML needs to be rolled back while committing only the error information row.
- When multiple DML statements need to be committed as a group in a single PL/SQL block. This means that one group of DML needs to be committed independent of a second group, but both are coded in the same PL/SQL subprogram. A good example is DML auditing, where it is needed to commit one group of audit records independent of any other DML.
- When performing DDL from within PL/SQL, because any DDL statement executed using dynamic SQL from within PL/SQL issues an implicit commit.
- When auditing SELECT statements.
- To perform a COMMIT or ROLLBACK inside a database trigger. This is needed in situations like providing a workaround for mutating table errors.

This section highlights, in a nutshell, the techniques involved in using autonomous transactions for error logging. The situations of DML auditing and performing DDL from PL/SQL are a special case of the first. A detailed account of error logging and DML auditing is presented in Chapter 9. The technique of auditing SELECTs is outlined in the next section. Regarding the use of COMMIT or ROLLBACK in a database trigger to provide a work-around for mutating table errors, using autonomous transactions to resolve mutating table errors is not always possible and I highlight here the possible scenarios when this can be done.

USING AUTONOMOUS TRANSACTIONS FOR ERROR LOGGING

As outlined previously, using autonomous transactions for error logging requires the primary DML statements to be rolled back, in case of failure, yet the information about the server error must be committed to an error log table. Because both DML statements are part of the same transaction, this is not possible with normal transaction processing.

Here are the steps involved in using autonomous transactions for error logging:

1. Create a packaged procedure that is declared autonomous using PRAGMA AUTONOMOUS_TRANSACTION and has formal parameters defined corresponding to the error information to be logged.
2. In the body of this procedure, log the error information about the failed DML row by inserting into an error log table using the actual parameters.
3. Perform a COMMIT inside this procedure. This is mandatory for autonomous transactions. In fact, this is what gives the autonomy to the spawned off (new) transaction.
4. Call this autonomous procedure in a calling PL/SQL program where the primary DML is being executed.

Listing 8.1 shows a skeleton of how the code looks.

LISTING 8.1   ERROR LOGGING CODE SNIPPET

```
CREATE OR REPLACE PACKAGE pkg_log_error
IS
   PROCEDURE log_error_info(
      p_application_name     IN error_log.application_name%TYPE,
      p_curr_program_name    IN error_log.current_program_name%TYPE,
      p_calling_program_name IN error_log.calling_program_name%TYPE,
      p_block_name           IN error_log.block_name%TYPE,
      p_description          IN error_log.description%TYPE,
      p_msg_no               IN error_log.message_no%TYPE,
      p_msg_type             IN error_log.message_type%TYPE,
      p_msg_desc             IN error_log.message_desc%TYPE,
      p_key_info             IN audit_detail.pk_fk_info%TYPE DEFAULT
                                NULL,
      p_comments1   IN  audit_detail.comments1%TYPE DEFAULT NULL,
      p_comments2   IN  audit_detail.comments2%TYPE DEFAULT NULL,
      p_comments3   IN  audit_detail.comments3%TYPE DEFAULT NULL,
      p_comments4   IN  audit_detail.comments4%TYPE DEFAULT NULL,
      p_comments5   IN  audit_detail.comments5%TYPE DEFAULT NULL
   );
......
END pkg_log_error;

CREATE OR REPLACE PACKAGE BODY pkg_log_error
IS
```

```
    PROCEDURE log_error_info(
      p_application_name     IN error_log.application_name%TYPE,
      p_curr_program_name    IN error_log.current_program_name%TYPE,
      p_calling_program_name  IN error_log.calling_program_name%TYPE,
      p_block_name           IN error_log.block_name%TYPE,
      p_description          IN error_log.description%TYPE,
      p_msg_no               IN error_log.message_no%TYPE,
      p_msg_type             IN error_log.message_type%TYPE,
      p_msg_desc             IN error_log.message_desc%TYPE,
      p_key_info             IN audit_detail.pk_fk_info%TYPE DEFAULT
                                 NULL,
      p_comments1            IN  audit_detail.comments1%TYPE DEFAULT NULL,
      p_comments2            IN  audit_detail.comments2%TYPE DEFAULT NULL,
      p_comments3            IN  audit_detail.comments3%TYPE DEFAULT NULL,
      p_comments4            IN  audit_detail.comments4%TYPE DEFAULT NULL,
      p_comments5            IN  audit_detail.comments5%TYPE DEFAULT NULL
    )
    IS
      PRAGMA AUTONOMOUS_TRANSACTION;
      ......
    BEGIN
      IF (<error_logging_turned_on> THEN

      INSERT INTO error_log(el_id, application_name,
      current_program_name, calling_program_name, unique_session_code,
      block_name, description, message_no, message_type, message_desc,
      key_info, comments1, comments2, comments3, comments4, comments5,
      date_created, user_created)
      VALUES (<new_seq_value>, p_application_name, p_curr_program_name,
      p_calling_program_name, SYS_CONTEXT('USERENV ', 'OS_USER'),
      p_block_name, p_description, p_msg_no, p_msg_type, p_msg_desc,
      p_key_info, p_comments1, p_comments2, p_comments3, p_comments4,
      p_comments5, SYSDATE, USER);

          COMMIT;
        END IF;
    EXCEPTION
      WHEN OTHERS THEN
          NULL;
    END log_error_info;
END pkg_log_error;
```

Here's how this procedure can be used in a calling program:

```
CREATE OR REPLACE PROCEDURE proc_test_error_logging(
  ip_input_source IN VARCHAR2
)
IS
  v_status NUMBER := 0;

  v_app_name VARCHAR2(100) := 'PLSQL';
  v_curr_prog_name VARCHAR2(100) := 'PROC_TEST_ERROR_LOGGING';
BEGIN

  BEGIN

    -- Insert1
    INSERT INTO ......

  EXCEPTION
    WHEN OTHERS THEN
     v_status := 1;
     pkg_log_error.log_error_info(v_app_name, v_curr_prog_name, NULL,
     'Insert1', NULL, NULL, pkg_log_error.c_error, SQLCODE, SQLERRM,
     ip_input_source);
  END;

  BEGIN
    -- Update1
    UPDATE......

  EXCEPTION
    WHEN OTHERS THEN
     v_status := 1;
     pkg_log_error.log_error_info(v_app_name, v_curr_prog_name, NULL,
     'Update1', NULL, NULL, pkg_log_error.c_error, SQLCODE, SQLERRM,
     ip_input_source);
  END;

  BEGIN

    -- Delete1
    DELETE......
```

```
    EXCEPTION
      WHEN OTHERS THEN
        v_status := 1;
        pkg_log_error.log_error_info(v_app_name, v_curr_prog_name, NULL,
        'Delete1', NULL, NULL, pkg_log_error.c_error, SQLCODE, SQLERRM,
        ip_input_source);
    END;


  EXCEPTION
    WHEN OTHERS THEN
      ROLLBACK;

      pkg_log_error.log_error_info(v_app_name, v_curr_prog_name, NULL,
      'Proc Test Error Logging', NULL, NULL, pkg_log_error.c_error,
      SQLCODE, SQLERRM, ip_input_source);
      RAISE;
  END proc_test_error_logging;
  /
```

The pkg_log_error.log_error_info procedure is defined as an autonomous transaction that inserts into the error_log table the appropriate error information based on its parameter input. This record gets committed independently of the main transaction record (initiated by the original DML statement) that failed. In this way, only the error information record is committed. Note that this procedure serves as the exception handler for each DML statement present in the code. This provides greater control as to how to deal with each such statement, such as stopping further processing when an error occurs.

USING COMMIT INSIDE A DATABASE TRIGGER

Using COMMIT inside a database trigger necessitates the use of an autonomous transaction inside the trigger body. Such a trigger is termed an autonomous trigger. A typical scenario when this might be used is while counteracting mutating table errors. Use the following guidelines when creating autonomous triggers to circumvent mutating table errors:

- Use autonomous transactions in database triggers only if the logic of the trigger is not dependent on the changes made by the triggering statement while it is executing.
- An autonomous trigger enables one to read the mutating table from within the trigger body. However, changes to the mutating table are not permitted.

TECHNIQUES FOR AUDITING QUERIES

This is often a requirement for the DBA/upper management interested in monitoring who is accessing what data. Although controlled by security measures implemented using pre-built features or otherwise, data from query audits can give you a comprehensive report of the data accessed.

This technique can be implemented by calling a function from the queries run by the various users. However, this function needs to insert the audit information into an audit table maintained for the purpose. Such audit information might include the user running the query, the date and time the query is run, and other application-specific statistics. This defies the restriction of calling user-defined functions from PL/SQL with DML inside them. This is where autonomous transactions come to the rescue—by allowing such functions to be called successfully from queries.

For the example here, I assume a data warehousing environment where there is a list of fact tables whose primary keys are surrogate IDs generated by sequences. These fact tables act as the driving tables for the queries to be audited.

Here are the steps involved in auditing queries:

1. Create two tables—A fact_tab table that has the actual data on which the queries are audited and an audit_tab_for_select table that stores the audit record for each row queried.
2. Create an autonomous function that inserts into the audit_tab_for_select table based on the table name of the query involved and the primary key column of this table.
3. Create a view that queries all the columns from the fact_tab along with the autonomous function as an additional column.
4. Run several queries against the view and check the number of records inserted into the audit_tab_for_select table.

Listing 8.2 shows the code for this process.

LISTING 8.2 AUDITING QUERIES

```
create table audit_tab_for_select
      (table_name varchar2(30) not null,
       pk_id      NUMBER       not null,
       audit_date DATE         not null,
       audit_by   VARCHAR2(30) not null)
  /
```

```
create or replace function audit_select
        (ip_tab_name VARCHAR2,
         ip_pk_id       NUMBER)
return number
is
  pragma autonomous_transaction;
begin
    insert into audit_tab_for_select values
        (ip_tab_name, ip_pk_id, SYSDATE, USER);
    commit;
    RETURN (0);
exception when others then
  return (-1);
end;
/

create table fact_tab
        (id    NUMBER not null,
         measure1 NUMBER not null,
         measure2 varchar2(20),
         measure3 date          )
/
begin
insert into fact_tab values
        (1001, 1000.20, 'TOTAL REVENUE', null);
insert into fact_tab values
        (1002, 5000.20, 'AS OF RVN', '01-MAR-07');
insert into fact_tab values
        (1003, 4000.00, null, null);
insert into fact_tab values
        (1004, 5800.25, 'AS OF', '01-JUL-07');
commit;
end;
/
```

Here's the code for the test queries:

```
SQL> alter system flush shared_pool;

System altered.
```

The following query initiates auditing the SELECT issued with a call to the audit_select function. As a result, four audit rows are inserted into the audit_tab_for_select table.

```
SQL> select a.*, audit_select('FACT_TAB',a.id)
  2  from   fact_tab a;

        ID   MEASURE1 MEASURE2                MEASURE3
---------- ---------- -------------------- ---------
AUDIT_SELECT('FACT_TAB',A.ID)
-----------------------------
      1001     1000.2 TOTAL REVENUE
                       0

      1002     5000.2 AS OF RVN            01-MAR-07
                       0

      1003       4000
                       0

      1004    5800.25 AS OF                01-JUL-07
                       0


SQL> select * from audit_tab_for_select;

TABLE_NAME                        PK_ID AUDIT_DAT
------------------------------ ---------- ---------
AUDIT_BY
-----------------------------
FACT_TAB                           1001 17-JAN-08
SCOTT

FACT_TAB                           1002 17-JAN-08
SCOTT

FACT_TAB                           1003 17-JAN-08
SCOTT

FACT_TAB                           1004 17-JAN-08
SCOTT
```

The following code creates a view using the SELECT issued earlier and issues a query against this view. As a result, four audit rows are inserted into the audit_tab_for_select table. (Note that this view is used in all subsequent tests for query auditing by running queries against the view.)

```
SQL> create view fact_tab_audit
  2  as
  3  select a.*, audit_select('FACT_TAB', a.id) audit_col
  4  from   fact_tab a;

View created.

SQL> truncate table audit_tab_for_select;

Table truncated.

SQL> select * from fact_tab_audit;

       ID   MEASURE1 MEASURE2                  MEASURE3  AUDIT_COL
---------- ---------- -------------------- --------- ----------
     1001     1000.2 TOTAL REVENUE                           0
     1002     5000.2 AS OF RVN            01-MAR-07          0
     1003       4000                                         0
     1004    5800.25 AS OF               01-JUL-07          0

SQL> select * from audit_tab_for_select;

TABLE_NAME                       PK_ID AUDIT_DAT
---------------------------- ---------- ---------
AUDIT_BY
-----------------------------
FACT_TAB                          1001 17-JAN-08
SCOTT

FACT_TAB                          1002 17-JAN-08
SCOTT

FACT_TAB                          1003 17-JAN-08
SCOTT

FACT_TAB                          1004 17-JAN-08
SCOTT
```

The following code issues a query using a summary on a column from the view that does not call the audit_select function. As a result, no new audit rows are inserted into the audit_tab_for_select table.

```
SQL> select sum(measure1) from fact_tab_audit;

SUM(MEASURE1)
-------------
    15800.65

SQL> select * from audit_tab_for_select;

TABLE_NAME                          PK_ID AUDIT_DAT
----------------------------- ---------- ---------
AUDIT_BY
-----------------------------
FACT_TAB                             1001 17-JAN-08
SCOTT

FACT_TAB                             1002 17-JAN-08
SCOTT

FACT_TAB                             1003 17-JAN-08
SCOTT

FACT_TAB                             1004 17-JAN-08
SCOTT
```

The following code issues a query using a summary on a column from the view based on row groupings, but this does not invoke the audit_select function. As a result, no new audit rows are inserted into the audit_tab_for_select table.

```
SQL> l
  1  select measure3, sum(measure1) from fact_tab_audit
  2* group by measure3
SQL> /

MEASURE3   SUM(MEASURE1)
--------- -------------
01-MAR-07        5000.2
01-JUL-07       5800.25
                 5000.2
```

```
SQL> select * from audit_tab_for_select;

TABLE_NAME                         PK_ID AUDIT_DAT
------------------------------ ---------- ---------
AUDIT_BY
------------------------------
FACT_TAB                             1001 17-JAN-08
SCOTT

FACT_TAB                             1002 17-JAN-08
SCOTT

FACT_TAB                             1003 17-JAN-08
SCOTT

FACT_TAB                             1004 17-JAN-08
SCOTT
```

The following code issues a query using a summary on a column from the view grouped by the audit_col column, which in turn invokes the audit_select function. As a result, four new audit rows are inserted into the audit_tab_for_select table—one new row for each row affected by the grouping and the summarization.

```
SQL> ed
Wrote file afiedt.buf

  1  select audit_col, sum(measure1) from fact_tab_audit
  2* group by audit_col
SQL> /

 AUDIT_COL SUM(MEASURE1)
---------- -------------
         0      15800.65

SQL> select * from audit_tab_for_select;

TABLE_NAME                         PK_ID AUDIT_DAT
------------------------------ ---------- ---------
AUDIT_BY
------------------------------
FACT_TAB                             1001 17-JAN-08
SCOTT
```

```
FACT_TAB                                      1002 17-JAN-08
SCOTT

FACT_TAB                                      1003 17-JAN-08
SCOTT

FACT_TAB                                      1004 17-JAN-08
SCOTT

FACT_TAB                                      1001 17-JAN-08
SCOTT

FACT_TAB                                      1002 17-JAN-08
SCOTT

FACT_TAB                                      1003 17-JAN-08
SCOTT

FACT_TAB                                      1004 17-JAN-08
SCOTT


8 rows selected.
```

The following code issues a query using a COUNT on the audit_col column of the view, which in turn invokes the audit_select function. As a result, four new audit rows are inserted into the audit_tab_for_select table—one new row for each row affected by the COUNT function.

```
SQL> select count(audit_col) from fact_tab_audit;

COUNT(AUDIT_COL)
----------------
              4

SQL> select * from audit_tab_for_select;

TABLE_NAME                           PK_ID AUDIT_DAT
------------------------------ ---------- ---------
AUDIT_BY
------------------------------
FACT_TAB                              1001 17-JAN-08
SCOTT
```

```
FACT_TAB                                    1002 17-JAN-08
SCOTT

FACT_TAB                                    1003 17-JAN-08
SCOTT

FACT_TAB                                    1004 17-JAN-08
SCOTT

FACT_TAB                                    1001 17-JAN-08
SCOTT

FACT_TAB                                    1002 17-JAN-08
SCOTT

FACT_TAB                                    1003 17-JAN-08
SCOTT

FACT_TAB                                    1004 17-JAN-08
SCOTT

FACT_TAB                                    1001 17-JAN-08
SCOTT

FACT_TAB                                    1002 17-JAN-08
SCOTT

FACT_TAB                                    1003 17-JAN-08
SCOTT

FACT_TAB                                    1004 17-JAN-08
SCOTT
```

```
12 rows selected.
```

The following code issues a query that simply selects a COUNT(*) from the view. This in turn does not invoke the audit_select function. As a result, no new audit rows are inserted into the audit_tab_for_select table, even though the count is for all the rows selected in the view.

```
SQL> select count(*) from fact_tab_audit;

  COUNT(*)
----------
         4

SQL> select * from audit_tab_for_select;

TABLE_NAME                        PK_ID AUDIT_DAT
------------------------------ ---------- ---------
AUDIT_BY
------------------------------
FACT_TAB                           1001 17-JAN-08
SCOTT

FACT_TAB                           1002 17-JAN-08
SCOTT

FACT_TAB                           1003 17-JAN-08
SCOTT

FACT_TAB                           1004 17-JAN-08
SCOTT

FACT_TAB                           1001 17-JAN-08
SCOTT

FACT_TAB                           1002 17-JAN-08
SCOTT

FACT_TAB                           1003 17-JAN-08
SCOTT

FACT_TAB                           1004 17-JAN-08
SCOTT

FACT_TAB                           1001 17-JAN-08
SCOTT

FACT_TAB                           1002 17-JAN-08
SCOTT
```

```
FACT_TAB                                1003 17-JAN-08
SCOTT


FACT_TAB                                1004 17-JAN-08
SCOTT


12 rows selected.
```

The following code issues a query using a COUNT on the ID column of the view, which in turn does not invoke the audit_select function. As a result, no new audit rows are inserted into the audit_tab_for_select table, even though the count affects all the rows selected in the view for which the ID column is not null.

```
SQL> select count(id) from fact_tab_audit;

 COUNT(ID)
----------
         4

SQL> select * from audit_tab_for_select;

TABLE_NAME                        PK_ID AUDIT_DAT
------------------------------ ---------- ---------
AUDIT_BY
------------------------------
FACT_TAB                          1001 17-JAN-08
SCOTT

FACT_TAB                          1002 17-JAN-08
SCOTT

FACT_TAB                          1003 17-JAN-08
SCOTT

FACT_TAB                          1004 17-JAN-08
SCOTT

FACT_TAB                          1001 17-JAN-08
SCOTT

FACT_TAB                          1002 17-JAN-08
SCOTT
```

```
FACT_TAB                                  1003 17-JAN-08
SCOTT

FACT_TAB                                  1004 17-JAN-08
SCOTT

FACT_TAB                                  1001 17-JAN-08
SCOTT

FACT_TAB                                  1002 17-JAN-08
SCOTT

FACT_TAB                                  1003 17-JAN-08
SCOTT

FACT_TAB                                  1004 17-JAN-08
SCOTT


12 rows selected.
```

The following query simply does a SELECT * from the view based on a WHERE clause. This in turn invokes the audit_select function for each row affected by the query. As a result, new audit rows are inserted into the audit_tab_for_select table (one for each row of the selected output).

```
SQL> select * from fact_tab_audit where measure2 like '%AS OF%';

        ID   MEASURE1 MEASURE2                MEASURE3  AUDIT_COL
---------- ---------- -------------------- ---------- ----------
      1002    5000.2 AS OF RVN             01-MAR-07           0
      1004   5800.25 AS OF                 01-JUL-07           0

SQL> select * from audit_tab_for_select;

TABLE_NAME                              PK_ID AUDIT_DAT
-------------------------------- ---------- ---------
AUDIT_BY
--------------------------------
FACT_TAB                                  1001 17-JAN-08
SCOTT

FACT_TAB                                  1002 17-JAN-08
SCOTT
```

```
FACT_TAB                              1003 17-JAN-08
SCOTT

FACT_TAB                              1004 17-JAN-08
SCOTT

FACT_TAB                              1001 17-JAN-08
SCOTT

FACT_TAB                              1002 17-JAN-08
SCOTT

FACT_TAB                              1003 17-JAN-08
SCOTT

FACT_TAB                              1004 17-JAN-08
SCOTT

FACT_TAB                              1001 17-JAN-08
SCOTT

FACT_TAB                              1002 17-JAN-08
SCOTT

FACT_TAB                              1003 17-JAN-08
SCOTT

FACT_TAB                              1004 17-JAN-08
SCOTT

FACT_TAB                              1002 17-JAN-08
SCOTT

FACT_TAB                              1004 17-JAN-08
SCOTT


14 rows selected.
```

The following query simply does a SELECT * from the view based on a WHERE clause that affects no rows. This in turn does not invoke the audit_select function. As a result, no new audit rows are inserted into the audit_tab_for_select table.

```
SQL> select * from fact_tab_audit where trunc(measure3)
                = trunc(sysdate);
```

no rows selected

```
SQL> select * from audit_tab_for_select;
```

TABLE_NAME	PK_ID	AUDIT_DAT
---------------------------	----------	---------
AUDIT_BY		

FACT_TAB	1001	17-JAN-08
SCOTT		
FACT_TAB	1002	17-JAN-08
SCOTT		
FACT_TAB	1003	17-JAN-08
SCOTT		
FACT_TAB	1004	17-JAN-08
SCOTT		
FACT_TAB	1001	17-JAN-08
SCOTT		
FACT_TAB	1002	17-JAN-08
SCOTT		
FACT_TAB	1003	17-JAN-08
SCOTT		
FACT_TAB	1004	17-JAN-08
SCOTT		
FACT_TAB	1001	17-JAN-08
SCOTT		
FACT_TAB	1002	17-JAN-08
SCOTT		
FACT_TAB	1003	17-JAN-08
SCOTT		

```
FACT_TAB                                      1004 17-JAN-08
SCOTT


FACT_TAB                                      1002 17-JAN-08
SCOTT


FACT_TAB                                      1004 17-JAN-08
SCOTT



14 rows selected.
```

The following query simply does a conditional SELECT * from the view based on a WHERE clause, which affects two rows. This in turn invokes the audit_select function for each row affected by the query. As a result, two new audit rows are inserted into the audit_tab_for_select table (one audit row for each row of the selected output).

```
SQL> select * from fact_tab_audit where measure3 between
                 sysdate-365 and sysdate;

        ID   MEASURE1 MEASURE2              MEASURE3   AUDIT_COL
---------- ---------- -------------------- ---------- ----------
      1002    5000.2 AS OF RVN             01-MAR-07           0
      1004   5800.25 AS OF                 01-JUL-07           0

SQL> select * from audit_tab_for_select;

TABLE_NAME                                PK_ID AUDIT_DAT
------------------------------ ---------- ---------
AUDIT_BY
------------------------------
FACT_TAB                                   1001 17-JAN-08
SCOTT


FACT_TAB                                   1002 17-JAN-08
SCOTT


FACT_TAB                                   1003 17-JAN-08
SCOTT


FACT_TAB                                   1004 17-JAN-08
SCOTT
```

FACT_TAB SCOTT	1001	17-JAN-08
FACT_TAB SCOTT	1002	17-JAN-08
FACT_TAB SCOTT	1003	17-JAN-08
FACT_TAB SCOTT	1004	17-JAN-08
FACT_TAB SCOTT	1001	17-JAN-08
FACT_TAB SCOTT	1002	17-JAN-08
FACT_TAB SCOTT	1003	17-JAN-08
FACT_TAB SCOTT	1004	17-JAN-08
FACT_TAB SCOTT	1002	17-JAN-08
FACT_TAB SCOTT	1004	17-JAN-08
FACT_TAB SCOTT	1002	17-JAN-08
FACT_TAB SCOTT	1004	17-JAN-08

```
16 rows selected.
```

The tests reveal the following observations:

- A SELECT * from fact_audit_tab view without any WHERE conditions uses the function and inserts one audit record for each row returned.

- A SELECT * from fact_audit_tab view with WHERE conditions that results in some rows returned uses the function and inserts as many audit records as the rows returned.
- A COUNT(*) from fact_audit_tab view without any WHERE conditions does not use the function.
- A SELECT COUNT on the additional column that represents the function return value inserts as many audit records as the COUNT value.
- A SELECT SUM on any appropriate column that does not make a reference to the function does not insert any audit records. However, a SELECT SUM on any appropriate measure column that groups by the additional audit column inserts as many rows as the number of rows returned by the query.

Summary

This chapter described application-management techniques in PL/SQL. Starting with the notion of asynchronous COMMIT, it touched upon the various techniques for using autonomous transactions. Finally, it dealt with the technique of auditing queries treated as a special case of using autonomous transactions. The next chapter deals with application development frameworks in PL/SQL.

Part III

Applying PL/SQL in the Real World

9 Application Development Frameworks Using PL/SQL

Application development frameworks provide for a standard template for implementing a particular task. Examples of PL/SQL tasks that call for such templates include error logging and performing ETL (Extract, Transform, Load) operations using PL/SQL. The framework provides both the design and code development features that can be used to implement the task in the best possible manner suitable for the application requirements (such as business or functional requirements that the application is targeted to) and criteria (such as functional and technical feature/product specific factors that need to be taken into consideration while implementing the business rules as per the application requirements) in question. The sections that follow discuss frameworks for four different tasks that are frequently implemented in most PL/SQL applications—error logging, DML auditing, ETL, and performance tuning.

ERROR-LOGGING FRAMEWORK

The error-logging framework refers to logging of SQL and/or PL/SQL errors occurring during program execution as well as customary error messages that are application-specific. Here, so-called logging refers to capturing the following information about each error:

■ An identifier pertaining to the code block where the error occurred
■ The actual error code and error message
■ The line number where the error occurred, including the error execution stack (the sequence of program steps that led to the error)

Error logging in this manner not only is useful for tracking runtime errors but also helps tremendously in later debugging as well as code correction. Error logging should be a must for all applications running interactively like OLTP applications. In batch mode, error logging can be enabled for programs that do incremental batch updates and disabled for those performing one-time massive loads.

While you are logging errors, be sure to consider the following factors:

■ The type of error being logged, like critical error, warning, or informational message. Errors can also fall into one of two categories: Oracle SQL or PL/SQL errors or application-specific errors.
■ The same program being executed multiple times, for example, in multiple sessions or by multiple programs in a single session.

Taking these factors into consideration, you can control error logging by using a control table and implement it using the two database tables. The control table can have a column to enable/disable error logging, and the implementation tables can be designed as an error information logging table and lookup table. The error information logging table can have additional columns to accommodate the information about the application and program being captured. A PL/SQL package provides the API for the implementation logic.

Here's the framework for such an implementation:

■ Error logging information is recorded in two database tables.
■ PL/SQL package API is used to program the logging process.
■ Error logging can be enabled/disabled using an audit control table. This is done at the application and/or current program levels. This table will always have a row for each application with current_program_name set to a single space.

Additional rows with valid current program names define the granularity of enabling/disabling and these rows take precedence over the single row with a blank current program name.

■ Each program is error-logged if error logging is turned on.

■ Application contexts can be used instead of a control table if the number of applications/modules needing error logging is not large. This makes control more secure and tightly integrated.

An application context is session-concerning information stored in secure data cache in UGA (or SGA) and can be used to incorporate access-control mechanisms. A context is specified as a set of attribute, value pairs that can be defined, set, and accessed using an associated package. They are used to make sure every DML is logged correctly, to turn off/on DML auditing/error logging, and to implement fine-grained security using application attributes to control what data users can access. Each application can have its own context with its own attributes. In each case, setting the application context attributes on a case-by-case need basis can enable some level of fine-grained security in your application.

For example, a library application can have a library context defined with an attribute called privileged_user whose value can be set to Yes for a specific group of users accessing the application. This value is set transparently once such a user logs in. This is secure because it is session-specific, is owned by SYS, and can only be set by the PL/SQL package associated with the context. This way is more secure and more tightly controlled than using packages. Also, multiple contexts, each specific to an application, can be created.

Here's the design of the data structures:

■ Error logging information table (ERROR_LOG table)—Its key information includes application name, calling program name, current program name, unique session code, block identifier name, message type, error code, error text and description, a key information column that captures the information about the transaction that caused the error, and miscellaneous comment columns.

■ Lookup table (CUSTOM_ERROR_MESSAGES table)—It contains application-specific messages. Its key information includes the message number, message text, and message type such as informational, warning, or critical error.

Listing 9.1 shows the code for this process.

LISTING 9.1 CREATING DATA STRUCTURES FOR ERROR LOGGING FRAMEWORK

```
DROP TABLE ERROR_LOG;

CREATE TABLE ERROR_LOG
(
    EL_ID                       NUMBER              NOT NULL
                        CONSTRAINT PK_ERROR_LOG PRIMARY KEY,
    APPLICATION_NAME        VARCHAR2(100)       NOT NULL,
    CURRENT_PROGRAM_NAME    VARCHAR2(100)       NOT NULL,
    CALLING_PROGRAM_NAME    VARCHAR2(100)       NULL,
    UNIQUE_SESSION_CODE     VARCHAR2(100)       NOT NULL,
    BLOCK_NAME              VARCHAR2(100)       NULL,
    DESCRIPTION             VARCHAR2(2000)      NULL,
    MESSAGE_NO              NUMBER,
    MESSAGE_TYPE            VARCHAR2(10)        NOT NULL,
    MESSAGE_DESC            VARCHAR2(4000)      NOT NULL,
    KEY_INFO                VARCHAR2(2000)      NULL,
    COMMENTS1               VARCHAR2(2000)      NULL,
    COMMENTS2               VARCHAR2(2000)      NULL,
    COMMENTS3               VARCHAR2(2000)      NULL,
    COMMENTS4               VARCHAR2(2000)      NULL,
    COMMENTS5               VARCHAR2(2000)      NULL,
    DATE_CREATED            DATE                NOT NULL,
    USER_CREATED            VARCHAR2(30)        NOT NULL
)
/

ALTER TABLE error_log ADD CONSTRAINT FK_ERROR_LOG
FOREIGN KEY MESSAGE_NO REFERENCES CUSTOM_ERROR_MESSAGES(MESSAGE_NO);

CREATE TABLE CUSTOM_ERROR_MESSAGES
(
    MESSAGE_NO          NUMBER                  NOT NULL,
    MESSAGE_TEXT        VARCHAR2(2000 CHAR)     NOT NULL,
    MESSAGE_TYPE        VARCHAR2(10 CHAR)       NOT NULL,
    DATE_CREATED        DATE                    NOT NULL,
    USER_CREATED        VARCHAR2(30)            NOT NULL
)
/

DROP TABLE audit_control;
```

```
CREATE TABLE audit_control
(APPLICATION_NAME          VARCHAR2(100) NOT NULL,
 CURRENT_PROGRAM_NAME      VARCHAR2(100) NOT NULL,
 RETENTION_PERIOD          NUMBER        NOT NULL,
 ERROR_LOGGING_ON          VARCHAR2(1)   DEFAULT 'Y' NOT NULL
                    CHECK (ERROR_LOGGING_ON IN ('Y','N'))
)
/

ALTER TABLE audit_control ADD CONSTRAINT PK_AUDIT_CONTROL
PRIMARY KEY (APPLICATION_NAME, CURRENT_PROGRAM_NAME);

DROP SEQUENCE seq_el_id;

CREATE SEQUENCE seq_el_id MINVALUE 1;
```

The design of the package API for the error logging framework consists of a package consisting of public constants for the completion status and three procedures, as described here for the pkg_log_error package.

- Public constants for the message type—M for informational message, E for error message, and W for warning message.
- Procedures such as log_error_info, which logs any Oracle Server/PL/SQL errors.
- The function get_message_text, which retrieves the message text for a given message number and type.

Listing 9.2 shows the code for this process.

LISTING 9.2 PACKAGE API OF ERROR LOGGING FRAMEWORK

```
CREATE OR REPLACE PACKAGE pkg_log_error
AS

    -- Public Message Types
    C_ERROR         CONSTANT CHAR   := 'E';
    C_WARNING       CONSTANT CHAR   := 'W';
    C_INFORMATION   CONSTANT CHAR   := 'I';

    PROCEDURE log_error_info(
      p_application_name    IN error_log.application_name%TYPE,
      p_curr_program_name   IN error_log.current_program_name%TYPE,
      p_calling_program_name IN error_log.calling_program_name%TYPE,
```

```
        p_block_name            IN error_log.block_name%TYPE,
        p_description           IN error_log.description%TYPE,
        p_msg_no                IN error_log.message_no%TYPE,
        p_msg_type              IN error_log.message_type%TYPE,
        p_msg_desc              IN error_log.message_desc%TYPE,
        p_key_info              IN audit_detail.pk_fk_info%TYPE DEFAULT
                                   NULL,
        p_comments1         IN  audit_detail.comments1%TYPE DEFAULT NULL,
        p_comments2         IN  audit_detail.comments2%TYPE DEFAULT NULL,
        p_comments3         IN  audit_detail.comments3%TYPE DEFAULT NULL,
        p_comments4         IN  audit_detail.comments4%TYPE DEFAULT NULL,
        p_comments5         IN  audit_detail.comments5%TYPE DEFAULT NULL
);

    FUNCTION get_message_text (p_message_no IN  NUMBER,
                     p_message_type   IN VARCHAR2) RETURN NUMBER;

END;
/

CREATE OR REPLACE PACKAGE BODY pkg_log_error
AS

    FUNCTION get_message_text (p_message_no NUMBER,
                       p_message_type IN  VARCHAR2)
    RETURN VARCHAR2
    IS
        v_message_text custom_error_messages.MESSAGE_TEXT%TYPE;

    BEGIN

        SELECT message_text
        INTO   v_message_text
        FROM   custom_error_messages
        WHERE  message_no = p_message_no
        AND    message_type = p_message_type;

        RETURN (v_message_text);

    EXCEPTION

        WHEN others THEN

            RETURN(NULL);
```

```
END get_message_text;

PROCEDURE log_error_info(
    p_application_name
        IN error_log.application_name%TYPE,
    p_curr_program_name
        IN error_log.current_program_name%TYPE,
    p_calling_program_name
        IN error_log.calling_program_name%TYPE,
    p_block_name
        IN error_log.block_name%TYPE,
    p_description
        IN error_log.description%TYPE,
    p_msg_no
        IN error_log.message_no%TYPE,
    p_msg_type
        IN error_log.message_type%TYPE,
    p_msg_desc
        IN error_log.message_desc%TYPE,
    p_key_info
        IN audit_detail.pk_fk_info%TYPE DEFAULT NULL,
    p_comments1
        IN  audit_detail.comments1%TYPE DEFAULT NULL,
    p_comments2
        IN  audit_detail.comments2%TYPE DEFAULT NULL,
    p_comments3
        IN  audit_detail.comments3%TYPE DEFAULT NULL,
    p_comments4
        IN  audit_detail.comments4%TYPE DEFAULT NULL,
    p_comments5
        IN  audit_detail.comments5%TYPE DEFAULT NULL
)
IS
  PRAGMA AUTONOMOUS_TRANSACTION;

 v_el_id                    error_log.el_id%TYPE;
 v_error_logging_on audit_control.error_logging_on%TYPE;
BEGIN
 BEGIN
        SELECT error_logging_on
        INTO   v_error_logging_on
        WHERE  application_name = p_app_name
        AND    current_program_name = p_curr_prog_name;
```

```
            EXCEPTION
                WHEN NO_DATA_FOUND THEN
                    BEGIN
                        SELECT error_logging_on
                        INTO   v_error_logging_on
                        FROM   audit_control
                        WHERE  application_name = p_app_name;
                    EXCEPTION
                        WHEN NO_DATA_FOUND THEN
                            NULL;
                            -- RAISE_APPLICATION_ERROR(
                            -- -20002,'Error Logging not set up for
                            --  application ' ||p_app_name);
                        WHEN OTHERS THEN
                            NULL;
                            -- RAISE_APPLICATION_ERROR(
                            -- -20003,'ERR getting setup info for
                            --  application ' ||p_app_name||': '||SQLERRM);
                    END;
                WHEN OTHERS THEN
                    NULL;
                    -- RAISE_APPLICATION_ERROR(
                    -- -20001, 'Error Logging not set up for '||
                    --         ||'(application, current program) ('||
                    --           p_app_name||', '
                    --         ||p_curr_prog_name||')'||SQLERRM);
            END;

    IF v_error_logging_on = 'Y' THEN
      SELECT seq_el_id.nextval
      INTO   v_el_id
      FROM   DUAL;

      INSERT INTO error_log(el_id, application_name,
      current_program_name, calling_program_name, unique_session_code,
      block_name, description, message_no, message_type, message_desc,
      key_info, comments1, comments2, comments3, comments4, comments5,
      date_created, user_created)
      VALUES (v_el_id, p_application_name, p_curr_program_name,
      p_calling_program_name, SYS_CONTEXT('USERENV ', 'OS_USER'),
      p_block_name, p_description, p_msg_no, p_msg_type, p_msg_desc,
      p_key_info, p_comments1, p_comments2, p_comments3, p_comments4,
      p_comments5, SYSDATE, USER);
```

```
      COMMIT;
   END IF;
  EXCEPTION
   WHEN OTHERS THEN
        NULL;
  END log_error_info;

END pkg_log_error;
/
```

Note how the unique session ID is derived from the OS_USER attribute of the system context USERENV.

Calling Program

Calling program invokes a call to log_error_info to log the error information based on the control parameter error_logging_on.

Listing 9.3 shows the code for a sample calling program using the error-logging framework.

Listing 9.3 Skeleton Code for Calling Program Using the Error-Logging Framework

```
CREATE OR REPLACE PROCEDURE proc_test_error_logging(
    ip_input_source IN VARCHAR2
)
IS
    v_status NUMBER := 0;

    v_app_name VARCHAR2(100) := 'PLSQL';
    v_curr_prog_name VARCHAR2(100) := 'PROC_TEST_ERROR_LOGGING';
BEGIN

    BEGIN

        -- Insert1
        INSERT INTO ......

    EXCEPTION
        WHEN OTHERS THEN
```

```
            v_status := 1;
            pkg_log_error.log_error_info(v_app_name,
                v_curr_prog_name, NULL,
            'Insert1', NULL, NULL, pkg_log_error.c_error,
                SQLCODE, SQLERRM,
            ip_input_source);
    END;

    BEGIN
        -- Update1
        UPDATE......

    EXCEPTION
        WHEN OTHERS THEN
            v_status := 1;
            pkg_log_error.log_error_info(v_app_name,
                v_curr_prog_name, NULL,
            'Update1', NULL, NULL, pkg_log_error.c_error,
                SQLCODE, SQLERRM,
            ip_input_source);
    END;

    BEGIN

        -- Delete1
        DELETE......

    EXCEPTION
        WHEN OTHERS THEN
            v_status := 1;
            pkg_log_error.log_error_info(v_app_name,
                    v_curr_prog_name, NULL,
            'Delete1', NULL, NULL, pkg_log_error.c_error,
                    SQLCODE, SQLERRM,
            ip_input_source);
    END;


EXCEPTION
    WHEN OTHERS THEN
        ROLLBACK;

        pkg_log_error.log_error_info(v_app_name,
                v_curr_prog_name, NULL,
```

```
            'Proc Test Error Logging', NULL, NULL,
                  pkg_log_error.c_error,
         SQLCODE, SQLERRM, ip_input_source);
         RAISE;
   END proc_test_error_logging;
   /
```

The pkg_log_error package can be further improved to include specifics for common pre-defined PL/SQL exceptions and non-pre-defined Oracle errors by defining public constants for them. Examples include NO_DATA_FOUND and TOO_MANY_ROWS exceptions. Also, customized exceptions can be defined for associating specific error codes with them so that they can be more meaningfully captured.

Secondly, the calling program had a RAISE in the final WHEN OTHERS exception handler. This kind of behavior is application specific and can be treated accordingly. For example, an additional parameter can be defined for the log_error_info procedure that directs whether to re-raise the exception.

DML Auditing Framework

The DML auditing framework refers to auditing of DML statements (INSERT, UPDATE, and DELETE statements) being executed within PL/SQL stored subprograms. Here, so-called auditing refers to capturing the following information about the execution or result of execution of each DML statement:

■ An identifier about the statement itself.
■ The number of rows affected by the statement.
■ The success or failure of the statement. This again is a special case of error logging and is captured by using the error-logging framework.

Auditing DML statements in this manner is useful in applications that run a multitude of transactions using programs having numerous INSERT, UPDATE, and DELETE statements. The criteria for DML auditing in such situations depends on the following factors:

■ The number of DML statements being executed in a single program
■ The same program being executed multiple times—for example, in multiple sessions or by multiple programs in a single session

Whether to audit DML also depends on where the application is running. If the application is mission-critical and is running in production in high priority mode, the failure of every DML needs to be trapped. In this case, DML auditing needs to be enabled. On the other hand, if the application is running in batch mode involving massive bulk loads, each DML operation need not be tracked and DML auditing can be disabled.

Taking these factors into consideration, you can control DML auditing by using a similar control table and implement it using the two similar database tables as in the error logging framework. The control table can have a column to enable/disable DML auditing, the master table can have the same structure as used in the error logging framework, and the detail table can have additional columns to accommodate the DML statistics. The package API changes accordingly to accommodate for the DML auditing framework.

Here's the framework for such an implementation:

- Audit and error logging information recorded in two database tables.
- PL/SQL package API used to program the logging process.
- Auditing, error logging, and DML auditing enabled/disabled using audit control table. This is done at the application and/or current program levels. This table will always have a row for each application with current_program_name set to a single space. Additional rows with valid current program names define the granularity of enabling/disabling and these rows take precedence over the single row with a blank current program name.
- Each program is audited if at least one DML statement is present and DML auditing is on, regardless of the number of rows affected by the DML.
- Application contexts can be used instead of a control table if the number of applications/modules needing DML auditing is not large. This makes control more secure and tightly integrated.

Here's the design of the data structures:

- Audit master (AUDIT_MASTER table)—Its key information includes the application name, calling program name, current program name, unique session code, start and end timestamps, completion status, information identified by a unique ID, and miscellaneous comment columns.
- Audit detail (AUDIT_DETAIL table)—Its key information includes block identifier name, description, number of records inserted/updated/deleted, PK/FK columns, and miscellaneous comment columns to record PK/FK/comment information of DML records. These records are identified by a load detail ID that points to an audit master record.

Listing 9.4 shows the code for this process.

LISTING 9.4 CREATING DATA STRUCTURES FOR DML AUDITING FRAMEWORK

```
DROP TABLE AUDIT_MASTER;

CREATE TABLE AUDIT_MASTER
(
    AM_ID                   NUMBER              NOT NULL
                    CONSTRAINT PK_AUDIT_MASTER PRIMARY KEY,
    APPLICATION_NAME        VARCHAR2(100)       NOT NULL,
    CURRENT_PROGRAM_NAME    VARCHAR2(100)       NOT NULL,
    CALLING_PROGRAM_NAME    VARCHAR2(100)       NULL,
    START_TIMESTAMP         TIMESTAMP           NOT NULL,
    END_TIMESTAMP           TIMESTAMP           NULL,
    COMPLETION_STATUS       VARCHAR2(100)       NULL,
    UNIQUE_SESSION_CODE     VARCHAR2(100)       NOT NULL,
    COMMENTS1               VARCHAR2(2000)      NULL,
    COMMENTS2               VARCHAR2(2000)      NULL,
    COMMENTS3               VARCHAR2(2000)      NULL,
    COMMENTS4               VARCHAR2(2000)      NULL,
    COMMENTS5               VARCHAR2(2000)      NULL,
    DATE_CREATED            DATE                NOT NULL,
    USER_CREATED            VARCHAR2(30)        NOT NULL
)
/

DROP TABLE AUDIT_DETAIL

CREATE TABLE AUDIT_DETAIL
(
    AD_ID         NUMBER              NOT NULL
                    CONSTRAINT PK_AUDIT_DETAIL PRIMARY KEY,
    AM_ID         NUMBER              NOT NULL,
    BLOCK_NAME    VARCHAR2(100)       NOT NULL,
    DESCRIPTION   VARCHAR2(2000)      NULL,
    RECS_INSERTED NUMBER              NULL,
    RECS_UPDATED  NUMBER              NULL,
    RECS_DELETED  NUMBER              NULL,
    RECS_ERRORED  NUMBER              NULL,
    PK_FK_INFO    VARCHAR2(2000)      NULL,
    COMMENTS1     VARCHAR2(2000)      NULL,
```

```
        COMMENTS2      VARCHAR2(2000)    NULL,
        COMMENTS3      VARCHAR2(2000)    NULL,
        COMMENTS4      VARCHAR2(2000)    NULL,
        COMMENTS5      VARCHAR2(2000)    NULL,
        DATE_CREATED   DATE              NOT NULL,
        USER_CREATED   VARCHAR2(30)      NOT NULL
)
/

ALTER TABLE audit_detail ADD CONSTRAINT
    FK1_AUDIT_DETAIL FOREIGN KEY AM_ID
    REFERENCES AUDIT_MASTER(AM_ID);


DROP TABLE audit_control;

CREATE TABLE audit_control
(APPLICATION_NAME       VARCHAR2(100) NOT NULL,
 CURRENT_PROGRAM_NAME   VARCHAR2(100) NOT NULL,
 RETENTION_PERIOD       NUMBER        NOT NULL,
 DML_AUDIT_ON           VARCHAR2(1)   DEFAULT 'Y' NOT NULL
             CHECK (DML_AUDIT_ON IN ('Y','N'))
)
/

ALTER TABLE audit_control ADD CONSTRAINT PK_AUDIT_CONTROL
PRIMARY KEY (APPLICATION_NAME, CURRENT_PROGRAM_NAME);

DROP SEQUENCE seq_am_id;

CREATE SEQUENCE seq_am_id MINVALUE 1;

DROP SEQUENCE seq_ad_id;

CREATE SEQUENCE seq_ad_id MINVALUE 1;
```

The design of the package API for the DML auditing framework consists of public constants for the completion status and three procedures, as described here for the pkg_audit package:

■ Public constants
Message types, such as M for informational message, E for error message, and W for warning message.
Final status, such as SUCCESS, SUCCESS WITH EXCEPTIONS, or FAILED.
Statement type, such as DML or ERR.

■ Procedures
Initialize—The very first statement after BEGIN for every calling program. It records the app name, the program name(s), and the kick-off time. Also returns DML audit control parameters (dml_audit_on and error_logging_on).
Log_audit_info—Logs Oracle Server/PL/SQL error or DML statement identifier message along with the audit statistics of the DML.
Finalize—The last statement before END; updates the completion time and final status.

Listing 9.5 shows the code for this package API.

LISTING 9.5 PACKAGE API OF DML AUDITING FRAMEWORK

```
CREATE OR REPLACE PACKAGE pkg_audit
AS

    -- Public Status Constants
    c_success                CONSTANT VARCHAR2(100)    := 'SUCCESS';
    c_success_with_exceptions    CONSTANT VARCHAR2(100)
                                    := 'SUCCESS WITH EXCEPTIONS';
    c_failed                 CONSTANT VARCHAR2(100)    := 'FAILED';

    PROCEDURE initialize(
        p_dml_audit_on       OUT
            audit_control.dml_audit_on%TYPE,
        p_am_id              OUT
            audit_master.am_id%TYPE,
        p_app_name           IN
            audit_master.application_name%TYPE,
        p_curr_prog_name     IN
            audit_master.current_program_name%TYPE,
        p_calling_prog_name IN
            audit_master.calling_program_name%TYPE
                                DEFAULT NULL
    );
```

```
        PROCEDURE log_audit_info(
            p_dml_audit_on      IN
                audit_control.dml_audit_on%TYPE,
            p_am_id             IN
                audit_master.am_id%TYPE,
            p_block_name        IN
                audit_detail.block_name%TYPE,
            p_description       IN
                audit_detail.description%TYPE,
            p_recs_inserted     IN
                audit_detail.recs_inserted%TYPE DEFAULT 0,
            p_recs_updated      IN
                audit_detail.recs_updated%TYPE DEFAULT 0,
            p_recs_deleted      IN
                audit_detail.recs_deleted%TYPE DEFAULT 0,
            p_recs_errored      IN
                audit_detail.recs_errored%TYPE DEFAULT NULL,
            p_pk_fk_info        IN
                audit_detail.pk_fk_info%TYPE DEFAULT NULL,
            p_comments1         IN
                audit_detail.comments1%TYPE DEFAULT NULL,
            p_comments2         IN
                audit_detail.comments2%TYPE DEFAULT NULL,
            p_comments3         IN
                audit_detail.comments3%TYPE DEFAULT NULL,
            p_comments4         IN
                audit_detail.comments4%TYPE DEFAULT NULL,
            p_comments5         IN
                audit_detail.comments5%TYPE DEFAULT NULL
        );
        PROCEDURE finalize(
            p_dml_audit_on      IN
                audit_control.dml_audit_on%TYPE,
            p_am_id             IN
                audit_master.am_id%TYPE,
            p_comp_status       IN
                audit_master.completion_status%TYPE
        );

END pkg_audit;
/

CREATE OR REPLACE PACKAGE BODY pkg_audit
AS
```

```
PROCEDURE initialize(
    p_dml_audit_on        OUT
        audit_control.dml_audit_on%TYPE,
    p_am_id               OUT
        audit_master.am_id%TYPE,
    p_app_name            IN
        audit_master.application_name%TYPE,
    p_curr_prog_name      IN
        audit_master.current_program_name%TYPE,
    p_calling_prog_name IN
        audit_master.calling_program_name%TYPE
                            DEFAULT NULL
)
IS
    PRAGMA AUTONOMOUS_TRANSACTION;
    v_dml_audit_on          audit_control.dml_audit_on%TYPE;

BEGIN
    BEGIN
        SELECT dml_audit_on
        INTO   v_dml_audit_on
        WHERE  application_name = p_app_name
          AND  current_program_name = p_curr_prog_name;
        p_dml_audit_on := v_dml_audit_on;
    EXCEPTION
        WHEN NO_DATA_FOUND THEN
            BEGIN
                SELECT dml_audit_on
                INTO   v_dml_audit_on
                FROM   audit_control
                WHERE  application_name = p_app_name;
                p_dml_audit_on := v_dml_audit_on;
            EXCEPTION
                WHEN NO_DATA_FOUND THEN


                    RAISE_APPLICATION_ERROR(
                    -20002,'Auditing parameters not set up for '
                    ||'application '||p_app_name);
                WHEN OTHERS THEN


                    RAISE_APPLICATION_ERROR(
                    -20003,'ERR getting auditing parameters for '
                    ||'application '||p_app_name||': '||SQLERRM);
```

```
          END;
          WHEN OTHERS THEN

               RAISE_APPLICATION_ERROR(
               -20001,'Auditing parameters not set up for '
               ||(application, current program) ('||
               p_app_name||', '||p_curr_prog_name||')'||SQLERRM);

     END;

     IF v_dml_audit_on = 'Y' THEN

          SELECT seq_am_id.nextval
          INTO p_am_id
          FROM DUAL;

          INSERT INTO audit_master(am_id, application_name,
          current_program_name, calling_program_name,
                              unique_session_code,
          start_timestamp, date_created, user_created)
          VALUES (p_am_id, p_app_name, p_curr_prog_name,
          p_calling_prog_name,SYS_CONTEXT('USERENV ', 'OS_USER'),
          SYSTIMESTAMP, SYSDATE, USER);

          COMMIT;
     END IF;
EXCEPTION

     WHEN OTHERS THEN
          p_am_id := to_number(to_char(SYSDATE, 'yyyymmddhh24miss'));
END initialize;


PROCEDURE log_audit_info(
     p_dml_audit_on
          IN  audit_control.dml_audit_on%TYPE,
     p_am_id
          IN  audit_master.am_id%TYPE,
     p_block_name
          IN  audit_detail.block_name%TYPE,
     p_description
          IN  audit_detail.description%TYPE,
     p_recs_inserted
          IN  audit_detail.recs_inserted%TYPE DEFAULT 0,
```

```
p_recs_updated
        IN   audit_detail.recs_updated%TYPE DEFAULT 0,
p_recs_deleted
        IN   audit_detail.recs_deleted%TYPE DEFAULT 0,
p_recs_errored
        IN   audit_detail.recs_errored%TYPE DEFAULT NULL,
p_pk_fk_info
        IN   audit_detail.pk_fk_info%TYPE DEFAULT NULL,
p_comments1
        IN   audit_detail.comments1%TYPE DEFAULT NULL,
p_comments2
        IN   audit_detail.comments2%TYPE DEFAULT NULL,
p_comments3
        IN   audit_detail.comments3%TYPE DEFAULT NULL,
p_comments4
        IN   audit_detail.comments4%TYPE DEFAULT NULL,
p_comments5
        IN   audit_detail.comments5%TYPE DEFAULT NULL
)
IS

    PRAGMA AUTONOMOUS_TRANSACTION;

    v_ad_id                    audit_detail.ad_id%TYPE;

BEGIN

    IF p_dml_audit_on = 'Y' THEN
        SELECT seq_ad_id.nextval
        INTO v_ad_id
        FROM DUAL;

        INSERT INTO audit_detail(ad_id, am_id, block_name,
            description, _inserted, recs_updated,
        recs recs_deleted, recs_errored, pk_fk_info, comments1,
        comments2, comments3, comments4, comments5,
        date_created, user_created)
        VALUES (v_ad_id, p_am_id, p_block_name, p_description,
        p_recs_inserted, p_recs_updated, p_recs_deleted,
        p_recs_errored, p_pk_fk_info, p_comments1,
        p_comments2, p_comments3, p_comments4,
        p_comments5, SYSDATE, USER);

        COMMIT;
    END IF;
```

```
    EXCEPTION
        WHEN OTHERS THEN
            NULL;
    END log_audit_info;

    PROCEDURE finalize(
        p_dml_audit_on      IN audit_control.dml_audit_on%TYPE,
        p_am_id             IN audit_master.am_id%TYPE,
        p_comp_status       IN audit_master.completion_status%TYPE
    )
    IS
        PRAGMA AUTONOMOUS_TRANSACTION;
    BEGIN

        IF p_dml_audit_on = 'Y' THEN
            UPDATE audit_master
            SET completion_status       = p_comp_status,
                end_timestamp = SYSTIMESTAMP
            WHERE am_id = p_am_id;
            COMMIT;
        END IF;
    EXCEPTION

        WHEN OTHERS THEN
            NULL;
    END finalize;

END pkg_audit;
/
```

Note how the unique session ID is derived from the OS_USER attribute of the system context USERENV.

CALLING PROGRAM

The calling program invokes calls to the packaged procedures pkg_audit.initialize(), pkg_audit.log_audit_info(), and pkg_audit.finalize() to store the audit information based on the control parameter dml_audit_on. The initialize procedure outputs the value of this control parameter that is used by the other two procedure calls.

Listing 9.6 shows the sample calling program code using the DML auditing framework.

LISTING 9.6   CALLING PROGRAM THAT USES THE DML AUDITING FRAMEWORK

```
CREATE OR REPLACE PROCEDURE proc_test_audit(
    ip_input_source IN VARCHAR2
)
IS
    v_am_id NUMBER;
    v_status NUMBER := 0;
    v_recs_count NUMBER := 0;
    v_recs_inserted NUMBER := 0;
    v_recs_updated NUMBER := 0;
    v_recs_deleted NUMBER := 0;
    v_recs_errored NUMBER;

    v_desc VARCHAR2(4000);

    v_success_status VARCHAR2(100);

    v_dml_audit_on       VARCHAR2(1);

    v_app_name VARCHAR2(100) := 'PLSQL';
    v_curr_prog_name VARCHAR2(100) := 'PROC_TEST_AUDIT';
BEGIN

    -- call initialize
    pkg_audit.initialize(v_dml_audit_on, v_am_id, v_app_name,
                         v_curr_prog_name);

    BEGIN
        -- Insert1
        INSERT......

        v_recs_inserted := SQL%ROWCOUNT;
        v_desc := v_recs_inserted || ' for insert1';
        pkg_audit.log_audit_info(v_dml_audit_on, v_am_id,
                         'Insert1', v_desc, v_recs_inserted);

    EXCEPTION
      WHEN OTHERS THEN
          v_status := 1;
    END;

    BEGIN
        --Update1
```

```
        UPDATE......
        v_recs_inserted := 0;
        v_recs_updated := SQL%ROWCOUNT;
        v_desc := v_recs_updated||' for update1';
        pkg_audit.log_audit_info(v_dml_audit_on, v_am_id,
                  'Update1', v_desc, v_recs_inserted, v_recs_updated);
    EXCEPTION
      WHEN OTHERS THEN
          v_status := 1;
    END;

    BEGIN

        -- Delete1
        DELETE......

        v_recs_inserted := 0;
        v_recs_updated := 0;
        v_recs_deleted := SQL%ROWCOUNT;
        v_desc := v_recs_deleted || ' for delete1';

        pkg_audit.log_audit_info(v_dml_audit_on, v_am_id,
                                ' Delete1', v_desc, v_recs_inserted,
                                v_recs_updated, v_recs_deleted);
    EXCEPTION
      WHEN OTHERS THEN
          v_status := 1;
    END;

    IF v_status = 0 THEN
        v_success_status := pkg_audit.c_success;
    ELSEIF v_status = 1 THEN
        v_success_status := pkg_audit.c_success_with_exceptions;
    ELSE
        v_success_status := NULL;
    END IF;
    pkg_audit.finalize(v_dml_audit_on, v_am_id, v_success_status);
EXCEPTION
  WHEN OTHERS THEN
      ROLLBACK;
      RAISE;
END;
/
```

The error-logging framework can be combined with the DML auditing framework to provide a robust and sophisticated audit and error logging framework. For example, the pkg_log_error.log_error_info procedure can be called in each of the exception handlers for the proc_test_audit procedure. This provides for a complete auditing and error-logging solution.

ETL FRAMEWORK

ETL processing is often required when a target database needs to be fed with data from an external source or from a different database than the target database that uses the data. One strong example where ETL processing can be employed is in populating a data warehouse. The need is more obvious when the source data is in an OLTP system and changes occasionally. In this case, not only does the initial load need to be performed, but the changed data should also be loaded on a periodic basis. The use of PL/SQL with its tight integration with SQL and the Oracle database along with its powerful features provides an efficient way to do the extract, transform, and load process when compared to using other methods like incorporating SQL*Loader to extract and load, or when using other BI tools. This section outlines the techniques of performing high-performance ETL using PL/SQL and the tips and traps involved therein. These techniques provide a framework for building ETL applications using PL/SQL.

TECHNIQUES FOR PERFORMING ETL USING PL/SQL

ETL processing can be broadly divided into three phases:

- Extract phase—This consists of reading the data source and storing it in an intermediate table, often called the staging table.
- Transform phase—This constitutes doing some processing on the extracted data like transforming the data into the format of the target database or splitting the data records or fanning multiple target records for each input record.
- Load phase—This phase finally loads the transformed data into the target database.

The next sections cover the methods for accomplishing these tasks using SQL-PL/SQL.

Extract Phase

The process of doing an extract operation depends on where the data is located, whether in an external file or in a source database. When it's in an external file, which is often the situation, the extract phase can be done either using SQL*Loader or using external tables.

Using SQL*Loader has certain limitations, processing-wise and performance-wise, as follows:

- Cannot be used as using a database table.
- Cannot access multiple tables while loading a particular table.
- Less flexibility in filtering data while loading with the WHEN clause.
- Very difficult to implement parallel processing.

Using external tables is an ideal method to do the load process. It circumvents all the limitations of SQL*Loader in addition to making the load process several times faster.

When the source data is located in a different source database, an initial load from the source can be done followed by a changed data load (if the source data is in an OLTP system). The ideal methods are as follows:

- Use a single SQL statement with INSERT...SELECT in the direct path mode to populate the intermediate tables for the initial load. This is faster than writing PL/SQL.
- Use CDC (Oracle's Change Data Capture) to populate the changing rows into the intermediate tables on a periodic basis.

TIP

*Use external tables to extract data in external files rather than using SQL*Loader. This provides a more elegant and efficient implementation than using SQL*Loader.*

Transform Phase

This is the phase where most of the logic in ETL processing is needed. It involves the following:

- Validation of input data before being loaded to the target tables.
- Transformation of input data into the format of the target database.
- Any additional processing.

If the validations or transformations are simple, they can be moved into SQL statements that will be used by the load process. If the validations and/or transformations are too complex to be incorporated into SQL, and/or additional processing needs to be done, the following PL/SQL techniques can be used:

- Bulk binds in PL/SQL
- Pipelined table functions

Using Bulk Binds

Bulk binds involve the following steps:

1. Use BULK COLLECT with the LIMIT clause in a loop to read the source data from the intermediate tables into a PL/SQL array.
2. Read the collection elements and perform the data transformations and any other processing.
3. Use the FORALL statement to load the transformed data into the target tables.

Here's a code snippet to illustrate these steps:

```
CREATE OR REPLACE PROCEDURE p_etl_insert(
    p_src_data SYS_REFCURSOR)
IS
    TYPE arr IS TABLE OF src_tab%ROWTYPE INDEX BY BINARY_INTEGER;
    arr1 arr;
BEGIN
    LOOP
        FETCH p_src_data BULK COLLECT INTO arr1 LIMIT 100;
        EXIT WHEN arr1.COUNT = 0;
        /* Perform some processing on the input rows in arr1 */
        FORALL i IN 1..arr1.COUNT
        INSERT INTO target_tab VALUES arr1(i);
        COMMIT;
    END LOOP;
END;
/
```

Using Pipelined Table Functions

Using pipelined table functions involves the following steps:

1. Define an object type having a structure equivalent to the source data record and a collection type of this object type at the schema level.
2. Create a pipelined table function in a package that returns the collection type. This function must have an input parameter of type REF CURSOR to have the source data pumped into it. Also define the function with the PARALLEL_ENABLE clause.

Using a table function accomplishes the following:

- It reduces the memory bottleneck to materialize the entire set of rows returned by the function in memory.
- It increases efficiency by not waiting for the function to execute completely.
- It enables parallel processing to be used thus further increasing speed by means of parallel query execution. This is a trade-off between the resources used to create the slave processes and the time taken to execute the function.

Here's a code snippet to illustrate pipelined table functions:

```
CREATE OR REPLACE FUNCTION f_etl_process(p_src_data SYS_REFCURSOR)
PIPELINED
IS
    TYPE arr IS TABLE OF src_tab%ROWTYPE INDEX BY BINARY_INTEGER;
    arr1 arr;
BEGIN
    LOOP
        FETCH p_src_data BULK COLLECTINTO arr1 LIMIT 100;
        EXIT WHEN arr1.COUNT = 0;
        /* Perform some processing on the input rows in arr1 */
        FOR i IN 1..arr1.COUNT LOOP
            /* Populate src_row_obj which is an element of a
               collection of objects corresponding to src_tab
               and defined in the database with input data read
               in the array arr1*/
            PIPE ROW (src_row_obj);
            /* Use multiple PIPE ROW statements to fan multiple
               records from a single source row */
        END LOOP;
    END LOOP;
    RETURN;
END;
/
```

TIP

Generally, the parallel pipelined table function approach leads to an order of magnitude faster than the bulk-binding approach. However, individual results may vary with the number of input records and the database resources available. For complex processing requirements such as fanning multiple rows for each input row, the pipelined table approach can prove beneficial as the bulk-binding approach requires FORALL to be used multiple times.

Always use schema-level types rather than PL/SQL types when defining the collection for the table function. This provides declarative control rather than programmatic control in addition to the ability of being stored as database row sets.

When defining the pipelined table function, always encapsulate it in a PL/SQL package. This way, it isolates it from database dependencies. Even a procedure in a package can be used for the bulk-binding approach using FORALL.

Load Phase

The way the load process is accomplished depends on how the transform process was done. Here are the techniques involved:

1. If the data validation and transformation can be moved into SQL itself, the load is simply an INSERT...SELECT into the target table. Here the DML error-logging facility with the LOG ERRORS clause introduced in Oracle 10g Release 2 can be used. Also, the multitable INSERT feature and the MERGE feature can be used to target the data load. This can be done in direct path mode.

   Here's a code snippet to illustrate this step of the load phase:

```
INSERT /*+ APPEND */ INTO target_tab
    SELECT <col_list> FROM src_tab
    LOG ERRORS
    REJECT LIMIT UNLIMITED;
```

2. If the processing required is mandating the use of PL/SQL logic, as with the table function approach, then using an INSERT...SELECT with a query to the table function using the TABLE operator is the optimal approach. This has to be done in direct path mode.

   Here's a code snippet to illustrate this step of the load phase:

```
INSERT /*+ APPEND */ INTO target_tab
    SELECT * FROM TABLE(f_etl_process(CURSOR
                        (SELECT * FROM src_tab)));
```

3. Using the FORALL statement to insert into target table is another way of accomplishing the load process. However, this method may not be optimal for complex processing situations that require multiple target records for each input record. This has been illustrated in the code for the p_etl_insert procedure in the "Using Bulk Binds" subsection presented earlier.

TIP

TIP

Always use direct-path inserts when performing the load process. If for any reason a direct-path insert cannot be used (for example, in cases where there may be unique constraint or index violations), resort to the bulk-binding approach using the BULK COLLECT and FORALL approach. This is faster than doing a conventional INSERT.

For complex processing requirements, use direct-path INSERT…SELECT with the parallel pipelined table function approach for doing the load process. This is probably the most efficient approach.

CASE STUDY–REPLACING STAGING TABLES USING TRANSFORMATION PIPELINE CHAIN

This case study outlines the use of pipelined table functions to create a transformation chain that can eliminate the need of staging tables. Consider the example of fanning multiple records from a single input row. This can be accomplished by means of a pipeline chain that queries the source table (either an external table or a database table), transforms the initial data, and fans out output records for each processed input row. A simple direct path INSERT…SELECT can be used to load the output rows returned by the pipeline chain into the target table. Here's the implementation process for this case study:

1. Query the external table and pass the SELECT as the input to the first pipelined table function that does the initial transformations:

```
f_pipelined1(CURSOR(SELECT * FROM external_tab))
```

2. Pass the output of f_pipelined1 as input to f_pipelined2 as a CURSOR expression using the TABLE operator. This second function fans the multiple output records for each input row:

```
f_pipelined2(CURSOR(SELECT * FROM TABLE
    (f_pipelined1(CURSOR(SELECT * FROM external_tab)))))
```

3. Load the target table using the output of f_pipelined2 with a direct path INSERT...SELECT:

```
INSERT /*+ APPEND */  INTO target_tab
SELECT * FROM TABLE(f_pipelined2(CURSOR
     (SELECT * FROM TABLE(f_pipelined1
     (CURSOR(SELECT * FROM external_tab))))))
```

This is more efficient than using a staging table and breaking the process of transformation chaining into multiple steps. Chapter 11 describes this technique in greater detail in the section "Simulating a Dataset Stage Using Pipelined Table Functions."

To summarize the ETL framework using PL/SQL in Oracle 10g, use EXTERNAL TABLES for EXTRACT phase, an INSERT...SELECT in direct-path mode with ERROR LOGGING for the LOAD phase, and a pipelined table function chain for the transformation phase. The solution of adopting the ETL framework discussed here is usually the optimal solution.

PERFORMANCE TUNING FRAMEWORK

Performance tuning is part and parcel of any application and PL/SQL is no exception. After all, the bottom line of an application running in production is that it needs to perform optimally. Optimally primarily refers to increased output response time for input (either from the user when the application is running interactively or otherwise), based on criteria such as load (number of users and operations), network traffic, and system resources.

From a PL/SQL perspective, performing tuning involves the following two aspects:

- Monitoring
- Tuning

Monitoring involves tracking the way the application is executing, including tracking the number of steps involved and the time taken and number of executions for each step.

Tuning involves tuning the SQL and the PL/SQL. SQL constitutes a significant portion of code for PL/SQL applications that are data intensive (which most of them are). Tuning of SQL queries (this comprises not only SELECTS but also UPDATES and DELETES) most often results in increased performance.

There are several factors you need to consider while tuning SQL:

- The size of the table
- The size of the resultset
- How often the table is updated
- The number of concurrent queries against the table

Tuning PL/SQL applies to both data-intensive and computationally intensive applications and depends on several factors, including:

- Data structures used
- Data management methods used
- How the application routines (mostly consisting of packages, standalone sub-programs, and trigger code) are coded
- How the application code is organized

These factors (for both SQL and PL/SQL) as a whole in turn depend on the type of application environment (such as OLTP, OLAP, and so on) and the resource's availability.

This section provides a performance framework in terms of SQL and PL/SQL monitoring and tuning from an application development perspective.

FRAMEWORK FOR MONITORING AND TUNING SQL

First let's discuss a framework for monitoring and tuning SQL. The most common performance bottleneck of a PL/SQL application is from the embedded SQL included in it. The first step is to monitor how the SQL is running so you can determine the cause of the poor performance. Once this is determined, the next step consists of determining how to improve the performance. Oracle, as of Release 10g, has provided several tools that help in monitoring and tuning SQL. The following steps provide a framework for monitoring and tuning SQL.

Monitoring the SQL

You should monitor the SQL used through tracing, SQL Tuning Advisor (as of Oracle 10g), SQL Access Advisor (as of Oracle 10g), SQL Performance Analyzer (as of Oracle 11g), Automatic WorkLoad Repository (AWR) (as of Oracle 10g), and Automatic Database Diagnostic Monitor (ADDM). Monitoring SQL consists of capturing and analyzing the SQL for the following criteria:

- Statistics about the parse, execute, and fetch phases, including the number of reads, gets, executions, parse calls, elapsed time, CPU time, memory usage, and I/O usage for each SQL statement in a single session.
- Execution plan for each SQL statement in a single session.

- Identification of long-running SQL at the session or instance level.
- Identification of problematic SQL at the instance level. This includes statistics about the various sessions in an instance such as number of reads (session logical reads and physical disk reads), executions, CPU load, long-running SQL, session and system events, locked objects, waits, I/O usage, database time, resource-intensive SQL (and PL/SQL), and any locked objects.

Statistics about the parse, execute, and fetch phases can be obtained easily by using tracing. Tracing can be done using SQL Trace, which you can enable using one of the following methods:

- The database parameter SQL_TRACE
- The packaged procedures DBMS_SESSION.set_sql_trace or DBMS_MONI-TOR.session_trace_enable (as of Oracle 10g). The DBMS_MONITOR package enables tracing on multiple sessions.

Once tracing is enabled and the SQL runs, the performance statistics are out-putted to a trace file on the database server that can be formatted and read using utilities like the tkprof utility. The trcsess utility (as of Oracle 10g) can be used for merging trace information from multiple trace files into a single file.

In addition to the previous statistics, the trace file also contains information about session waits.

Execution plans for each SQL statement can be obtained using EXPLAIN PLAN (that can be used at the client level) or the packaged function dbms_xplan.display (as of Oracle 9iR2). The trace file generated by SQL Trace also contains an execution plan for the SQL statement if necessary.

Long-running SQL pertains to SQL that is taking an unusually long time and can be obtained using dynamic performance views v$session and v$session_longops. Also, long-running SQL can be monitored asynchronously (that is, in real-time), as it is being executed using two new views, V$SQL_MONITOR and V$SQL_PLAN_MON-ITOR (as of Oracle 11g). Both I/O and execution statistics are recorded. The Active Session History statistics can also be used to identify the cause for the delay by obtain-ing a phase-by-phase breakup of SQL execution based on row-level activity informa-tion for the SQL statement in question.

Problematic SQL pertains to identifying SQL problem areas at the instance level. Dynamic performance views, AWR (queried using views), and ADDM (using an AWR snapshot and generating reports from the analyzed output) can be used to identify such problem areas. Even AWR baselines can be employed and automatic performance statistics can be obtained for this SQL.

Improving the SQL

You can now begin to improve the SQL using the output from monitored analysis. The key elements in determining the bad performance are the reads, gets, executions, parse calls, and shareable statements, as well as the CPU time, elapsed time, execution plans, and resource-intensive SQL. Based on these elements, you can make an approach to tuning the SQL in the following ways:

1. Analyze the execution plan. This helps in finding any SQL not using indexes where required. Implementing the required indexing speeds the query. The execution plan also helps in determining the access paths such as the join methods used that can be improved by using hints or otherwise. Caching the results of SQL statements (via hints available as of Oracle 11g) also helps in speeding up queries. SQL Execution Plan baselines can be used to capture and reuse existing plans and improve these plans based on analyzed criteria.
2. Find out if any locks exist on the database objects being used. Also find out if any system waits are blocking resources. This can be done using dynamic performance views and AWR. Resolving object and resource contention helps in minimizing execution time.
3. Analyze whether already parsed SQL statements can be shared and reused by deciding on the use of bind variables, especially when using dynamic SQL. The use of bind variables reduces instance memory in the SGA.
4. Analyze the database initialization parameters to determine whether they are set optimally. For example, the parameter OPEN_CURSORS, when set to a high value, is useful for soft parsing avoidance and improves runtime performance of embedded SQL in PL/SQL.
5. Determine whether object statistics are available for use by SQL execution. Slow running SQL can be ferreted out by analyzing the underlying tables and/or indexes. This can be done using the DBMS_STATS.GATHER_SCHEMA_STATS procedure. The cost-based optimizer uses these statistics to determine the cost of the SQL statement.

The SQL tuning process can also be configured to run automatically in Oracle 11g by automatic scheduling of SQL Tuning Advisor tasks to run at specific time periods. The Automatic Tuning Optimizer along with the SQL Tuning Sets, Profiles, and Tuning Information Views can provide recommendations on how to tune the SQL involved to perform optimally.

FRAMEWORK FOR MONITORING AND TUNING PL/SQL

This framework has a broader scope with regard to application performance tuning and involves a considerable effort on the part of both the developer and the administrator.

Although most of PL/SQL monitoring occurs at execution time, some aspects of bad performance can be identified at compile-time. This can be done using compile-time warnings. These are warning messages generated during compile-time that notify you about potential performance-related problems during runtime. These are applicable to stored PL/SQL program units and named PL/SQL blocks.

A standard framework for PL/SQL monitoring and tuning is outlined here:

1. Use compile-time warnings to identify potential runtime performance issues. This can be done by setting the PLSQL_WARNINGS parameter or by using the DBMS_WARNING built-in package. Stored programs can be compiled with warnings enabled in a development environment, modified as per the warning messages, and then compiled in production with warnings turned off. A good example is the warning generated when a WHEN OTHERS clause does not have a RAISE or RAISE_APPLICATION_ERROR (in Oracle 11g).

2. Monitor PL/SQL code at runtime for the four criteria—the order of code execution, the overall execution time, the number of executions and time taken for each execution, and the resource-intensive PL/SQL in terms of memory, I/O, and CPU usage.

   The order of code execution can be obtained by using PL/SQL tracing. This can be implemented using the DBMS_TRACE package. PL/SQL tracing can be enabled or disabled using the PLSQL_DEBUG parameter.

   The overall execution time and number of executions and time taken for each execution can be obtained using the PL/SQL profiling. This can be implemented using the DBMS_PROFILER package. Dynamic execution profiles about dependent subprograms (both called and calling) of a particular PL/SQL program can be obtained using the DBMS_HPROF package (as of Oracle 11g).

   The resource-intensive PL/SQL can be obtained using AWR and ADDM. This provides an overall impact of badly performing PL/SQL code in an application.

3. Audit PL/SQL program units to capture the start time, end time, status of completion (success, failure, or abnormal termination), unique ID identifying the program unit invoker (useful in case of the same program unit being called by multiple users or multiple times), the number of database records processed, and the key data involved.

This combined with error logging provides for a flexible tracing of application logic that helps in monitoring PL/SQL execution.

You can audit PL/SQL program units by writing a standard auditing package along with audit control mechanisms that enable/disable auditing at the application/program level. The audit control can be done using application contexts (more fine-grained) or regular database tables. A discussion of this type of auditing is presented in DML auditing and error-logging framework sections of this chapter.

4. Tune PL/SQL code commensurate with the findings of the monitoring. This can be done using the following approach:

- Using optimal data structures involved, such as by using PL/SQL cache tables.
- Using optimal application program structures involved, such as packages (and pinning them if necessary).
- Using other PL/SQL performance-specific features, such as NOCOPY hint, caching function resultsets (as of Oracle 11g), enhanced native compilation (useful for compute-intensive programs), efficient array processing (for performing batch-DML in PL/SQL), pipelined and/or parallelized table functions, fine-grained dependency tracking (as of Oracle 11g), invoker rights (useful for writing dynamic utilities, centralization of code, and decentralization of data), and definer rights (useful for sharing SQL, database-driven application security, decentralization of code, and centralization of data).
- Using optimal application logic, such as optimizing loops and function calls, using application contexts as an alternative for bind variables in dynamic SQL, and the like.
- Using default PL/SQL code optimization based on initialization parameters such as PLSQL_OPTIMIZE_LEVEL (when set to 2, the default in Oracle 10g, it provides aggressive optimization; when set to 3 as of Oracle 11g, it provides for automatic intra-unit inlining of code).
- Tuning Oracle memory specific to PL/SQL execution such as the SGA in the shared pool.

A discussion of performance-tuning PL/SQL features is found in Chapter 12 of this book.

SUMMARY

This chapter described application development frameworks using PL/SQL. It touched upon the error-handling framework, DML auditing framework, ETL framework, and performance-tuning framework from the perspective of PL/SQL application construction and development. The next chapter deals with techniques for applying PL/SQL in 3GL and Web environments, specifically those for extending PL/SQL to use Java, C, C++ and HTML, and emailing from PL/SQL.

10 Applying PL/SQL in 3GL and Web Environments

In This Chapter

- Extending PL/SQL to use Java
- Extending PL/SQL to use HTML
- HTML in PL/SQL versus PL/SQL in HTML
- Emailing techniques in PL/SQL
- Using UTL_MAIL versus UTL_SMTP

Applying PL/SQL in a non-Oracle world primarily deals with using PL/SQL in conjunction with 3GL/OOP languages such as Java, C, C++, and C# and Web-enabling PL/SQL. This is what the word "extending" means—you have to expand its use beyond SQL and the Oracle database. This chapter outlines and discusses the techniques involved in applying PL/SQL in Java, HTML, and Web environments. Rather than describing the beginning-to-end method involved in each of these, the chapter exposes the tried-and-true methods in each that most often are stronger candidates in real-world projects.

EXTENDING PL/SQL TO USE JAVA

Java within the database is a choice when any of the following situations exist:

- The processing involved is computation-intensive, from moderately complex to highly complex.
- The processing involved cannot be optimally performed in PL/SQL. Examples include when it mandates using rich features like a safer type system, automatic garbage collection, dynamic polymorphism, inheritance, multi-threading, and fine-grained security, as well as intra-, inter-, and extra-net portability across multiple tiers and platforms.
- The Java method is required to be called from SQL and PL/SQL (achieved through seamless integration with the database via Java stored procedures and PL/SQL calling Java methods).
- Your database needs access to system resources outside of the database such as operating system (OS) commands, files, and so forth.
- You require functionality not available in PL/SQL such as OS commands, fine-grained security policies, and easy sending of emails with attachments using JavaMail.
- You are looking for database independence in addition to the platform independence provided by Java stored procedures.

The framework for extending PL/SQL to use Java is based on a load-publish-call model that makes it as seamless as a PL/SQL subprogram. This model enables a Java class method to be treated as a PL/SQL subprogram that can interact with the database, return resultsets, or transparently be a part of transaction processing.

Figure 10.1 illustrates the load-publish-call model.

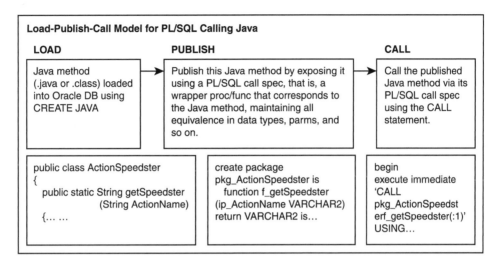

FIGURE 10.1
Load-publish-call model for PL/SQL calling Java.

The following sections cover the steps involved in the load-publish-call model.

LOADING THE JAVA CLASS (SOURCE OR BINARY)

The Java class source or the compiled Java binary should be loaded into the RDBMS before it can be used in PL/SQL. A Java class method can be uploaded to the database as a libunit using the CREATE JAVA statement. Here's an example code snippet:

```
CREATE OR REPLACE AND COMPILE JAVA SOURCE NAMED "ActionSpeedster" AS
import java.io.*;
import java.sql.*;
import oracle.sql.*;
import oracle.jdbc.driver.*;
public class ActionSpeedster
{
public static oracle.sql.ARRAY SpeedsterList(String ActionName)
// Logic involved……
  }
 }
/
```

Alternatively, an existing Java class method compiled as a .class binary object can be loaded into the database using the CREATE JAVA CLASS statement. Here's a code snippet of the same:

```
CREATE JAVA CLASS USING BFILE (bfile_dir, 'ActionSpeedster.class');
```

This creates a database object of type JAVA CLASS in the data dictionary.
In case the Java class resides in a BLOB, it can be loaded using this statement:

```
create or replace and resolve Java class using blob
(select blob_data from blob_tab where id = ...);
/
```

Here it is assumed that the referenced class is stored in a database table using a column of type BLOB.

Additionally, Java classes of all of these categories can be loaded using a command-line utility called loadjava.

PUBLISHING THE JAVA METHOD

Once a Java libunit is created in the database corresponding to a Java class, the class methods have to be exposed to the SQL (and PL/SQL environment) in a way familiar to a standard PL/SQL procedure or function. This ensures that the calling SQL or PL/SQL code can "understand" the external Java class method and interpret it as if it were calling a true PL/SQL subprogram. This method of registering a Java class method to be able to be callable by SQL and PL/SQL is called publishing. This is done by writing a call spec (short for call specification) that is a PL/SQL equivalent of the Java method. It is similar to a PL/SQL subprogram in its header, but with its body (the local declarations and the BEGIN…END section) being replaced by an AS LANGUAGE JAVA statement. Here's an example:

```
CREATE OR REPLACE TYPE list_arr_type IS TABLE OF VARCHAR2(512);
/

CREATE OR REPLACE PACKAGE pkg_ActionSpeedster
AUTHOD CURRENT_USER
IS

    FUNCTION f_SpeedsterList(ip_ActionName VARCHAR2)
       RETURN list_arr_type;

END pkg_ActionSpeedster;
```

```
/

CREATE OR REPLACE PACKAGE BODY pkg_ActionSpeedster
AUTHOD CURRENT_USER
IS
    FUNCTION f_SpeedsterList(ip_ActionName VARCHAR2)
        RETURN list_arr_type;
    AS LANGUAGE JAVA
    NAME 'ActionSpeedster.SpeedsterList(String ActionName)
        return oracle.sql.ARRAY';

END pkg_ActionSpeedster;
/
```

Notice how the Java class oracle.sql.Array is mapped to the nested table type list_arr_type created as a schema-level type.

The following points hold good in regard to call specifications:

- The call spec maps the Java method names, parameter types, and return types to their SQL counterparts. This involves mapping the data types and parameter modes between SQL and Java. To minimize loss of information and mapping of NULL values during these conversions, it is recommended to use the oracle.sql package that provides Java wrapper classes for SQL native types. Parameters of the IN mode can be mapped one-to-one, whereas parameters of the OUT or IN OUT modes should be mapped to a one-element array declaration of the equivalent type. However, the String[] parameter of the main() method can map to multiple parameters of VARCHAR2.

- Automatic memory allocation and de-allocation is done, as is the case with PL/SQL subprograms. This allocates memory for static variables and memory-resident programs as well as dynamically created ones including those requiring on-demand. It also frees memory of variables and data structures that are out of scope or no longer needed. It also takes care of the garbage in/garbage out process automatically on the Java side in a manner similar to that done on the PL/SQL side.

- A PL/SQL call spec can be defined as a standalone subprogram or as part of a package (specification only or both specification and body) and object type spec and/or body. A Java method with a return type should be published as a function and void method as a procedure. Also, static methods should be published as STATIC member methods while choosing an object type as a call spec. To be published as member methods of an object type, the Java class containing the Java methods must implement the java.sql.SQLData interface or the oracle.sql.ORAData interface. The SQLData interface is a Java interface for accessing the object attributes of an object type. This requires the implementation of two methods named readSQL() and writeSQL(), which are defined in the SQLData interface. These methods have to be defined in the Java class and are executed by the JDBC driver to read values from and write values to the database and the instance of the Java class.

CALLING THE JAVA METHOD VIA ITS CALL SPEC

Once published, the Java method can be executed from within SQL and/or PL/SQL via its call spec using the CALL statement. The CALL statement can be in stand-alone and packaged subprograms, database triggers, and object type methods. The published Java method can also be called from a SQL statement but only if it is defined as a packaged function.

Here's how the pkg_ActionSpeedster.f_SpeedsterList function can be called from PL/SQL:

```
DECLARE
    list_arr list_arr_type;
    v_ActionName VARCHAR2(20) := 'RangeRun';
BEGIN
        EXECUTE IMMEDIATE
        'CALL pkg_ActionSpeedster.f_SpeedsterList(:1)
         INTO :2' USING v_ActionName, list_arr;
END;
/
```

The following points are worth noting:

- The EXECUTE privilege should be granted to the caller of the call spec, as is done when calling an ordinary PL/SQL subprogram.
- It is best to use the CALL statement to execute the call spec instead of directly calling it. This can be done by using the NDS statement EXECUTE IMMEDIATE within a PL/SQL block. Its direct use is not allowed within a BEGIN…END.

I'll now discuss two special techniques that often don't figure in available texts or documentation. These are

- Using external Java methods to pass data between applications
- Auto-generating call specs using the loadjava utility

USING EXTERNAL JAVA METHODS TO PASS DATA BETWEEN APPLICATIONS

Chapter 7 illustrated how to pass data between applications by using packaged procedures and functions. (Refer to the section "Coding Packages to Pass Data Between Applications" in Chapter 7 for a review.) This section discusses this process from a Java standpoint.

Similar to a PL/SQL function, an external Java method published in PL/SQL can be made to pass data between application subprograms by making it return the results of a multi-row query to the calling environment. In PL/SQL, this can be done using REF CURSORS or collections. When Java is interacting with the database, a REF CURSOR is the most viable and performance-centric data structure available for this purpose. A Java method can use the JDBC resultset feature on the Java side that is mapped to a REF CURSOR on the equivalent call spec. This mapping in Java of the type ResultSet->REF CURSOR enables the Java method to return a resultset via a function return value or as an OUT parameter to a procedure defined in PL/SQL. This conversion also uses the JDBC API and is made possible by using a special procedure setCreateStatementAsRefCursor(true) (introduced as of Oracle 9iR2).

The steps involved in using a Java method to pass data between applications by having it return a resultset are outlined in the next sections.

Coding the Java Method That Returns a Resultset

You code a Java method that returns a resultset using the JDBC API to access the database and return a set of rows from a multi-row query. This involves the following steps:

1. Import the JDBC-specific packages such as java.sql.*, oracle.jdbc.driver.*, and oracle.sql.*

2. Get the default server-side Oracle connection:

   ```
   Connection conn = new OracleDriver().defaultConnection();
   ```

3. Create the Statement or PreparedStatement as a REF CURSOR by calling the method setCreateStatementAsRefCursor(true) on the Connection object cast to an OracleConnection object:

   ```
   ((OracleConnection)conn).setCreateStatementAsRefCursor(true);
   ```

4. Define the Statement object:

   ```
   Statement sql_stmt = conn.createStatement();
   ```

5. Define a ResultSet object to execute the appropriate query. This query returns the desired resultset:

```
ResultSet rset = sql_stmt.executeQuery
    ("SELECT hrc_descr, org_long_name " +
"FROM org_tab o, hrc_tab h where
    o.hrc_code = h.hrc_code");
```

6. Return the ResultSet object as a REF CURSOR:

```
return rset;
```

Listing 10.1 shows the complete program (saved as ApplDataShare.java).

LISTING 10.1 JAVA METHOD RETURNING A RESULTSET

```
CREATE OR REPLACE AND COMPILE JAVA SOURCE NAMED "ApplDataShare" AS
//Import JDBC packages
import java.sql.*;
import oracle.jdbc.driver.*;
import oracle.sql.*;
public class RefCursor {
public static ResultSet DataShare() throws SQLException {
try {
Connection conn = new OracleDriver().defaultConnection();
((OracleConnection)conn).setCreateStatementAsRefCursor(true);
//Create a Statement object
Statement sql_stmt = conn.createStatement();
//Create a ResultSet object, execute the query and return a
// resultset
ResultSet rset = sql_stmt.executeQuery
    ("SELECT hrc_descr, org_long_name " +
"FROM org_tab o, hrc_tab h where o.hrc_code = h.hrc_code");
return rset;
} catch (SQLException e) {System.out.println
    (e.getMessage()); return null;}
}
}
/
```

The Java method, if it's a function, should return a resultset of type java.sql.ResultSet. If it's a procedure, the Java method should be declared as a parameter of type java.sql.ResultSet[] (that is, an array of type java.sql.ResultSet).

Only OUT parameters in the call spec are allowed. You can't use IN or IN OUT parameters because there's no mapping from REF CURSOR to ResultSet.

Publishing the Java Program

Once this Java program is defined, compiled into a .class file, and uploaded into the database, it can be published by defining the corresponding call spec as a packaged function to correspond to the Java function.

Listing 10.2 shows the code for this process.

LISTING 10.2 PL/SQL CALL SPECS FOR THE APPLDATASHARE JAVA CLASS METHOD(S)

```
CREATE OR REPLACE PACKAGE pkg_ApplDataShare AS
    TYPE rc_ds IS REF CURSOR;
    FUNCTION f_DataShare RETURN rc_ds;
END pkg_ApplDataShare;
/
CREATE OR REPLACE PACKAGE BODY pkg_ApplDataShare AS
    FUNCTION f_DataShare return rc_ds
    IS LANGUAGE JAVA
    NAME 'ApplDataShare.DataShare() return java.sql.Resultset';
END pkg_ApplDataShare;
/
```

Note that the fully qualified type name java.sql.ResultSet is specified for the return type.

Invoking the Java Method

As a final step, the Java method is invoked using its call spec. Here's the code:

```
DECLARE
  v_rc_ds pkg_ApplDataShare.rc_ds;
  v_hrc_descr varchar2(20);
  v_org_long_name varchar2(60);
BEGIN
  EXECUTE IMMEDIATE
     'CALL pkg_ApplDataShare.f_DataShare INTO :1' USING v_rc_ds;
     dbms_output.put_line('Hierarchy Org Long Name');
  dbms_output.put_line('---------------');
```

```
      FETCH v_rc_ds INTO v_hrc_descr, v_org_long_name;
      WHILE v_rc_ds%FOUND LOOP
        dbms_output.put_line(rpad(v_hrc_descr, 9)||
                       ' '||v_org_long_name);
        FETCH v_rc_ds INTO v_hrc_descr, v_org_long_name;
      END LOOP;
      CLOSE v_rc_ds;
    END;
    /
```

AUTOGENERATING CALL SPECS USING LOADJAVA

By default, loaded methods aren't automatically published. However, as of Oracle 9i Release 2, the loadjava utility has a –publish option that auto-generates call specs as part of a package. You can specify the package name to be generated along with the –publish option.

As an example, the ActionSpeedster class can be modified to add a new Java method called DeleteAction, which deletes a particular action identified by the ActionName parameter.

Here's the modified code:

```
import java.io.*;
import java.sql.*;
import oracle.sql.*;
import oracle.jdbc.driver.*;
public class ActionSpeedster
{
public static oracle.sql.ARRAY SpeedsterList(String ActionName)
// Logic involved……
  }
public static void DeleteAction(String ActionName)
// Logic involved……
  }

  }
```

This contains the same method as the original class along with an additional one. To demonstrate the auto-generation capability, this ActionSpeedster.java file is compiled and uploaded into the database using the loadjava command with the –publish option.

Here's the code:

```
loadjava —user plsql9i/plslq9i
    —r —publish pkg_Action_Speedster
     ActionSpeedster.class
```

where the name pkg_Action_Speedster immediately following the option –publish specifies that a call spec of type package should be auto-generated with the same name as the package name. This command loads the ActionSpeedster.class file into the database, creating a schema object named ActionSpeedster of type JAVA CLASS and a call spec named pkg_Action_Speedster of type PACKAGE. No package body is created. The contents of this package specification can be obtained by querying the USER_SOURCE data dictionary view. Here's the code:

```
SELECT TEXT
FROM USER_SOURCE
WHERE NAME = 'PKG_ACTION_SPEEDSTER'
AND TYPE = 'PACKAGE'
ORDER BY LINE;
```

Here's the output of this query:

```
TEXT
--------------------------------------------------
PACKAGE PKG_ACTION_SPEEDSTER AUTHID CURRENT_USER AS
PROCEDURE DELETE_ACTION(arg0 VARCHAR) AS LANGUAGE JAVA NAME
'ActionSpeedster.DeleteAction(java.lang.String )';
```

Once the packaged call specs have been generated, they can be called in a similar manner as explicitly coded call specs. No call spec was generated for the SpeedsterList() method, because the –publish option doesn't generate call specs for methods returning collections. In fact, object types, collections, and OUT and IN OUT parameters are exceptions to the rules for auto-generating call specs.

Call specs are generated for only those methods that meet the following criteria:

- The method is defined in a public class.
- The method is defined as public and static.
- The method arguments or return types are byte, int, long, float, double, char, or java.lang.String.
- Arguments or return types of byte, int, long, float, and double types are mapped to NUMBER. Arguments or return types of char and java.lang.String are mapped to VARCHAR.
- Void methods are created as procedures, and methods with return values are created as functions.

Auto-generating call specs in this manner can help develop a template that can be used as a starting point for the final version. However, before loading the final version of the call spec, the originally loaded Java class must be dropped.

EXTENDING PL/SQL TO USE HTML

PL/SQL applications can be made globally accessible by deploying them on the Web. Web-enabling a PL/SQL application involves the use of HTML and/or XML and requires deployment using a Web server. The combination of PL/SQL and HTML/XML brings an altogether new technology to the world of PL/SQL. The method using XML with Oracle is also possible.

Web enabling PL/SQL essentially consists of coding PL/SQL subprograms (mostly encapsulated in a package) that generate Web content for back-end and front-end application processing. This in turn involves the following:

- Generating the GUI using HTML forms
- Generating the interaction logic for database processing and presentation services

The client (typically a Web browser) interacts with the database over an HTTP communication channel. Traditionally, this is done using CGI, with each HTTP request being handled by a new forked CGI process. Using PL/SQL over CGI eliminates this in addition to providing the power and efficiency of the Oracle database in terms of features that can be used and the optimizations that can be done. You can use PL/SQL in conjunction with HTML via one of two methods:

- Using HTML in PL/SQL
- Using PL/SQL in HTML

To distinguish between the two methods, I specify examples that illustrate how the basic code looks when implementing each method. Here's an example of code that uses HTML in PL/SQL:

```
CREATE OR REPLACE PROCEDURE p_html_in_plsql
IS
BEGIN
    htp.p('<HTML>');
    htp.p('<HEAD>');
    htp.p('<TITLE>Organization Records</TITLE>');
    htp.p('</HEAD>');
    htp.p('<BODY>');
```

```
    htp.p('<H1>Organization Records</H1>');
    htp.p('<TABLE BORDER="1 ">');
    htp.p('<TR><TH>Hierarchy</TH><TH>Org Long Name</TH></TR>');
    FOR idx IN (SELECT h.hrc_descr, d.div_long_name
                FROM   div_tab d, hrc_tab h
                WHERE  d.hrc_code = h.hrc_code
                ORDER BY h.hrc_code ) LOOP
        htp.p('<TR>');
        htp.p('<TD>'||idx.hrc_descr||'</TD>');
        htp.p('<TD>'||idx.div_long_name||'</TD>');
        htp.p('</TR>');
    END LOOP;
    htp.p('</TABLE>');
    htp.p('</BODY>');
    htp.p('</HTML>');
END;
/
```

Here's an example of code that uses PL/SQL in HTML:

```
<%@ page language="PL/SQL"%>
<%@ plsql procedure="p_plsql_in_html_psp"%>
<HTML>
<HEAD>
<TITLE>Corporate Records</TITLE>
</HEAD>
<BODY>
<H1>Division Records</H1>
<TABLE BORDER="1 ">
<TR><TH>Hierarchy</TH><TH>Div Long Name</TH></TR>
<%
    FOR idx IN (SELECT h.hrc_descr, d.div_long_name
                FROM   div_tab d, hrc_tab h
                WHERE  d.hrc_code = h.hrc_code
                ORDER BY h.hrc_code ) LOOP
%>
<TR>
<TD> <%= idx.hrc_descr %> </TD>
<TD> <%= idx.org_long_name %> </TD>
</TR>
<% END LOOP; %>
</TABLE>
</BODY>
</HTML>
```

The first method involves using HTML in PL/SQL by means of a generic API provided as a PL/SQL Web toolkit. This finally generates HTML output (including dynamic HTML) that is executed on the Web client. A stored procedure written using the API is invoked as a URL (with parameters) that gets translated by the PL/SQL gateway and is processed to return database information combined with HTML to the client. This method is suited only for PL/SQL-intensive applications, because the generation of HTML is from within PL/SQL code.

Note that most of the Web applications are highly HTML-intensive and mandate the use of dynamic content. This combined with the need to include the results of SQL queries and PL/SQL logic inside Web pages calls for a fast and convenient method to Web-enable a PL/SQL application.

The second method of using PL/SQL in HTML is a second way of Web-enabling PL/SQL applications. This is done by embedding PL/SQL within HTML using special PL/SQL tags. This kind of Web page is called a PL/SQL Server Page (PSP). PL/SQL is placed within special script tags known as PSP tags. These are similar to scriptlets in a Java Server Page with the only difference being that they are written in PL/SQL. A PSP can be written in HTML or XML.

The primary advantage of a PL/SQL Server Page is that it enables inclusion of dynamic content within static HTML to produce cutting-edge Web pages. The dynamic content is generated using PL/SQL logic that is executed on the server-side (that is, the database server) when the PSP page is submitted by a Web browser. This is more powerful than Dynamic HTML and also minimizes network roundtrips, thus increasing efficiency. The rich dynamic content gives more flexibility in Web-enabling the application.

The techniques of coding these two methods are simples task involving following the requisite steps and are well-documented in both the Oracle docs and the on-line Oracle-related sites. What is important is how the critical areas are addressed while doing the two. Here are some guidelines:

- Passing parameters from the Web client to the database can be done using HTML forms or URL links with hard-coded parameter values. The former is a rich and more flexible method that enables input validation and user selection.
- Parameter values can be reused by storing in non-display parameters in the HTML form or in cookies. The PL/SQL Web toolkit has API to set and get cookie information. An alternative to this is a database solution that involves storing these parameters in tables or PL/SQL structures. However, this requires user-concurrency issues to be resolved.
- SQL resultsets can be processed dynamically and returned to the Web client using these methods. The PSP technique adds more flexibility to this, as the output can be directly included in the enclosing HTML without any overhead.

■ File I/O (uploading and such) can be done to a certain degree using the Oracle database storage features for large objects and external binary files.

■ The Web-enabling process is a two-task process with the HTML taking care of the presentation services and the underlying PL/SQL package taking care of the processing logic. This segmentation provides for inclusion of robust authentication logic of data being input to the subprograms including missing, NULL, wrong, and too many values. OUT parameters can be used internally within the PL/SQL layer, with the calling subprogram decoding the same before transferring the data to the Web client.

■ Error messages from the PL/SQL code can be propagated to the Web client using the HTP.P procedure. However, the PL/SQL subprogram should ensure that effective exception handling is in place so as to prevent inadvertent calls to subsequent procedures or DML from taking place. Unhandled-exceptions in a PSP can be displayed on the Web client as an error PSP by including a definition in the original PSP using the errorPage attribute of the page directive. Current state of data in dynamic Web pages can be preserved by using hidden parameters.

■ HTML pages generated by either of these methods can be invoked by external Web programs like JavaScript or CGI. Passing of data between the various layers should be in strict conformity with SQL and PL/SQL requirements in terms of data type, parameter, and return value mappings.

HTML IN PL/SQL VERSUS PL/SQL IN HTML

The choice of using HTML in PL/SQL or PL/SQL in HTML (via a PSP) is governed by the following points:

■ If the application to be Web-enabled is HTML-intensive, use a PL/SQL Server Page. If it is PL/SQL-intensive, use HTML in PL/SQL.

■ If the application to be Web-enabled requires lot of dynamic content (especially database-dependent content) within static HTML, using a PSP provides the optimal solution. Even dynamic HTML cannot handle all cases of dynamic content to be embedded within PL/SQL. This is probably the biggest plus in choosing PSP over HTP.

■ A PSP can be deployed with only the Web browser on the client, making it a handy and easy tool as a front-end for any database application. The inherent PL/SQL code can take care of all other interfacing, database processing, and interaction processes. This gains an edge over using the HTML in PL/SQL method.

■ A PSP allows for PL/SQL code that is pluggable after the HTML has been generated. This makes it handy for its use with Web authoring tools that mostly generate pure HTML. The HTP way of Web-enabling requires the HTML to be generated out of existing PL/SQL code, which most Web authoring tools cannot interpret. However, the latter technique comes as a boon when converting existing PL/SQL applications to a Web-enabled mode.

EMAILING TECHNIQUES IN PL/SQL

As a recap, PL/SQL provides two ways of emailing from within the database:

■ Using UTL_SMTP
■ Using UTL_MAIL

These are pre-built packages that provide functional API to connect to a mail server and send messages, including text and binary attachments. UTL_MAIL is available as of Oracle 10g.

This section discusses the technique of emailing from PL/SQL with large binary attachments.

EMAILING FROM PL/SQL WITH LARGE BINARY ATTACHMENTS

This technique is highlighted using a PL/SQL packaged procedure and a standalone calling procedure that calls the former procedure. An implementation package pkg_email is defined that provides the API. A standalone testing procedure proc_test_email is used to test the emailing capability using a large PDF file as an attachment.

Here are the steps involved:

1. Open an SMTP connection to the outgoing mail server, register the domain of the sender, register the sender and receiver, start the mail process by registering the header (including the mail boundary), specify the from, to, subject, and actual mail body, and register the body details (such as content type and encoding method used) and the attachment details (such as content type, encoding method, and content disposition).
2. Locate the attachment file on the server using a BFILE locator, open the input BFILE, create a temporary BLOB, and populate it with the whole bfile data. Obtaining the length of the populated BLOB gives the size of the attachment file.

3. Stream the binary data from the BLOB in chunks of 57 after encoding it in base64 format to the email server. The number 57 is chosen to enable easy encoding in the said format using the UTL_ENCODE built-in package.

Listing 10.3 shows the code for this process.

LISTING 10.3   EMAILING FROM PL/SQL WITH LARGE BINARY ATTACHMENTS

```
CREATE OR REPLACE PROCEDURE proc_send_email (
    ip_sender VARCHAR2,
    ip_receiver VARCHAR2,
    ip_subject VARCHAR2,
    ip_body VARCHAR2 DEFAULT NULL,
    ip_filename VARCHAR2)
IS

    conn UTL_SMTP.CONNECTION;

    bfile_loc BFILE;
    blob_loc BLOB;
    bfile_offset NUMBER := 1;
    blob_offset NUMBER := 1;
    tot_len INTEGER;
    raw_chunk RAW(57);
    buffer_chunk INTEGER := 57;

    invalid_filename EXCEPTION;

    cannot_open EXCEPTION;

    boundary_tag VARCHAR2(78)
        := '-------411d51fd411d51fd-------';
BEGIN

    --Open SMTP connection to outgoing mail server
    conn := UTL_SMTP.OPEN_CONNECTION('mail.coinfo.com');

    --Register domain of sender
    UTL_SMTP.HELO(conn, 'coinfo.com');

    --Initialize the mail by specifying a sender
    UTL_SMTP.MAIL(conn, ip_sender);
```

```
--Register receiver
UTL_SMTP.RCPT(conn, ip_receiver);

--Start the mail header
UTL_SMTP.OPEN_DATA(conn);

-- Specify From:, To:, Subject: and the actual mail body
UTL_SMTP.WRITE_DATA(conn, 'From: ' || ip_sender || utl_tcp.crlf);
UTL_SMTP.WRITE_DATA(conn, 'To: ' || ip_receiver || utl_tcp.crlf);
UTL_SMTP.WRITE_DATA(conn, 'Subject: '
    || ip_subject || UTL_TCP.CRLF);
UTL_SMTP.WRITE_DATA(conn, 'Content-Type: multipart/mixed;
    boundary="'||boundary_tag ||'"'|| UTL_TCP.CRLF||
    UTL_TCP.CRLF);

-- Register body details
UTL_SMTP.WRITE_DATA(conn, '--'||boundary_tag || UTL_TCP.CRLF);
UTL_SMTP.WRITE_DATA(conn, 'Content-Type: text/plain'
    || UTL_TCP.CRLF);
UTL_SMTP.WRITE_DATA(conn, 'Content-Transfer-Encoding: 7bit' ||
    UTL_TCP.CRLF|| UTL_TCP.CRLF );
UTL_SMTP.WRITE_DATA(conn,  ip_body|| UTL_TCP.CRLF||
    UTL_TCP.CRLF);
UTL_SMTP.WRITE_DATA(conn, UTL_TCP.CRLF );

-- Register attachment details
UTL_SMTP.WRITE_DATA(conn, '--'||boundary_tag || UTL_TCP.CRLF);
UTL_SMTP.WRITE_DATA(conn, 'Content-Type: application/pdf;
    name="'||ip_filename||'"'|| UTL_TCP.CRLF);
UTL_SMTP.WRITE_DATA(conn, 'Content-Transfer-Encoding: base64' ||
    UTL_TCP.CRLF);
UTL_SMTP.WRITE_DATA(conn, 'Content-Disposition: attachment;
    filename="' || ip_filename || '"' || UTL_TCP.CRLF||
    UTL_TCP.CRLF);

-- Obtain the BFILE locator
bfile_loc := BFILENAME('BFILE_DIR',ip_filename);
IF (DBMS_LOB.FILEEXISTS(bfile_loc)=0) THEN
    RAISE invalid_filename;
END IF;
-- Open the input BFILE
DBMS_LOB.FILEOPEN(bfile_loc, DBMS_LOB.FILE_READONLY);
```

```
IF (DBMS_LOB.FILEISOPEN(bfile_loc)=0) THEN
    RAISE cannot_open;
END IF;

-- Initialize the BLOB locator;
DBMS_LOB.CREATETEMPORARY(blob_loc, TRUE);

-- Open the BLOB
DBMS_LOB.OPEN(blob_loc, DBMS_LOB.LOB_READWRITE);
-- Populate the blob with the whole bfile data

DBMS_LOB.LOADBLOBFROMFILE(blob_loc, bfile_loc, DBMS_LOB.LOBMAXSIZE,
                          bfile_ offset, blob_offset) ;
-- Obtain length of the populated BLOB
tot_len := DBMS_LOB.GETLENGTH(blob_loc);
-- Display the length of the BLOB
DBMS_OUTPUT.PUT_LINE(
'The length of the BLOB after population is: '||
TO_CHAR(tot_len));

-- Stream the binary data in chunks of 57 to the email server
blob_offset := 1;

WHILE blob_offset < tot_len LOOP
    DBMS_LOB.READ(blob_loc, buffer_chunk, blob_offset, raw_chunk);
    UTL_SMTP.WRITE_RAW_DATA(conn,
        UTL_ENCODE.BASE64_ENCODE(raw_chunk));
    blob_offset := blob_offset + buffer_chunk;
END LOOP;

UTL_SMTP.WRITE_DATA(conn, UTL_TCP.CRLF||UTL_TCP.CRLF||
                    '--'||boundary_tag||'--');
UTL_SMTP.CLOSE_DATA(conn);
UTL_SMTP.QUIT(conn);

-- Release the BLOB
DBMS_LOB.FREETEMPORARY(blob_loc);

-- Close the BFILE
DBMS_LOB.FILECLOSE(bfile_loc);

EXCEPTION
    WHEN invalid_filename THEN
        UTL_SMTP.QUIT(conn);
```

```
                RAISE_APPLICATION_ERROR(-20001, 'Invalid filename '
                                    ||ip_filename);
        WHEN cannot_open THEN
            UTL_SMTP.QUIT(conn);
            RAISE_APPLICATION_ERROR(-20002, 'Error opening
                                    filename '||ip_filename);
        WHEN UTL_SMTP.TRANSIENT_ERROR OR UTL_SMTP.PERMANENT_ERROR THEN
            UTL_SMTP.QUIT(conn);
            DBMS_OUTPUT.PUT_LINE(DBMS_UTILITY.FORMAT_ERROR_BACKTRACE);
--          RAISE;
        WHEN OTHERS THEN
            DBMS_OUTPUT.PUT_LINE(DBMS_UTILITY.FORMAT_ERROR_BACKTRACE);
--          RAISE;
END proc_send_email;
/
```

Here's the code to test this process:

```
BEGIN
    proc_send_email('lb@coinfo.com',
                    'bl@coinfo.com',
                    'Requested Report details',
                    'Herewith the details. Pls see attached PDF.,
                    'Thanks. doc1.pdf');
END;
/
```

The following points are worth noting:

- The email specification is set as multipart/mixed, meaning the email has a body part in text format and an attachment in PDF format. Each of the parts is separated by a boundary including a starting and end boundary. This is required as per the MIME standards.
- The attachment is sent as streamed output from the BLOB to the email server. This facilitates one-on-one transfer from source to the email client.
- The procedure checks for the existence and validity of the file before sending it as an attachment.

Using UTL_MAIL versus UTL_SMTP

The choice of using UTL_MAIL or UTL_SMTP is governed by the following points:

■   UTL_MAIL is a one-line API for sending emails and is simpler to use as it eliminates the steps of formatting the message body in proper target-compatible format and the explicit coding of details required by SMTP protocol such as content type, encoding, disposition, boundary, and mime type. It is quite handy once properly configured. However, attachments larger than 32KB cannot be emailed using UTL_MAIL and it allows specifying name aliases in conjunction with the actual email address.

As an example, an email with text attachment can be sent by means of a single call, as follows:

```
BEGIN
  UTL_MAIL.SEND_ATTACH_VARCHAR2(
      sender=>' "Lakshman Bulusu" lb@coinfo.com',
      recipients=>' BL bl@coinfo.com',
      subject=>'From Lakshman Bulusu',
      message=>'This is a test from LB',
      att_mime_type=>'text/plain',
      attachment=>'Hi Hello……',
      att_inline=>FALSE,
      att_filename=>'c.txt');
END;
/
```

■   UTL_SMTP is a more fine-grained API that enables attachments of any arbitrary size (up to the limit restricted by the SMTP server) to be emailed from PL/SQL. This is the only direct way to email such attachments from within PL/SQL without resorting to using external programs. However, it requires the SMTP-specific and email-specific details to be coded along with the emailing logic in addition to the piecewise writing of the attachment data to the outgoing email server. This makes it more cumbersome to code.

SUMMARY

This chapter described techniques in PL/SQL relating to extending its use with Java and HTML. With regard to extending PL/SQL to use HTML, the chapter compared the technologies available. Finally, you learned about the emailing techniques available from within the Oracle database using PL/SQL, with special reference to sending emails with large binary attachments. The next chapter deals with certain miscellaneous techniques in PL/SQL relating to simulating dataset stages, auto-generating PL/SQL code, and hiding statically and dynamically generated PL/SQL code.

11 Miscellaneous Techniques

In This Chapter

- Simulating a dataset stage using pipelined table functions
- Auto-generating code using dynamic SQL and/or PL/SQL
- Hiding statically written and dynamically generated PL/SQL code

This chapter highlights and discusses some miscellaneous techniques and practices involved in writing PL/SQL code, including simulating a dataset stage using pipelined functions, auto-generating code, and hiding statically written code and dynamically generated code.

SIMULATING A DATASET STAGE USING PIPELINED TABLE FUNCTIONS

Recall that a table function is implemented by creating a function that takes the incoming data as a REF CURSOR parameter, applies processing logic to each record, and outputs the transformed record(s) as a collection via the function return value. With a pipelined table function, the streaming is done on a record-by-record basis, by applying a technique called pipelining, whereby the input dataset is processed record by record. This in turn enables asynchronously streaming of function output on a row-by-row basis that allows for "real-time" availability. This is a benefit most often needed for OLTP and OLAP applications.

As mentioned in Chapter 7 in the section "Coding Packages to Pass Data Between Applications," the use of pipelined table functions is performance-efficient in at least four cases:

- When you need to stream data in on a row-by-row basis rather than load it all at once.
- To pass huge datasets between PL/SQL programs (when combined with bulk array processing).
- When you need to funnel multiple output rows from a single input row. In this case, table functions are the optimal choice.
- When there is a need to return the first n rows from an input dataset involving complex transformations that otherwise cannot use direct SQL. This makes it somewhat similar to getting the FIRST n ROWS in a SQL SELECT statement.

This section highlights a technique of streaming that relates to eliminating intermediate staging tables in ETL processing.

Dataset staging is often a requirement in ETL processing when the target database needs to be fed with data available in an external source or in a different database than the target database that uses the data. One strong example where ETL processing can be employed is in populating a data warehouse. The need is even more critical when the source data is in an OLTP system and changes occasionally. In this case, not only does the initial load need to be performed, but the changed data should also be loaded on a periodic basis. Table functions have a tight integration with SQL and hence with the Oracle database. When you use table functions, coupled with pipelining and parallelization, you have an efficient way to do the extract, transform, and load processes when compared to using other methods such as incorporating SQL*Loader to extract and load or using other BI tools. This high-performance technique eliminates the need for intermediate dataset staging tables by virtue of its streaming capabilities.

Figures 11.1 and 11.2 depict the basic ETL processing overview and how it can be simulated using pipelined table functions to increase efficiency.

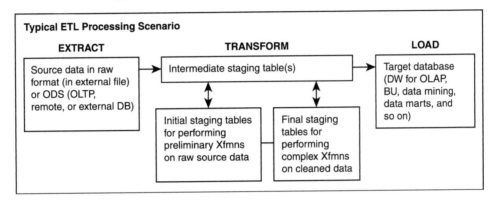

FIGURE 11.1
ETL processing overview.

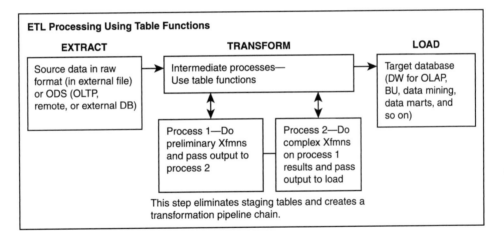

FIGURE 11.2
Using table functions to simulate dataset stage in ETL processing.

To understand where a dataset comes into the picture in ETL, it pays to first get an outline of what ETL processing involves and how it is accomplished. This outline can determine how the dataset stage can be simulated by means of pipelined table functions.

ETL processing can be broadly divided into three phases:

- Extract phase—Consists of reading the data source and storing it in an intermediate table, often called the *staging table.*
- Transform phase—Constitutes doing some processing on the extracted data like transforming the data into the format of the target database, splitting the data records, or fanning multiple target records for each input record.
- Load phase—Loads the transformed data into the target database.

EXTRACT PHASE

The intermediate dataset stage is where the raw data from an ODS is stored so that it can be converted into a more "target-friendly" format. This stage might involve operations like data type conversion, extraction, and/or concatenation, splitting, funneling, wrapping, and other complex transformations as needed.

Here are some ways the data gets into the staging table:

- With external data, this is done using external tables, which is an ideal method to do the load process. Using external tables allows you to circumvent all the limitations of traditional methods, like using SQL*Loader. It also makes the load process much faster.
- When the source data is located in a different source database, an initial load from the source can be done followed by a changed data load if the source data is in an OLTP system. There are two ideal methods to do this. You can use a single SQL statement with INSERT...SELECT in the direct path mode, which populates the intermediate tables for the initial load. This is faster than writing PL/SQL. Also, you can use CDC (Oracle's Change Data Capture) to populate the changing rows into the intermediate tables on a periodic basis.

TRANSFORM PHASE

This is the phase where most of the logic in ETL processing is needed. It involves the following steps:

- Validation of input data before being loaded to the target tables.
- Transformation of input data into the format of the target database.
- Any additional processing.

If the validations and transformations are simple, they can be moved into SQL statements that will be used by the load process. If the validations and/or transformations are too complex to be incorporated into SQL, and/or additional processing needs to be done, the following PL/SQL techniques can be used:

- Bulk binds in PL/SQL
- Pipelined table functions

Using Bulk Binds

The use of bulk binds involves the following steps:

1. Use BULK COLLECT with the LIMIT clause in a LOOP to read the source data from intermediate tables into a PL/SQL array.
2. Read the collection elements and perform the data transformations and any other processing.
3. Use the FORALL statement to load the transformed data into the target tables.

Listing 11.1 shows a code snippet that illustrates the process of using bulk binds.

LISTING 11.1 USING BULK BIND AND **FORALL**

```
CREATE OR REPLACE PROCEDURE p_etl_insert(
    p_src_data SYS_REFCUROSR)
IS
  TYPE src_arr IS TABLE OF src_tab%ROWTYPE
      INDEX BY BINARY_INTEGER;
   src_arr1 src_arr;
  TYPE tgt_arr IS TABLE OF target_tab%ROWTYPE
      INDEX BY BINARY_INTEGER;
   tgt_arr1 tgt_arr;

BEGIN
  LOOP
    FETCH p_src_data BULK COLLECT INTO src_arr1 LIMIT 100;
    EXIT WHEN src_arr1.COUNT = 0;
       /* Perform some processing on the input
       /* rows in src_arr1 and perform assignments
       /* to tgt_arr1 corresponding to the target table */

       FORALL i IN 1..tgt_arr1.COUNT
       INSERT INTO target_tab VALUES tgt_arr1(i);
  COMMIT;
END;
/
```

Using Pipelined Table Functions

The use of pipelined table functions involves the following steps:

1. Define an object type having a structure equivalent to the source data record and a collection type of this object type at the schema level.
2. Create a pipelined table function in a package that returns the new collection type. This function must have an input parameter of type REF CURSOR to have the source data pumped into it. Also define the function with the PARALLEL_ENABLE clause.

Using a table function accomplishes the following:

- Reduces the memory bottleneck to materialize the entire set of rows returned by the function in memory.
- Increases efficiency by not waiting for the function to execute completely. This is a great saving for retrieving the first rows.
- Enables parallel processing to be used, thus further increasing speed by means of parallel query execution. This, however, is a trade-off between the resources used to create the slave processes and the time taken to execute the function.

Listing 11.2 shows a code snippet to illustrate this process.

LISTING 11.2 USING PIPELINED TABLE FUNCTIONS

```
CREATE OR REPLACE FUNCTION f_etl_process
     (p_src_data SYS_REFCURSOR) RETURN tgt_row_obj_arr
PIPELINED
IS
  TYPE src_arr IS TABLE OF src_tab%ROWTYPE
       INDEX BY BINARY_INTEGER;
   src_arr1 src_arr;
  TYPE tgt_arr IS TABLE OF target_tab%ROWTYPE
       INDEX BY BINARY_INTEGER;
   tgt_arr1 tgt_arr;
BEGIN
    LOOP
    FETCH p_src_data BULK COLLECTINTO src_arr1 LIMIT 100;
    EXIT WHEN src_arr1.COUNT = 0;
        /* Perform some processing on the input
           rows in src_arr1 and perform assignments to
           tgt_arr1 corresponding to the target table */
```

```
        FOR i IN 1..tgt_arr1.COUNT LOOP
            /* Populate tgt_row_obj which
               is an element of a collection of
               objects corresponding to target_tab and
               defined in the database with input data
               read in the array tgt_arr1*/
             PIPE ROW (tgt_row_obj);
            /* Use multiple PIPE ROW statements to fan multiple
               records from a single source row */
        END LOOP;
    END LOOP;
    RETURN;
END;
/
```

This means the get-transform-stream processing chain is done incrementally without needing the entire function to complete execution and also without having to materialize the entire output dataset. Also note how the retrieval process is optimized by employing bulk set-at-a-time array processing. This implementation of combining bulk array processing with pipelining provides optimal performance in terms of both execution time and memory consumption.

Note that the incoming data is "streamed" row-by-row and not "loaded" in its entirety using this technique. The outputted rows can be queried as an inline view in a SELECT…FROM clause that can directly be used to perform DML to the target location (as illustrated in the load phase, covered next). This integration with SQL gives it added flexibility for its use in PL/SQL. Also, the table function can be parallel-enabled to further enhance its performance.

TIP

Generally, the parallel pipelined table function approach is an order of magnitude quicker than the bulk-binding approach. However, individual results may vary with the number of input records and the database resources available. For complex processing requirements such as fanning multiple rows for each input row, the parallel pipelined table function approach can prove beneficial, as the bulk-binding approach requires FORALL to be used multiple times.

Always use schema-level types rather than PL/SQL types when defining the collection for the table function.

When defining the pipelined table function, always encapsulate it in a PL/SQL package. This way it isolates it from database dependencies. Even a procedure in a package can be used for the pure bulk-binding approach using FORALL.

LOAD PHASE

The way the load phase is accomplished depends on how the transform process was done. Here are the steps involved:

1. If the data validation and transformation can be moved into SQL itself, the load is simply an INSERT...SELECT into the target table. Here, you can use the DML error-logging facility with the LOG ERRORS clause introduced in Oracle 10g Release 2. You can also use the multi-table INSERT feature and the MERGE feature to the target data load. This can be done in direct path mode.

    Here's a code snippet to illustrate this:

    ```
    INSERT /*+ APPEND */ INTO target_tab
      SELECT <col_list> FROM src_tab
      LOG ERRORS
      REJECT LIMIT UNLIMITED;
    ```

2. If the processing required is mandating the use of PL/SQL logic, use the table function approach. By using an INSERT...SELECT with a query to the table function (using the TABLE operator), you get the optimal approach. This has to be done in direct path mode.

    Here's a code snippet to illustrate this:

    ```
    INSERT /*+ APPEND */ INTO target_tab
      SELECT * FROM TABLE(f_etl_process(CURSOR(SELECT * FROM
    src_tab)));
    ```

Using the FORALL statement to insert into target table is another way of accomplishing the load process. However, this method might not be optimal for complex processing requirements that require multiple target records for each input record.

TIP

Always use direct-path inserts when performing the load process. If for any reason a direct-path insert cannot be used (for example, when there are unique constraint or index violations), use the bulk-binding approach using BULK COLLECT and FORALL. This is faster than doing a conventional INSERT.

For complex processing requirements, use direct-path INSERT...SELECT with the parallel pipelined table function for the load process. This is probably the most efficient approach.

Now that you have the foundation for implementing a data stage, the following section explains how you can eliminate the actual staging table by using a transformation pipeline chain.

REPLACING STAGING TABLES USING A TRANSFORMATION PIPELINE CHAIN

This section outlines the use of pipelined table functions to create a transformation chain that can eliminate the need of staging tables. Consider the example of fanning multiple records from a single input row. This can be accomplished by means of a pipeline chain that queries the source table (either an external table or a database table), does the initial data transforms, and fans out output records for each processed input row. A simple direct path INSERT...SELECT can be used to load the output rows returned by the pipeline chain into the target table. The following sections explain the implementation process.

Query the External Table and Pass the Source SELECT as Input

So, first you query the external table and pass the source SELECT as input to the first pipelined table function that does the initial transformations, as follows:

```
f_pipelined1(CURSOR(SELECT * FROM external_tab))
```

Here's a skeleton implementation of the f_pipelined1 function:

```
CREATE OR REPLACE FUNCTION f_pipelined1
      (p_src_data SYS_REFCURSOR) RETURN src_row_obj_arr
PIPELINED
IS
  TYPE src_arr IS TABLE OF src_tab%ROWTYPE
      INDEX BY BINARY_INTEGER;
    src_arr1 src_arr;
    xfrm_arr1 src_arr;
BEGIN
    LOOP
    FETCH p_src_data BULK COLLECTINTO src_arr1 LIMIT 100;
    EXIT WHEN src_arr1.COUNT = 0;
        /* Perform some initial processing on the input
           rows in src_arr1 and perform assignments to
           xfrm_arr1 corresponding to the target table */
        FOR i IN 1..xfrm_arr1.COUNT LOOP
           /* Populate xfrm_row_obj which is an element
              of a collection of objects corresponding to
              src_tab and defined in the database with input
              data read in the array xfrm_arr1*/
```

```
                    PIPE ROW (xfrm_row_obj);
                END LOOP;
            END LOOP;
            RETURN;
    END f_pipelined1;
    /
```

Pass the Output of f_pipelined1 as Input to f_pipelined2

Next, you pass the output of f_pipelined1 as input to f_pipelined2 as a CURSOR expression using the TABLE operator. This second function fans the multiple output records for each input row.

```
    f_pipelined2(CURSOR(SELECT * FROM TABLE
        (f_pipelined1(CURSOR(SELECT * FROM
        external_tab)))))
```

Here's a skeleton implementation of the f_pipelined2 function:

```
CREATE OR REPLACE FUNCTION f_pipelined2
        (p_init_xfrm_ddata SYS_REFCURSOR)
        RETURN tgt_row_obj_arr
PIPELINED
IS
    TYPE src_arr IS TABLE OF src_tab%ROWTYPE
        INDEX BY BINARY_INTEGER;
    init_xfmd_arr1 src_arr;
    TYPE tgt_arr IS TABLE OF target_tab%ROWTYPE
        INDEX BY BINARY_INTEGER;
    tgt_arr1 tgt_arr;
BEGIN
    LOOP
    FETCH p_init_xfrmd_data BULK COLLECTINTO
            init_xfrmd_arr1 LIMIT 100;
    EXIT WHEN init_xfrmd_arr1.COUNT = 0;

        FOR i IN 1..init_xfrmd_arr1.COUNT LOOP
        /* Perform some additional processing on the input rows
            in init_xfrmd_arr1 to split one input record into
            multiple output records in the format of the target
            table. Populate tgt_row_obj which is an element of a
            collection of objects corresponding to target_tab
```

```
                    followed by a PIPE ROW statement. This leads to an
                    assignment as per the target table format followed by
                    a PIPE ROW for each such output record to be fanned from
                    one source record in init_xfmd_arr1 */

 -- Assign tgt_row_obj here as per the first output fanned -- record
                PIPE ROW (tgt_row_obj);
                    -- change some fields to get a second (different)
                    -- output fanned record
                PIPE ROW (tgt_row_obj);
                    -- ...... /* Repeat this for each additional fanned
                                 record needed */
            END LOOP;
        END LOOP;
        RETURN;
END f_pipelined2;
/
```

Load the Target Table

Finally, you load the target table using the output of f_pipelined2 with a direct path INSERT...SELECT statement, as follows:

```
        INSERT /*+ APPEND */  INTO target_tab
                SELECT * FROM TABLE(f_pipelined2(CURSOR(SELECT * FROM
 TABLE(f_pipelined1(CURSOR(SELECT * FROM external_tab))))))
```

This is much more efficient than using a staging table and breaking up into multiple steps.

As a result, the entire ETL process eliminated the use of a physical intermediate staging table without compromising on any other functionality. Starting with the EXTERNAL TABLE for EXTRACT phase, an INSERT...SELECT in direct-path mode with ERROR LOGGING for the LOAD phase, and a pipelined table function chain for the transformation phase, this technique of ETL processing is the optimal solution.

AUTO-GENERATING CODE USING DYNAMIC SQL AND/OR PL/SQL

One of the more common examples of auto-generating code is generating SQL scripts that perform functions such as granting privileges to or disabling all triggers on all the tables in a particular schema. This is achieved by concatenating the command text with the table name and spooling the output to a text file.

Here's an example of a SELECT statement:

```
SQL> SELECT 'GRANT SELECT, INSERT, UPDATE ON
        '||table_name||' TO DVLP;'
  2  FROM   user_tables
  3  ORDER  BY 1;
```

The output of the spooled file is as follows:

```
GRANT SELECT, INSERT, UPDATE ON ODS_TAB1 TO DVLP;
GRANT SELECT, INSERT, UPDATE ON ODS_TAB2 TO DVLP;
GRANT SELECT, INSERT, UPDATE ON ODS_TAB3 TO DVLP;
GRANT SELECT, INSERT, UPDATE ON ODS_TAB4 TO DVLP;
GRANT SELECT, INSERT, UPDATE ON ODS_TAB5 TO DVLP;
```

This is just a simple example of how code can be auto-generated with the help of SQL. In fact, there is some primitive use of dynamic SQL in this because the table_name is specified as a non-hard-coded value. The table name can also be specified as a substitution variable or as a parameter at runtime. This dynamism can be extended to auto-generate code ranging from PL/SQL blocks and stored procedure definitions to SQL and PL/SQL that can be executed dynamically. This means that the EXECUTE IMMEDIATE statements can also be auto-generated. The code for enclosing the PL/SQL block or the subprogram can also be auto-generated.

The techniques for auto-generating static and dynamic PL/SQL code are discussed in the subsections that follow.

Consider an application that involves different regions of a country and contains a list of multiple users, each having a set of tables pertaining to a particular region. The application also contains a global region table that has records of all the regions. The individual region tables have to be populated from the global region table. There are two scenarios here:

- A global user wants to populate individual region tables created in a centralized schema.
- Each of the individual users wants to populate his or her own region table from the global region table.

This section makes use of native dynamic PL/SQL to demonstrate auto-code generation of static and dynamic PL/SQL for implementation of each of these scenarios, although it can be accomplished with other methods.

Auto-Generating Static PL/SQL Code

The first scenario involves generating auto-code for creating as many single procedures as there are regions, but all in the centralized schema. This makes use of static PL/SQL code. Listing 11.3 shows the code listing for this process.

LISTING 11.3 AUTO-GENERATING STATIC PL/SQL CODE

```
CREATE OR REPLACE PROCEDURE auto_gen_static_plsql
                            (ip_region_name VARCHAR2)
AUTHID CURRENT_USER
IS
  v_dyn_string VARCHAR2(32767);
BEGIN
  v_dyn_string :=
  'CREATE OR REPLACE PROCEDURE p_ppl_region_'||ip_region_name||'
   IS
      TYPE t_region_names IS TABLE OF
         global_region_tab.region_name%TYPE;
         global_region_names t_region_names;
   BEGIN
      SELECT region_name BULK COLLECT INTO
         global_region_names FROM global_region_tab;
      FORALL i global_region_names.FIRST..global_region_names.LAST
         INSERT INTO region_'||ip_region_name||'_tab
         SELECT * FROM global_region_tab
            WHERE region_name = global_region_names(i);
      COMMIT;
   EXCEPTION WHEN OTHERS THEN
      RAISE_APPLICATION_ERROR(-20001,
         ''Error in creating proc for region
         '||ip_region_name||': ''||SQLERRM);
   END p_ppl_region_'||ip_region_name||';'
   ;
--    EXECUTE IMMEDIATE v_dyn_string;
   DBMS_OUTPUT.PUT_LINE(v_dyn_string);
   DBMS_OUTPUT.NEW_LINE;
EXCEPTION WHEN OTHERS THEN
  RAISE_APPLICATION_ERROR(-20002,
     'Error in proc auto_gen_static_sql: '||SQLERRM);
END auto_gen_static_plsql;
/
```

Here's the output of executing the procedure in Listing 11.3:

```
SQL> exec auto_gen_static_plsql('EAST');

CREATE OR REPLACE PROCEDURE p_ppl_region_EAST
IS
  TYPE t_region_names IS TABLE OF
      global_region_tab.region_name%TYPE;

  global_region_names t_region_names;
BEGIN
  SELECT region_name BULK COLLECT INTO
     global_region_names FROM global_region_tab;

  FORALL i global_region_names.FIRST..
     global_region_names.LAST
   INSERT INTO region_EAST_tab
     SELECT * FROM global_region_tab
     WHERE region_name = global_region_names(i);
   COMMIT;
EXCEPTION WHEN OTHERS THEN
  RAISE_APPLICATION_ERROR(-20001, 'Error in
      creating proc for region EAST: '||SQLERRM);
END p_ppl_region_EAST;
```

Notice how the code for the procedure p_ppl_region_EAST is auto-generated and it contains static SQL to be executed. The procedure auto_gen_static_plsql calls an enclosing PL/SQL block that takes the region names from an outer implicit cursor loop. Here's the code to demonstrate this:

```
BEGIN
  FOR idx IN (SELECT region_name FROM global_region_tab) LOOP
    auto_gen_static_plsql(idx.region_name);
  END LOOP;
END;
/
```

Auto-Generating Dynamic PL/SQL Code

The second scenario involves creating one procedure for each individual user in his or her schema that uses his or her version of the region table. This involves creating these procedures with invoker rights. This example also uses native dynamic SQL to execute the INSERT for populating the region-specific table.

Now let's convert the auto_gen_static_plsql procedure to auto-generate PL/SQL that is dynamically executed. Listing 11.4 shows the code for this process.

LISTING 11.4 AUTO-GENERATING DYNAMICALLY EXECUTABLE PL/SQL CODE

```
CREATE OR REPLACE PROCEDURE auto_gen_dynamic_plsql
                         (ip_region_name VARCHAR2)
AUTHID CURRENT_USER
IS
  v_dyn_string VARCHAR2(32767);
BEGIN
  v_dyn_string :=
  'CREATE OR REPLACE PROCEDURE p_ppl_region_'||ip_region_name||'
  AUTHID CURRENT_USER
   IS
     TYPE t_region_names IS TABLE OF
        global_region_tab.region_name%TYPE;
        global_region_names t_region_names;
    BEGIN
      SELECT region_name BULK COLLECT INTO
        global_region_names FROM global_region_tab;
      FORALL i global_region_names.FIRST..global_region_names.LAST
        EXECUTE IMMEDIATE
           ''INSERT INTO region_'||ip_region_name||'_tab
               SELECT * FROM global_region_tab WHERE
                  region_name = :1'' USING global_region_names(i);
      COMMIT;
  EXCEPTION WHEN OTHERS THEN
     RAISE_APPLICATION_ERROR(-20001, ''Error in creating
        proc for region '||ip_region_name||': ''||SQLERRM);
  END p_ppl_region_'||ip_region_name||';'
  ;
--    EXECUTE IMMEDIATE v_dyn_string;
  DBMS_OUTPUT.PUT_LINE(v_dyn_string);
  DBMS_OUTPUT.NEW_LINE;
EXCEPTION WHEN OTHERS THEN
  RAISE_APPLICATION_ERROR(-20002, 'Error in proc
        auto_gen_dynamic_sql: '||SQLERRM);
END auto_gen_dynamic_plsql;
/
```

Here's the output of executing the procedure shown in Listing 11.4:

```
SQL> exec auto_gen_dynamic_plsql('EAST');

CREATE OR REPLACE PROCEDURE p_ppl_region_EAST
AUTHID CURRENT_USER
IS
    TYPE t_region_names IS TABLE OF
        global_region_tab.region_name%TYPE;

    global_region_names t_region_names;
BEGIN
    SELECT region_name BULK COLLECT INTO global_region_names
        FROM global_region_tab;

    FORALL i global_region_names.FIRST..global_region_names.LAST
        EXECUTE IMMEDIATE
            'INSERT INTO region_EAST_tab
                SELECT * FROM global_region_tab
                    WHERE region_name = :1'
                    USING global_region_names(i);
    COMMIT;
EXCEPTION WHEN OTHERS THEN
    RAISE_APPLICATION_ERROR(-20001, 'Error in creating
        proc for region EAST: '||SQLERRM);
END p_ppl_region_EAST;

PL/SQL procedure successfully completed.
```

The following points are worth mentioning regarding the dynamic version of the auto-generated code:

- The dynamic PL/SQL code generated by using the EXECUTE IMMEDIATE statement made use of bind variables in the INSERT statement to pass the value of region name to it. However, the values for generating the table name and procedure name made use of simple concatenation.
- The auto-generated procedure in this case is defined as an invoker rights procedure.

These are very good practices in coding dynamic SQL statements using NDS.

Also, the parent procedures auto_gen_static_plsql and auto_gen_dynamic_plsql are both defined as invoker rights procedures. This, again, conforms to the two criteria for using NDS—using bind variables for data and using invoker rights for the enclosing procedure.

HIDING STATICALLY WRITTEN AND DYNAMICALLY GENERATED PL/SQL CODE

This process deals with making the source code unavailable to clients, customers, or third parties. Up until Oracle 10g, there was only one way of hiding such code—using a PL/SQL binary version of the source code. As of Oracle 10g, a new technique of obfuscating source code that is dynamically generated has been introduced. This section describes both of these techniques.

WRAPPING THE PL/SQL SOURCE FILE TO A PL/SQL BINARY FILE

This process enables PL/SQL code in a source file to be wrapped into a binary version of the source code. The output produced is a file with .plb extension. This is done with the help of the WRAP utility. Consider the following example.

Assume the file Hide1.sql contains the following source code:

```
CREATE OR REPLACE PROCEDURE p_hide1
IS
  TYPE t_dept_arr IS TABLE OF dept%ROWTYPE;
  depts_arr t_dept_arr;
BEGIN
  SELECT * BULK COLLECT INTO depts_arr FROM dept;
EXCEPTION WHEN OTHERS THEN
    DBMS_OUTPUT.PUT_LINE(SQLERRM);
END p_hide1;
/
```

This file can be wrapped using the following command (executed from the OS prompt):

```
WRAP INAME=hide1.sql
```

It produces a corresponding hide1.plb file whose contents can be viewed as text and appear as follows:

```
CREATE OR REPLACE PROCEDURE p_hide1 wrapped
a000000
b2
abcd
abcd
abcd
abcd
abcd
abcd
abcd
abcd
abcd
abcd
abcd
abcd
abcd
abcd
abcd
7
db f7
4OvjfoxGcVEFFVjlZmIzro1zri4wgy7wLcsVfHSiWPiUh8ip+
    ybH6BtS3qKrW8bzfAH7vd/5
qhXN4dYBTxC7blh2kpfnTzMjJEEQH/Jbyv5fytcLp998hBbK
    1vDnIRXCaGVMH9DMu1HZ/JL7
6AMwnqFkRO97Nx2Oq3KPFuJlFGskuJHs6t57NK3NN9NxSVlnZ
    agex5AqdDSQDIzFvpfMCpXI
uOrR81jB7RX6hEhepbQT1x/qMntM


/
```

As is evident, the source code is unreadable and hence unavailable. The hide1.plb file can then be run in a schema to create the p_hide1 procedure that can be called like a normal standalone procedure.

The text column in user_source view contains the wrapped binary version of the code instead of the original source code. Here's a query to illustrate this:

```
SQL> select * from user_source where name = 'P_HIDE1';

NAME                             TYPE           LINE
-------------------------------- -------------- ----------
TEXT
-----------------------------------------------------------
P_HIDE1                          PROCEDURE         1
```

```
PROCEDURE p_hide1 wrapped
a000000
b2
abcd
abcd
abcd
abcd
abcd
abcd
abcd
abcd
abcd
abcd
abcd
abcd
abcd
abcd
abcd
7
db f7
4OvjfoxGcVEFFVjlZmIzro1zri4wgy7wLcsVfHSiWPiUh8ip+
    ybH6BtS3qKrW8bzfAH7vd/5
qhXN4dYBTxC7blh2kpfnTzMjJEEQH/Jbyv5fytcLp998hBbK
    1vDnIRXCaGVMH9DMu1HZ/JL7
6AMwnqFkRO97Nx2Oq3KPFuJlFGskuJHs6t57NK3NN9NxSVlnZ
    agex5AqdDSQDIzFvpfMCpXI
uOrR81jB7RX6hEhepbQT1x/qMntM
```

Now let's wrap a procedure that contains dynamically generated PL/SQL code. Here's the source for this:

```
create or replace procedure p_hide2
authid current_user
is
  v_str varchar2(2000);
begin
v_str := '
create or replace procedure p2
authid current_user
is
begin
  execute immediate ''insert into dept (deptno) values (1)'';
  commit;
```

```
end p2;';
execute immediate v_str;
end p_hide2;
/
```

Wrapping it using the following command:

```
WRAP INAME=hide2.sql
```

produces the following binary code:

```
create or replace procedure p_hide2 wrapped
a000000
b2
abcd
abcd
abcd
abcd
abcd
abcd
abcd
abcd
abcd
abcd
abcd
abcd
abcd
abcd
abcd
7
107 144
ifX8NkiIAJuASiVOSm/qbccvxOgwg2zQfyBGfHQC2vjqMJl+
    IQvMW57MlmqzXqleeKK2CvD1
No7x5SSdvJ8tQeTk5DEfTjzlSGWe/jrZ2vFQWYahv7Tc1EO
    /brA1iFAd4QYyHGDWsdSgsNSF
5itcXDylUYcyKLUZ64KeS/enolPpX6CabwxTxtfx2feNRmx
    JOWvXfwlaxyIWrCSP1iIQcOdz
yNd2/h7y/5ofve4dKGzSqHl9Ea5UaPaO8uSHSFjLVhwMqC
    fcBXlMEOU3rAsr1wCB4oPewO1y
FzOpQD2aJn7SpIfJP1z6ku4fmbCuGg==
/
```

Wrapped code is parsed by the PL/SQL compiler; however, syntax and semantic error checking is deferred until the .plb file is run. It is a good practice to leave package and object type specifications unwrapped so that the source code definitions contained in them are accessible to other PL/SQL programs (or external programs).

The wrapping of source code works in the following instances:

- The source code is in an OS file and is not stored in the data dictionary.
- The source code is not an anonymous PL/SQL block or trigger code.
- The project-specific requirements are met with regard to source-code availability given the fact that the translated binary version is not query-able using the data dictionary views DBA_SOURCE, ALL_SOURCE, and USER_SOURCE to get the source code. This means that the wrapped procedure code is stored in its binary version in these data dictionary views. An exception to this is dynamically generated source code.

To illustrate the second point, let's execute the file hide2.plb and query the USER_SOURCE view for the TEXT column for the P_HIDE2 and P2 procedures. Note that P_HIDE2 is created using the wrapped version of the code, whereas the source code for P2 is generated dynamically in the body of P_HIDE2.

```
SQL> @hide2.plb

Procedure created.

SQL> exec p_hide2

PL/SQL procedure successfully completed.

SQL> select text from user_source where name = 'P_HIDE2';

TEXT
-----------------------------------------------------
procedure p_hide2 wrapped
a000000
b2
abcd
abcd
abcd
abcd
abcd
abcd
abcd
```

```
abcd
abcd
abcd
abcd
abcd
abcd
abcd
abcd
7
107 144
ifX8NkiIAJuASiVOSm/qbccvxOgwg2zQfyBGfHQC2vj
      qMJl+IQvMW57MlmqzXqleeKK2CvD1
No7x5SSdvJ8tQeTk5DEfTjzlSGWe/jrZ2vFQWYahv7
      Tc1EO/brA1iFAd4QYyHGDWsdSgsNSF
5itcXDylUYcyKLUZ64KeS/enolPpX6CabwxTxtfx2fe
      NRmxJOWvXfwlaxyIWrCSP1iIQcOdz
yNd2/h7y/5ofve4dKGzSqH19Ea5UaPaO8uSHSFjLVhw
      MqCfcBXlMEOU3rAsr1wCB4oPewO1y
FzOpQD2aJn7SpIfJP1z6ku4fmbCuGg==


SQL> select text from user_source where name = 'P2';

TEXT
------------------------------------------------------
procedure p2
authid current_user
is
begin
  execute immediate 'insert into dept (deptno) values (1)';
  commit;
end p2;

7 rows selected.
```

As is evident, the source code for P_HIDE2 is stored as a binary version, whereas the source code for P2 is stored as the original source code.

To avoid this limitation, PL/SQL 10g introduced a new technique that enables storing of dynamically generated code in wrapped binary form. The next subsection discusses this technique.

Obfuscating Dynamically Generated PL/SQL Source Code

You hide dynamically generated PL/SQL source code using two packaged subprograms—DBMS_DDL.WRAP (a function) and DBMS_DDL.CREATE_WRAPPED. These are new in Oracle 10g.

First, you assign the dynamically generated source code to a string variable. Then, you use the DBMS_DDL.WRAP function to return wrapped binary PL/SQL code with the assigned variable as the actual parameter value. *This step does not execute the generated binary code.*

Listing 11.5 shows the code for these steps.

LISTING 11.5 USING THE DBMS_DDL.WRAP FUNCTION

```
create or replace procedure p_hide2_new
authid current_user
is
  v_str varchar2(2000);
begin
v_str := '
create or replace procedure p2_new
authid current_user
is
begin
  execute immediate ''insert into dept (deptno) values (1)'';
  commit;
end p2_new;';
dbms_output.put_line(SYS.DBMS_DDL.WRAP(v_str));
end p_hide2_new;
/

SQL> exec p_hide2_new

create or replace procedure p2_new wrapped

a000000
b2
abcd
abcd
abcd
abcd
abcd
abcd
```

```
abcd
abcd
abcd
abcd
abcd
abcd
abcd
abc
d
abcd
7
80
c6
uUDiJQYgDRXOzqx8Krn/JQ5PP5cwg5TZLcusfI5gOME
     ilVWpzDzctPmz2qDIJWDE1NvLFOgv
JqWS
BsCbYhe47azLy6Cgf7BM9a+aVLee/6+SBGBXr4xTj5crL+
     77lHrj8DeLuWkqQyoQni6+
R9LyDGuSmnp
4oACamqAJEEjFQjTleEDtjkvsQN+jaEMpW2n7FBc=


PL/SQL procedure successfully completed.
```

Note that the source code for P2_NEW that is being dynamically generated is wrapped but not executed. This can be verified as follows:

```
SQL> select text from user_source where name = 'P2_NEW';
no rows selected
```

In the final step, you use the DBMS_DDL.CREATE_WRAPPED function to wrap the PL/SQL code being dynamically generated and then execute it. This step stores the dynamically generated source code in wrapped form in the data dictionary.

Listing 11.6 shows the code for this step.

LISTING 11.6 USING THE **DBMS_DDL.CREATE_WRAPPED** FUNCTION

```
create or replace procedure p_hide2_new2
authid current_user
is
  v_str varchar2(2000);
begin
```

```
v_str := '
create or replace procedure p2_new
authid current_user
is
begin
  execute immediate ''insert into dept (deptno) values (1)'';
  commit;
end p2_new;';
SYS.DBMS_DDL.CREATE_WRAPPED(v_str);
end p_hide2_new2;
/

SQL> exec p_hide2_new2

PL/SQL procedure successfully completed.

SQL> select text from user_source where name = 'P_HIDE2_NEW2';

TEXT
---------------------------------------------------------
procedure p_hide2_new2
authid current_user
is
  v_str varchar2(2000);
begin
v_str := '
create or replace procedure p2_new
authid current_user
is
begin
  execute immediate ''insert into dept (deptno) values (1)'';
  commit;
end p2_new;';
SYS.DBMS_DDL.CREATE_WRAPPED(v_str);
end p_hide2_new2;

15 rows selected.

SQL> select text from user_source where name = 'P2_NEW';

TEXT
---------------------------------------------------------
procedure p2_new wrapped
a000000
```

```
b2
abcd
abcd
abcd
abcd
abcd
abcd
abcd
abcd
abcd
abcd
abcd
abcd
abcd
abcd
7
80 c6
uUDiJQYgDRXOzqx8Krn/JQ5PP5cwg5TZLcusfI5gOMEil
     VWpzDzctPmz2qDIJWDE1NvLFOgv
JqWSBsCbYhe47azLy6Cgf7BM9a+aVLee/6+SBGBXr4xT
     j5crL+77lHrj8DeLuWkqQyoQni6+
R9LyDGuSmnp4oACamqAJEEjFQjTleEDtjkvsQN+jaEMpW2n7FBc=
```

The following points are worth noting:

- Neither the DBMS_DDL.WRAP function nor the DBMS_DDL.CREATE_WRAPPED procedure wraps the source code of the enclosing procedure in which they are called. They wrap only the dynamically generated code contained in the enclosing procedure. The DBMS_DDL.CREATE_WRAPPED procedure, in addition to wrapping, also executes the dynamically generated code, so that it is stored in wrapped binary form inside the data dictionary.
- The call to the SYS.DBMS_DDL.WRAP function can be executed using native dynamic SQL (with the EXECUTE IMMEDIATE statement) to simulate the functionality of DBMS_DDL.CREATE_WRAPPED.

Using the WRAP Utility in Conjunction with DBMS_DDL.CREATE_WRAPPED

You can combine the WRAP utility with the DBMS_DDL.CREATE_WRAPPED procedure to wrap the dynamically generated source code as well as its enclosing procedure source code together and store them in the same form in the data dictionary.

Consider the file hide3_new.sql containing the following source code:

```
create or replace procedure p_hide3_new
authid current_user
is
  v_str varchar2(2000);
begin
v_str := '
create or replace procedure p3_new
authid current_user
is
begin
  execute immediate ''insert into dept (deptno) values (1)'';
  commit;
end p3_new;';
SYS.DBMS_DDL.CREATE_WRAPPED(v_str);
end p_hide3_new;
/
```

This can be wrapped using the following command:

```
WRAP INAME=hide3_new.sql
```

to produce the binary hide3_new.plb containing the wrapped version:

```
create or replace procedure p_hide3_new wrapped
a000000
b2
abcd
abcd
abcd
abcd
abcd
abcd
abcd
abcd
abcd
abcd
abcd
abcd
abcd
abcd
abcd
7
```

```
122 15c
```
AL37zYzF7kdr53Spxx6QhyJBWFcwg2LQNSDWfHQCv/9
    kpbJTw6Dtss1n9A1meXRsUCew4OQK
bcPhnvphT531VZXC5Ir+OgOGO+YZmUbpEOz3M5cleNX
    4uVTHTSOoSynDlsxLo+EdVz4xvVeN
UXun4Jy5m3pynp/dwUU4v8OIvdPopLJBcJ+PEb7L7HB
    SA+h/U7RViIS18+d7V4A8CkvxC8kB
LPV/36x9B/Xjb8nsESF4AxR/39FCfDxyfCUGqO1c2
    helKnEdO8hIAxQ+Bg1BsPrOrPektULp
btm/vu4H6iZXqjHD4dnLPZOJeW16cxIiYK9AhArgI2
    gKOXKVapYFjpMq

```
/

SQL> @hide3_new.plb

Procedure created.

SQL> exec p_hide3_new

PL/SQL procedure successfully completed.

SQL> select text from user_source where name='P_HIDE3_NEW';

TEXT
----------------------------------------------------------
procedure p_hide3_new wrapped
a000000
b2
abcd
abcd
abcd
abcd
abcd
abcd
abcd
abcd
abcd
abcd
abcd
abcd
abcd
abcd
abcd
```

```
7
122 15c
AL37zYzF7kdr53Spxx6QhyJBWFcwg2LQNSDWfHQCv/9
     kpbJTw6Dtss1n9A1meXRsUCew40QK
bcPhnvphT531VZXC5Ir+OgOGO+YZmUbpEOz3M5cle
     NX4uVTHTSOoSynDlsxLo+EdVz4xvVeN
UXun4Jy5m3pynp/dwUU4v80IvdPopLJBcJ+PEb7
     L7HBSA+h/U7RViIS18+d7V4A8CkvxC8kB
LPV/36x9B/Xjb8nsESF4AxR/39FCfDxyfCUGq01
     c2helKnEdO8hIAxQ+Bg1BsPrOrPektULp
btm/vu4H6iZXqjHD4dnLPZOJeW16cxIiYK9AhArgI2gKOXKVapYFjpMq
```

```
SQL> select text from user_source where name = 'P3_NEW';

TEXT
-------------------------------------------------------
procedure p3_new wrapped
a000000
b2
abcd
abcd
abcd
abcd
abcd
abcd
abcd
abcd
abcd
abcd
abcd
abcd
abcd
abcd
abcd
abcd
7
80 c6
9nBpGubd7GdZ3LZ2QOvCUDlPv8owg5TZLcusfI5gOMEilV
     Wps3yfFTPQGWsCid9FKhufyn8C
WgKxH5y3IK3WHpT1uA5j8K3NUZn51OzDuMs8xnwVvRyVRO
     phrOcoTY81fnQhvwflPmQpXhGX
Aejqo549tYu+a806+eiN/Mde+oZc7X+KY6k9IaCzBtGuJGkQFN4=
```

This way, both the statically and dynamically generated code are stored in wrapped form in the data dictionary.

SUMMARY

This chapter described miscellaneous techniques in PL/SQL relating to simulating the dataset stage using pipelined table functions, auto-generating code using dynamic SQL and PL/SQL, and hiding statically written and dynamically generated PL/SQL code. The next chapter deals with PL/SQL tuning and debugging.

12

PL/SQL Tuning and Debugging

In This Chapter

- Tuning data structures
- Tuning procedural code
- Techniques for debugging PL/SQL

Tuning and debugging are indispensable for any software application, regardless of the language and software used in developing the application. Applications coded using PL/SQL as the development language for the database and/or other tiers also mandate that these exercises be performed before and after deployment in production environments. In fact, tuning and debugging are both critical to the performance of the application and directly affect its productivity in terms of performance, scalability, and throughput. Tuning and debugging should be initiated as the application is run in test environments, which should typically simulate a production scenario. This prepares the application to be performance-centric in terms of efficiency, productivity, and scalability.

The tuning and debugging procedures have been simplified, enhanced, and even automated to a certain extent with the help of tools, utilities, pre-built packages, and incorporated features through version 11g of the Oracle database. With minimum effort and time, the code can be tweaked, tried, and tested to meet the performance-centric metrics. The following sections discuss the primary techniques for tuning PL/SQL code in two broad categories—tuning data structures and tuning application logic (which in turn uses these data structures). In the final section, the primary debugging techniques are highlighted.

The spectrum of performance tuning of PL/SQL code encompasses the following primary areas:

- Parsing, which consumes resources like memory from the library cache and the dictionary cache and the latching involved in locking these memory structures from being modified while parsing is going on. In instances where shared SQL is not a reality, this can result in waits, with parsing requests from multiple sessions being enqueued.
- Execution time
- Context switching
- Extra writes: undo and redo
- CPU usage
- Memory usage, including RAM memory (PGA memory) used by data structures as well as SGA used (like when pinning packages in the shared pool, using bind variables, and so on). The memory used by a PL/SQL procedure during its execution can be calculated from the dynamic performance views v$mystats to get session PGA memory usage and v$sgastat to get SGA memory usage.

Tuning PL/SQL code (which often has SQL embedded in it) consists of optimizing the code so that the impact of each of the factors mentioned here is minimal. The goal is to reduce parsing and execution time, minimize context switching, and maintain a balance between memory usage, CPU usage, and execution time.

The majority of the techniques described in the previous chapters incorporate these performance-centric measures. The next two sections summarize these techniques in the context of tuning data structures and procedural code.

TUNING DATA STRUCTURES

Recall that various data structures are used in coding PL/SQL applications, including records, collections (associative arrays, nested tables, and VARRAYS), and object types. These are both PL/SQL memory structures and schema-level objects stored using the corresponding type definitions. Of these, PL/SQL memory structures are primarily defined in PL/SQL programs and schema-level objects are defined in the database with the application logic, which often references them for read/write purposes. Optimal use of these two types of data structures contributes to the performance benefit of the application and in turn requires their tuning to meet this goal in terms of parsing, redo, memory consumption, CPU usage, and execution count and time. Here are some guidelines to help tune data structures in regard to their use in PL/SQL application programs:

- Encapsulate commonly accessed record, table, and collection type definitions in a package for global access. This derives the performance benefits of packages.
- Use aggregate assignment wherever possible instead of individual field assignment. This saves code and time. The first advantage of saving code comes as a performance enhancer in saving execution time given the fact that "less code is optimal" in PL/SQL (even while natively compiling).
- Use table-oriented records or cursor-oriented records wherever possible. Table-oriented records can be used when there is a need to include all the columns in the underlying database table as fields in the record. This way, any changes are automatically reflected in the table-oriented record when the structure of the table is altered. You can use cursor-oriented records when you require a greater degree of flexibility—for example, when you're choosing columns from multiple tables. This insulates the application code from dependency invalidations and saves execution time.
- Use entire records in INSERT and UPDATE statements to eliminate execution errors arising out of underlying table structure changes, like dropping or adding a column after the code has been compiled. Including an entire PL/SQL record in an INSERT or UPDATE statement (with the SET ROW clause) prevents the excessive recompilations (which are resource-intensive) typically needed after fixing the code. However, with an UPDATE statement, you use entire records in case of asynchronous COMMIT or only if all the columns are being changed. This is because an UPDATE incurs additional resources like redo information to be generated for each column being changed. This saves overall memory consumption and execution time.
- Use collections sparingly but smartly in terms of their usage mandates, memory consumption, and execution profiles. Use associative arrays to cache lookup tables that are small to moderately sized. When populating these arrays, use a cursor FOR loop instead of BULK COLLECT. This enables using the lookup table PK column as the associative array index variable while writing and reading the array. VARCHAR2 indexes help navigate through string data faster.

- Use nested tables and variable arrays. They are beneficial in scenarios requiring array processing (single or multi-dimensional), when returning resultsets from subprograms (especially when the resultset returned is not conformable to data returned by a SELECT query), when streaming data using table function, and when storing array-like lists inside the database. All of these contribute to the memory reduction and faster execution criteria of performance tuning. A good scenario is to use table functions with bulk array processing to pass large datasets between applications.

- Use the collection operations on nested tables for null checking, comparison, member existence (and non-existence), and set functions such as UNION, INTERSECT, and MINUS.

- Use object types as data structures. This process involves extra overhead in terms of administrative, programmatic, and processing power while accessing member data and methods. This makes them solely suitable for applications designed for OOP requiring them as data structures combining code. Exceptions to this rule are when they return datasets using table functions involving composite record structures, which involves creating the record as a schema-level object type. A second example is a call spec to a Java stored procedure that returns a linear array that requires the corresponding collection (nested table or VARRAY) to be created as a schema-level type.

TUNING PROCEDURAL CODE

All the code between BEGIN and END—including code in local subprograms, standalone subprograms, packages, and triggers written for the purposes of functional logic implementation—is categorized as procedural code. This code in turn uses data structures that also need to be tuned according to the guidelines outlined in the preceding section. The tuning criteria applicable here are parsing (including reuse of parsed SQL), the ability of code to be shared, memory consumption, CPU usage, and execution count and time. The primary areas of focus are cursor management, use of dynamic SQL and PL/SQL, coding of procedures and functions and their modularization (and encapsulation) into a package, using definer and invoker rights, and efficient transaction management (along with triggers). Certain guidelines enable efficient code to be written in terms of improving memory reduction and execution time without compromising on scalability. The next sections cover those guidelines.

CURSOR MANAGEMENT

Consider the following guidelines for efficient cursor management:

- Use a cursor FOR loop when processing *all* the rows in a cursor unconditionally and when there is no additional SQL processing involved inside the body of the loop. One use of a cursor FOR loop is to populate an associative array for caching lookup tables.
- Avoid coding SQL inside a cursor loop. Instead, code it in an explicit loop by first transferring the cursor rows into a bulk collection that can be used for processing them.
- Use implicit cursors in preference to explicit cursors. They are always faster, even when using native compilation, than explicit cursors. It is recommended to place a single-row SELECT...INTO in a packaged function to achieve reusability and greater performance, provided it will not be used repeatedly in a loop.
- Use the SELECT FOR UPDATE cursor only when you want to update the table that you're selecting from. In this case, specify the column names being updated. Doing so not only locks the rows after the cursor is opened and the resultset rows are identified for update, but it also eliminates a second fetch of the rows for doing the update and preserves the current row by the WHERE CURRENT OF clause. Don't commit or roll back inside the cursor loop while processing a SELECT FOR UPDATE cursor. Do so after the loop. *Always access rows by ROWID than by primary key when you are using SELECT...FOR UPDATE to retrieve, process, and then update the same row. This is faster than using the primary key.* Note the phrase *retrieve, process, and then update*. This means that a direct update without the rows being retrieved first does not benefit from this technique.
- Choose between coding independent cursors and dependent cursors with parameters. The latter might involve nested loops for processing that might degrade performance. It also matters how the data from the cursors is selected and processed by each of the cursors so defined.
- Use cursor variables when passing huge datasets. Also, use this approach to return resultsets to and from subprograms in environments that are mostly external to PL/SQL, such as Java and C++.
- Use cursor variables to take advantage of the dynamism provided by them—for passing multi-type data using a single cursor variable, executing multiple queries with the same cursor variable, and inter-program resultset sharing.
- Cursor expressions are efficient for retrieval of multi-row data for which a join is too complex or for which a join will not suffice (like data combining two independent n:n relationships). This, however, comes at an execution

cost involving additional logical I/O, recursive calls, and avoidance of implicit array processing. However, this can be compromised in cases that mandate their use, such as using them in PL/SQL (as of Oracle 9iR2) and in non-PL/SQL environments such as Java.

- Use cursor variables in conjunction with cursor expressions to optimize n:n queries into a single query that can be passed to the calling program. This results in a multi-fold performance gain in terms of parsing, memory usage, and execution speed.

ARRAY PROCESSING

Consider the following guidelines for implementing array processing in PL/SQL:

- Use array processing in PL/SQL only if using pure SQL is not viable. If PL/SQL is a viable option, array processing can be used to improve any SQL (not bulk SQL) that is being used iteratively in a cursor loop.
- Using bulk binds improves performance with respect to overall PL/SQL parsing and execution and also context switching when processing sets of DML statements in PL/SQL such as multi-row inserts, updates, and deletes.
- Leverage the use of native dynamic SQL with bulk binding. Using bulk binding with dynamic SQL combines the performance advantage of using bulk binds to reduce context switching with the ability to execute quickly using native dynamic SQL statements, wherever appropriate. The word *leverage* implies that the disadvantages of using dynamic SQL should be kept in mind while choosing to use native dynamic SQL with bulk SQL.
- Use the RETURNING clause with bulk binds to output information from INSERT and UPDATE statements into collections.
- Don't mistake a FORALL statement with a cursor FOR loop. They are quite different. When deciding whether to use a cursor FOR loop (or for that matter, any cursor loop) or an implicit query with BULK COLLECT, keep these points in mind. A cursor FOR loop can be used to work on only a subset of the total resultsets identified by the cursor (which might depend on runtime conditions) on a row-by-row fetch basis. An implicit query used with BULK COLLECT can unconditionally fetch *all* the rows, provided the memory requirement is met. Even when using an explicit cursor with a FETCH...BULK COLLECT INTO...LIMIT statement, a minimum amount of fetches cannot be eliminated in each iteration. However, a cursor FOR loop is handy in order to unconditionally process all the rows (fetched so far). Note the phrases *unconditionally fetch* and *unconditionally process*. A good use of BULK COLLECT in preference to a cursor FOR loop is to populate arrays defined as nested table and VARRAY types.

One very strong use of BULK COLLECT is to retrieve n rows, process n rows and INSERT/UPDATE/DELETE/MERGE these processed n rows into a target—so use BULK COLLECT...LIMIT... along with FORALL.

■   The performance benefit of array processing in PL/SQL is primarily due to reduced parsing and execution in addition to context switching. FORALL is a glaring example. The DML in FORALL is parsed and executed only once.

■   Use record types with caution when dealing with bulk DML and bulk dynamic SQL. Individual record fields cannot be referenced in the WHERE clause of the DML involved in FORALL. This holds true also when using them in bulk query if the populated collection is used as input for the FORALL DML operation (not the FORALL driving collection) and dynamic SQL is being used.

■   Use the SAVE EXCEPTIONS clause only when the driving collection is not sparse. Otherwise, use the VALUES OF clause. Always allow the bulk process to continue when you have row-wise exceptions and track exceptions in bulk DML, even when you're using INDICES OF and VALUES OF clauses.

USE OF DYNAMIC SQL AND PL/SQL

Consider the following guidelines for efficient use of dynamic SQL and PL/SQL:

■   Do not use dynamic SQL when you can use static SQL. Dynamic SQL is costlier than static SQL and also has the disadvantages of deferred dependency checking and compile-time error checking until runtime.

■   Use native dynamic SQL over DBMS_SQL to perform dynamic SQL operations on the server side. This improves performance because execution is faster. However, such use is restricted to the fact that the SQL statement is not being executed a large number of times, like iteratively in a loop. Use DBMS_SQL over native dynamic SQL when the same SQL statement is executed multiple times in the same session. *However, the techniques for interoperating NDS and DBMS_SQL—using TO_REFCURSOR and TO_CURSOR_NUMBER functions (as of Oracle 11g)—allow you to bend these rules a bit, because a DBMS_SQL cursor can be converted to a REF CURSOR and vice-versa, depending on the runtime criteria.*

■   Use only weak REF CURSORS for processing multi-row queries using native dynamic SQL.

■   Use bind variables when defining dynamic SQL statements only if their number is limited. Using bind variables for data values in native dynamic SQL makes the code execute faster and also makes the code easier to maintain. It's faster because the same SQL statement is executed with different values of the bind variables so that a single cursor is shareable by multiple SQL statements. Also, binding takes care of data type conversion implicitly because native data types are involved. Use bind variables only for data values and not for values that hold metadata values such as table names, column names, and SQL statement clauses. Use PL/SQL variables to hold metadata values. Using bind variables for specifying schema object names can result in errors that can cause confusion.

■ Always use invoker rights when using dynamic SQL and dynamic PL/SQL.

■ Use dynamic PL/SQL to simulate method 4 Dynamic SQL, a situation where the number and data types of the dynamic input are not available at compile-time. This is also possible with native dynamic SQL. Using contexts to replace bind variables to achieve the "soft-parse" benefit comes in handy in cases similar to those involving method 4 Dynamic SQL. When the number of bind variables to be used is unknown during compile-time, the USING clause in case of NDS also becomes dynamic. This cannot be part of the SQL statement that is constructed dynamically. The use of contexts comes to the rescue in such situations by eliminating the use of the USING clause. Soft-parse refers to the matching of the submitted SQL statement (when specified with bind variables) with those already parsed and available in the shared pool, so that a re-parse of the submitted SQL can be avoided.

Coding of Procedures and Functions and Their Modularization (and Encapsulation) into a Package

Consider the following guidelines for design-centric and performance-centric coding of procedures and functions:

■ Use a package to insulate code from other programs, to provide a greater degree of modularity, and to increase performance by eliminating the need for referencing programs to be recompiled when the package body changes. This in turn breaks the dependency chain and avoids cascading invalidations when a single invalid object exists in the chain.

■ Do not use a package for coding functions that are used in function-based indexes. However, function-based indexes render optimal calling of PL/SQL functions from SQL by eliminating re-execution of the function being called.

■ Pin frequently used packages in memory to optimize their load time. Pinning refers to caching of the entire package in the shared pool so that it is not aged out after completing execution or session expiration. It can be removed from memory only by undoing the pinning operation.

■ Use SQL and PL/SQL resultset caching by specifying the RESULT_CACHE hint for SQL and the RESULT_CACHE clause for functions (available as of Oracle 11g). This way, you gain added performance for output-reusable functions and queries inside them. The results of the previous execution are cached in the data buffer instead of the data block. This enables inter-session sharing of function resultset output, as it is stored on SGA. For calling functions from SQL, follow these steps:

1. Tweak the query so that the called function operates on a minimal set of rows for which the computation of the function result is relevant. All other rows can be exempted from making use of the function call. Using function-based indexes can eliminate execution of the function being called for each row returned by the query.

2. Cache the function resultset in the shared pool using the RESULT_CACHE clause for functions that execute SQL within them. This provides additional performance gain by reducing the context switches involved even if the individual SQL queries are result cached.

■ When coding cursor variables to return resultsets, always use weak cursor variables. This ensures that the definition of the cursor variable isn't constrained.

■ Use parameter passing by reference using NOCOPY when passing huge sets of data as parameters. This improves performance.

■ Use package variables to define PL/SQL globals and always define get and set methods that use native dynamic SQL to retrieve and populate these globals. Use a package initialization section to initialize any package variables needed for a session's duration.

■ Use native compilation of PL/SQL code when writing compute-intensive PL/SQL subprograms that perform database-independent tasks. In this case, native compilation results in faster execution of PL/SQL.

INVOKER AND DEFINER RIGHTS

Consider the following guidelines for choosing between invoker and definer rights:

■ Leverage the use of invoker and definer rights to take care of centralization/localization of code and data. Invoker rights provide centralization of code and decentralization of data but come with a disadvantage. Using invoker rights does not help in sharing the SQL involved, whereas in a definer-rights scenario, the SQL can be shared. Always use invoker rights for coding generic routines (using dynamic SQL) and on object member methods. This provides a greater degree of flexibility to be used by a larger number of users.

■ Always use invoker rights when using dynamic SQL and dynamic PL/SQL. Always implement customized access control tailored toward the specific application by using invoker rights in addition to the default authentication and authorization schemes provided by Oracle.

■ Use NDS so that PL/SQL subprogram references are resolved with invoker rights in the invoker rights' procedures/functions.

EFFICIENT TRANSACTION MANAGEMENT

Consider the following guidelines for efficient transaction management:

■ Minimize code containing SQL in triggers by modularizing the code into subprograms to reduce parsing. SQL in triggers is parsed once for each execution of the triggering statement.
■ It's good practice to analyze the schema after logon using a user-event trigger to estimate statistics on the tables in the schema.
■ Use the asynchronous COMMIT feature for transactions that are not recovery-based.
■ When using autonomous transactions to partition transactions, the focus areas should be to avoid deadlocks with the main transaction for resources and locks, and smart selection of scenarios to use them, such as when using autonomous transactions to avoid side effects of functions callable from SQL or counteracting trigger issues.
■ Avoid using autonomous transactions when auditing queries that are based purely on aggregate functions. An audit record for each of the rows affected will be created in this case.
■ Use autonomous transactions in database triggers only if the logic of the trigger is not dependent on the changes made by the triggering statement while it is executing.
■ Use autonomous transactions to perform DDL from PL/SQL (possible when used with native dynamic SQL).

TECHNIQUES FOR DEBUGGING PL/SQL

Debugging involves tracing the source and cause of any errors that occur during runtime. Debugging differs from error-handling, which consists of trapping of these errors. Debugging comes into picture after the code has run and aids in troubleshooting the application. Runtime errors can occur due to exceptions raised by the Oracle Server (due to failure of SQL and/or PL/SQL code) or can be logical errors that affect the functionality of the application. Exceptions raised by the Oracle Server are more visible in the sense that they are thrown to the calling environment in the form of error messages trapped by the code and customized or in un-handled form. Logical errors are less visible because they are inherent in or dependent on the data or results from the application. Only after careful analysis can logical errors reveal a functional glitch in the application and hence in the underlying code.

Debugging and error-handling go hand in hand and in fact complement each other. An efficient error-handling mechanism in place enables easy, smart, and quick debugging. However, not all errors can be debugged using error-handlers alone. There are certain scenarios where the execution of the PL/SQL code needs to traced line-by-line to determine the location of an error or its cause. This is true in case of un-handled exceptions and logical errors. In certain situations, the actual error occurring in a production system needs to be simulated in a test environment to determine the real problem. This is turn depends on the input dataset that might vary from production to test environments and hence the so-called simulation might not always be possible. However, simulating the test data first as per production can help solve this problem in most cases.

Whatever the scenario, implementation of a debugging framework helps enable efficient debugging. Retaining the implemented debugging framework (along with the code for debug message logging) while deploying the code in production environments is recommended as it ensures a fairly easy and efficient way of troubleshooting a live problem that can otherwise cause unnecessary delays in fixing it.

Although it seems to affect performance, this impact will be minimal if proper care is taken in implementing the framework on an on-demand basis based on criteria, such as by individual user, application module, program, or even table level; an access-analysis interface for the debug information being stored; and periodic purging of unnecessary debug data.

The design of any debugging framework consists of three essential tasks:

- Putting a robust error-handling mechanism in place (before running the application). This will serve as the base for trapping any errors.
- Introducing debug messages as part of the code asynchronously. This can operate on a flip-flop basis with debug messages being logged transparently on demand.
- Monitoring the code to get the execution profile.

PUTTING A ROBUST ERROR-HANDLING MECHANISM IN PLACE

The first step in error handling has been discussed in detail in Chapter 5 and in the section "Error-Logging Framework" in Chapter 9. A combination of the techniques described in both of these sections provides for a rich set of error-handling routines that encompass both error trapping and error logging.

INTRODUCING DEBUG MESSAGES AS PART OF THE CODE ASYNCHRONOUSLY

With error-handling implemented, the second step starts the debugging process by following a similar mechanism to log any debug messages (in contrast to error messages). A debug message is simply a string of text that tags the location and position of a line or portion of code in a subprogram. It is specified just before the code snippet that it refers to. The code snippet can have a second debug message tagged to it to indicate its end point. Likewise, a particular subprogram can be host to a number of such debug messages. Any debug logging framework can be devised to generate and log debug messages inside areas of code that are identifiable as important and/or critical. Here's a brief outline of the steps involved:

1. Create two tables called DEBUG_LOG and CUSTOM_DEBUG_MESSAGES (similar to the ERROR_LOG and CUSTOM_ERROR_MESSAGES tables). The second table defines a master list of all possible debug messages to be pooled together and is optional. If the second table is omitted, the first table can serve as the central repository of all debug messages in place.

2. You can flip-flop the logging of the debug messages using an audit control table. The audit control table used for error logging can be modified to add another column called DEBUG_ON, which turns debugging on and off in a session on an individual application/module/program basis. Each program is debug-logged only if debugging is turned on. Application contexts can be used instead of a control table if the number of applications/modules needing debugging is not large so that control is more secure and tightly integrated. This table can also be used to control on-demand debugging based on external criteria, such as user authentication, in addition to that at the application/subprogram level. Situations that demand debugging to be turned off include batch programs (especially when processing huge number of rows) and initial loads to ETL processes.

3. You can implement concurrency control while logging debug messages by capturing the unique OS user of the current session rather than the application user login or the database user login in conjunction with the calling/called program information. This allows you to log information about users executing a program with maximum accuracy, in case the same program is being called by multiple sessions or multiple times in the same session.

4. To implement the debug logging mechanism, you can use a simple API similar to the pkg_log_error code (see Chapter 9). In addition, you can add a new function to this API that generates the debug message dynamically based on specified parameters. Listing 12.1 shows an example of such a function.

5. Code a subprogram that returns the debug message information for the main program unit being called as formatted output.

6. Purge the debug logs periodically based on criteria such as retention period, application cut-off dates, and so forth.

LISTING 12.1 GENERATING A DEBUG MESSAGE DYNAMICALLY

```
FUNCTION f_gen_debug_msg(
    p_application_name       IN debug_log.application_name%TYPE,
    p_curr_program_name      IN debug_log.current_program_name%TYPE,
    p_calling_program_name   IN debug_log.calling_program_name%TYPE,
    p_block_name             IN debug_log.block_name%TYPE,
    p_description            IN debug_log.description%TYPE,
    p_msg_no                 IN debug_log.message_no%TYPE,
    p_msg_desc               IN debug_log.message_desc%TYPE,
    p_key_info               IN VARCHAR2 DEFAULT NULL,
    p_include_header         IN VARCHAR2 DEFAULT 'N')
RETURN VARCHAR2
IS
    v_debug_msg VARCHAR2(2000);
    FUNCTION header RETURN VARCHAR2
    IS
    BEGIN
      RETURN('In APP: '||p_application_name||
             ' PROG: '||p_curr_program_name||
             ' Called By: '||p_calling_program_name||';');
    END;
BEGIN
    IF p_message_no IS NOT NULL THEN
        v_debug_msg :=
        pkg_log_debug.get_message_text (p_message_no);
    END IF;
    RETURN ((CASE WHEN p_include_header = 'Y' THEN header
         ELSE NULL END)||
          ' This code identifies '||p_block_name||
          '-'||p_description||
          ': '||(CASE WHEN v_debug_msg IS NOT NULL THEN v_debug_msg
               ELSE p_msg_desc END)||
          '(KEY INFO: '||p_key_info||')');
END f_gen_debug_msg;
/
```

Implementing such debug message logging provides the first level of monitoring code execution by revealing the control points in the code at which the execution faltered or stopped. The third step of monitoring the code to get the dynamic execution profile augments this step by tracing the finer granular details about code execution.

In addition to using database tables in conjunction with autonomous transactions, asynchronous debug messages can be logged using file I/O, pipelined table functions, or the DBMS_APPLICATION_INFO packaged routines. The last one offers limited flexibility as far as the message text is concerned.

MONITORING THE CODE TO GET THE EXECUTION PROFILE

This primarily involves tracking the order of execution of code. You track the count, time, and execution of each individual execution unit within the program (this may be a single line or another subprogram call); the same statistics for each of the descendent subprograms of the calling subprogram and the caller and called subprogram information; and finally the resources used in executing the program.

A detailed procedure for monitoring PL/SQL is outlined in Chapter 9 under the subsection "Framework for Monitoring and Tuning PL/SQL." A combination of the techniques presented there provides a rich set of tools to monitor the code execution profile, with breakup of SQL and PL/SQL executions.

The debugging framework presented here can be automated by constructing a generic debug utility as part of a code library that incorporates this framework. The design and coding steps for such a utility can be derived from those built in this debugging framework.

SUMMARY

This chapter described techniques for tuning and debugging PL/SQL applications. The key concepts for tuning data structures and procedural code along with several debugging solutions available were discussed. The next chapter deals with PL/SQL coding standards.

13

PL/SQL Coding Standards

In This Chapter

- Data structure management
- Error management
- Data management
- Application management
- Transaction management
- Using PL/SQL in 3GL and the Web

Any software application calls for the use of proper guidelines to write the code. These guidelines form a blueprint for the code to be written and adhere to certain rules that primarily pertain to syntax and semantic usage, proper formatting, and use of optimal code structures. Optimal code that's well documented enables effective maintenance and debugging in addition to reduced errors, improved performance, and readability. These guidelines are accepted as coding standards and are generally outlined before beginning the development phase of the software development lifecycle. They serve as rules of thumb while coding and should be followed to enable standardized and efficient code to be developed. These standards also incorporate tried-and-true techniques that expose ignored facts and provide solutions to technical problems, saving time and effort on the part of developers in addition to providing well-written, well-maintained, and efficient PL/SQL code.

This chapter provides certain guidelines for PL/SQL coding practices. This list should be augmented by a design document with proper design criteria, identified inputs and outputs to the application being coded, along with information to be logged or audited. The application might also be partitioned into several modules, each tailored to a specific task. Most of these guidelines outline the more in-depth rules that address expert techniques rather than concentrating on general guidelines like those of formatting and using basic PL/SQL features.

DATA STRUCTURE MANAGEMENT

Encapsulate record and table type definitions in a package for global access.

While accessing the individual elements of a record, use the record variable name and not the record type name.

Use aggregate assignment wherever possible instead of individual field assignment. This saves code and time.

Use a table-oriented record when there is a need to include all the columns in the underlying database table as fields in the record. This ensures that the changes are automatically reflected in the table-oriented record when the structure of the table is altered.

Make use of user-defined data types, subprograms, and user-defined exceptions.

Use cursor-oriented records when a greater degree of flexibility is desired—for example, when you're choosing columns from multiple tables.

TIP

Use entire PL/SQL records in INSERT and UPDATE statements with caution. With an UPDATE statement, use entire records only if an asynchronous COMMIT is being issued or if all the columns are being changed. This is because an update incurs additional resources like undo information to be generated for each column being changed.

Use associative arrays to transform database table data into PL/SQL structures, like lookup table caching.

Use a loop to populate an associative array when it's required to create the rows sequentially.

Check for the existence of an associative array element before referencing it for the first time in PL/SQL control structures for reading its value. Use a WHILE loop with the FIRST, LAST, and NEXT methods to access the elements in an associative array.

Simulate multi-dimensional arrays using multiple associative arrays.

Use character indexes for associative arrays when dealing with VARCHAR2 data. This improves performance by enabling fast lookup of individual array elements, eliminates the need to know the position of the individual element, and avoids looping through all array elements.

Encapsulate collection type definitions in a package when defining them in PL/SQL.

Use nested tables and variable arrays to return resultsets from subprograms, especially when the resultset returned is not conformable to data returned by a SELECT query. Using table functions enables one way of returning resultsets from subprograms. When you use table functions, pipeline them to incrementally return data for maximum efficiency.

Always use a PL/SQL collection only after initializing it. An associative array is an exception to this rule.

Leverage the advantage of nested tables and variable arrays. These can be stored in the database to efficiently store list data in the form of arrays, including multidimensional arrays using multilevel collections.

Don't try to manipulate VARRAY elements in PL/SQL. Doing so can result in illegal program termination.

Use the SQL TABLE operator to retrieve the individual elements of a nested table.

It's recommended that you include multilevel collection type definitions of the PL/SQL type in a package so that they're available persistently across sessions.

Use objects to model real-world entities in PL/SQL. The inherent advantages of object orientation help leverage objects in PL/SQL, such as richer encapsulation and binding of methods to data.

Use GET and SET methods to retrieve and populate attributes of an object type. Use user-defined constructors to customize object initialization enabling added flexibility, ease of use, and proper validation of attribute data.

Use type hierarchies to model hierarchical relationships involving objects. Features such as superclass and subclass definition, substitutability, and dynamic method dispatch enable you to model efficiently with ease.

Use object views to present an object relational view of relational table data using INSTEAD-OF triggers on these views.

For more information on how some of these guidelines can be applied in PL/SQL development, see Chapters 4 and 6.

ERROR MANAGEMENT

Classify error messages into information, warning, and error messages, and handle each in a proper way. Also, you can categorize the messages based on their severity level:

- Messages of type *error* are actual application/code failure messages resulting at runtime and should be handled by propagating them to the calling environment or halting further processing. The severity level parameter can help in this process.
- Messages of type *warning* are specific alerts cautioning a deviation of the application from its normal behavior but can still be ignored. Examples include "The value of credit level assigned is out of sync with his/her actual credit history; change it unless override allowed" and "Current limit is nearing the maximum limit." These messages can be propagated to the calling environment.
- Messages of type *information* simply convey general, hint, or successful status information, such as about a particular input value. Examples include "You can use any value less than 100 for input," "Use this checkbox to override the earlier selections," and "The file creation process terminated successfully." These can be handled as per application- and user-specific needs by outputting them in the manner desired without disturbing the application execution flow.

Categorize errors in an application by segregating them into predefined exceptions, non-predefined Oracle errors, user-defined exceptions, and user-defined PL/SQL error messages. For all of these types of errors, write generic error-handling routines that separate error processing from business logic processing.

Throw, trap, and handle customized error messages based on application-specific requirements. This also includes associating programmer-defined exceptions with these customized error messages that correspond to logical errors.

Audit errors in an error table with complete error information such as the error code, the error message text, the error line number where the error first occurred, and the error execution stack.

Customize error information returned by SQLERRM and DBMS_UTILIT.FORMAT_ERROR_STACK (to get only the error message text) or DBMS_UTILITY.FORMAT_ERROR_BACKTRACE (to get only the error line number).

Use EXCEPTION_INIT to associate a non-predefined Oracle error with a user-defined exception. Although you can also use EXCEPTION_INIT to associate user-defined error messages with user-defined exceptions, don't use it for this purpose. Instead, code an error-raising procedure that makes a call to RAISE_APPLICATION ERROR within it for providing user-defined error messages in PL/SQL. For messages of type error, you can use this method. Code examples illustrating such use have been provided in Chapter 5 in the subsection "Throwing, Trapping, and Handling Customized Errors."

Determine when to halt processing, ignore and continue program execution, or let the exception fall through after an exception occurs. For informative and warning messages, the messages can be ignored. In the case of error messages, the normal behavior should be to halt program execution at that point. However, a careful analysis can reveal when to continue after errors in some exceptional cases. Also, don't let exceptions fall through. Code an exception handler exclusively for each PL/SQL block or subprogram defined in the application. Define a WHEN OTHERS handler in each exception handling section. This traps any errors not handled explicitly or otherwise. In this case, trap the Oracle error raised using SQLCODE and SQLERRM.

Don't forget the benefit of using RAISE_APPLICATION_ERROR. It not only raises the customized error and stops further execution, but it also returns the customized error number and error message as the SQLCODE and SQLERRM to the calling environment.

Define user-defined exceptions in a package for global access. Don't define duplicate user-defined exceptions while dealing with nested blocks. Handle all user-defined exceptions explicitly by coding an exception handler for each of them. Don't try to associate more than one user-defined exception with the same error number. Don't declare user-defined exceptions with the same names as the predefined ones. Always follow a naming pattern when you define user-defined exceptions.

Be careful about exceptions raised in declaration and exception-handling sections of a PL/SQL block. In the case of nested blocks, always include a WHEN OTHERS handler in the top-most level of every PL/SQL program.

For more information on how some of these guidelines can be applied in PL/SQL development, see Chapters 5 and 9.

DATA MANAGEMENT

Always use cursors for dealing with multi-row SELECTS. In this way, you can process the results of multi-row SELECTS, row by row, in a PL/SQL block.

Always check for implicit cursor attributes with SQL% after performing a DML inside a PL/SQL block. Also, use the RETURNING clause to output information inserted or updated by the DML statement. Using SQL%FOUND, SQL%NOT-FOUND or SQL%ROWCOUNT replaces a SELECT COUNT(*). Even if a SELECT COUNT(*) isn't used, at least a SELECT...INTO should be used instead. Using implicit cursor attributes saves this overhead.

Use a cursor FOR loop when processing *all* the rows in a cursor unconditionally and when there is no additional SQL processing involved inside the body of the loop. Also, use this FOR loop to populate an associative array used for caching lookup values.

Use implicit cursors rather than explicit cursors. They are always faster, even when used with native compilation, than explicit cursors. It is a good idea to place a single-row SELECT...INTO in a packaged function to achieve reusability and greater performance, provided it will not be used repeatedly in a loop.

Use the SELECT FOR UPDATE cursor only when you want to update the table that you're selecting from. In this case, specify the column names being updated. Doing so not only locks the rows after the cursor is opened and the resultset rows are identified for update, but it also eliminates a second fetch of the rows for doing the update and preserves the current row by the WHERE CURRENT OF clause. Don't commit or roll back inside the cursor loop while processing a SELECT FOR UPDATE cursor. Do so after the loop.

TIP

Always access rows by ROWID rather than by primary key when you are using SELECT...FOR UPDATE to retrieve, process, and then update the same row. This is faster than using the primary key.

Make use of dynamism in cursor variables by reusing the same cursor variable for opening multiple queries or assigning different queries to the same cursor variable depending on runtime conditions.

Make use of cursor variables to return resultsets from subprograms in environments that are mostly external to PL/SQL, such as Java, C++, and so on.

Make use of cursor expressions to facilitate retrieval of multi-row data for which a join is too complex or a join will not suffice at all (such as with data combining two independent n:n relationships). This, however, comes at an execution cost involving additional logical I/O, use of recursion internally and avoidance of implicit array processing.

Use array processing in PL/SQL only if using pure SQL is not viable. If PL/SQL is a viable option, array processing can be used to improve SQL (not bulk SQL) that is being used iteratively in a cursor loop.

Using bulk binds improves performance with respect to overall PL/SQL parsing and execution and also context switching when processing sets of DML statements in PL/SQL such as multi-row inserts, updates, and deletes.

Leverage the use of native dynamic SQL with bulk binding. Using bulk binding with dynamic SQL combines the performance advantage of using bulk binds to reduce context switching with the ability to execute quickly using native dynamic

SQL statements, wherever appropriate. The word "leverage" implies that the disadvantages of using dynamic SQL should be kept in mind while choosing to use native dynamic SQL with bulk SQL.

Use the RETURNING clause with bulk binds to output information from INSERT and UPDATE statements into collections.

Don't mistake a FORALL statement with a cursor FOR loop. They are quite different concepts.

Use record types with caution when dealing with bulk DML and bulk dynamic SQL. Individual record fields cannot be referenced in the WHERE clause of the DML involved in FORALL. This is also an implication for using them in a bulk query if the populated collection is used as input for the FORALL DML operation (not the FORALL driving collection) and dynamic SQL is being used.

Use the SAVE EXCEPTIONS clause only when the driving collection is not sparse. Otherwise, use a VALUES OF clause. Always track exceptions in bulk DML, even when using INDICES OF and VALUES OF clauses.

TIP

Do not use dynamic SQL when you can use static SQL. Dynamic SQL is costlier than static SQL in terms of parsing and execution and also has the disadvantages of loss of dependency checking and compile-time error checking.

Use native dynamic SQL over DBMS_SQL to perform dynamic SQL operations on the server-side. This improves performance because execution is faster. However, such use is restricted to the fact that the SQL statement is not being executed a large number of times, like iteratively in a loop.

Use only weak REF CURSORS for processing multi-row queries using native dynamic SQL.

Use bind variables when defining dynamic SQL statements only if their number is limited. Using bind variables for data values in native dynamic SQL makes the code execute faster and also makes the code easier to maintain. It's faster because the same SQL statement is executed with different values of the bind variables so that a single cursor is shareable by multiple SQL statements. Also, binding takes care of data type conversion implicitly because native data types are involved. Only use bind variables for data values and not for values that hold metadata values such as table names, column names, and SQL statement clauses. Use PL/SQL variables to hold metadata values. Using bind variables for specifying schema object names can result in errors that can cause confusion.

Always use invoker rights when using dynamic SQL and dynamic PL/SQL.

When using native dynamic SQL, always define an exception-handling section by specifying it in an enclosing PL/SQL block.

Use DBMS_SQL over native dynamic SQL when the same SQL statement is executed multiple times in the same session.

Leverage the interoperability of native dynamic SQL and DBMS_SQL to increase flexibility of coding and achieve desired functionality.

Use dynamic PL/SQL to implement method 4 dynamic SQL, a situation of dynamic SQL where the number of inputs and their types are unknown at compile-time. This can be done using native dynamic SQL statements for dynamic PL/SQL. Using contexts to replace bind variables to achieve the "soft-parse" benefit comes in handy in cases similar to those involving method 4 Dynamic SQL.

Use native dynamic SQL with objects. This produces the same performance benefits as when you use relational tables that execute code involving objects in the database efficiently.

For more information on how some of these guidelines can be applied in PL/SQL development, see Chapters 6 and 11.

APPLICATION MANAGEMENT

Leverage the use of packages to globalize data and code and also to localize data and privatize code. This comes as an implication of modularity. Even in the case of a single program unit, if it performs huge tasks and is compute-intensive, or if it processes multiple SQL statements, it's good practice to place it in a package.

TIP

Do not use a package for coding functions that are used in function-based indexes. However, function-based indexes render optimal calling of PL/SQL functions from SQL by eliminating re-execution of the function being called.

Packages insulate code from other programs, provide a greater degree of modularity, and increase performance. Also, packages have the advantage that referencing programs need not be recompiled when the package body changes. They also break the dependency chain by avoiding cascading invalidations when there's a single invalid object in the chain.

Pin frequently used packages in memory to optimize performance of the shared pool.

Overload similarly functioning subprograms that differ only in their parameter types or number of parameters.

Use SQL and PL/SQL resultset caching by specifying the RESULT_CACHE hint with SQL and the RESULT_CACHE clause with functions (available as of Oracle 11g) to gain added performance for output-reusable functions and queries inside them.

This way the results of the previous execution are cached in the data buffer instead of the data block.

Leverage the use of user-defined operators over functions if the project-specific design-specific guidelines mandate it. Design-specific refers to converting a complex computing function to a built-in operator that can be called declaratively. Such a scheme can be used as part of template construction in large PL/SQL applications. This access can be provided to such functions that can be safely used within SQL. User-defined operators are handy in building code libraries but might involve an additional administration overhead.

When coding cursor variables to return resultsets, always use weak cursor variables. This ensures that the definition of the cursor variable isn't constrained.

Use parameter passing by reference using NOCOPY when passing huge sets of data as parameters. This improves performance.

Leverage the use of invoker and definer rights to take care of centralization/localization of code and data. Using invoker rights provides centralization of code and decentralization of data but comes with a disadvantage. Using invoker rights does not help in sharing the SQL involved whereas in a definer rights scenario, the SQL can be shared. Always use invoker rights for coding generic routines and on object member methods. This provides a greater degree of flexibility to be used by a large number of users.

Always implement customized access control tailored toward the specific application by using invoker rights in addition to the default authentication and authorization schemes provided by Oracle.

Use package variables to define PL/SQL globals and always define GET and SET methods that use native dynamic SQL to retrieve and populate these globals. Use a package initialization section to initialize any package variables needed for a session's duration.

Use native compilation of PL/SQL code when writing compute-intensive PL/SQL subprograms that perform database-independent tasks. In this case, native compilation results in faster execution of PL/SQL.

Use a customized error-reporting mechanism when defining errors from triggers.

Use system-event and user-event trigger attributes to reference system events, object owner, or object name when a system-level trigger fires. These are available through the SYS.% attributes or by means of public synonyms named ORA_%.

Make use of the new compound trigger introduced in Oracle 11g.

Code DML operations on a view by means of INSTEAD-OF triggers. It's a good practice to analyze schema after logon using a user-event trigger to estimate statistics on the tables in the schema.

For more information on how some of these guidelines can be applied in PL/SQL development, see Chapter 7.

TRANSACTION MANAGEMENT

Use the asynchronous COMMIT feature for transactions that are not recovery-based.

When using autonomous transactions to partition transactions, make sure to avoid deadlocks with the main transaction for resources and locks. Code an explicit COMMIT or ROLLBACK in an autonomous transaction program to end it normally. Don't attempt to jump to ROLLBACK to a save point issued in the main transaction from inside the autonomous transaction.

In case of a package, each individual subprogram should be defined as autonomous.

Use autonomous transactions to avoid side effects of functions callable from SQL.

TIP

Avoid using autonomous transactions when auditing queries that are based purely on aggregate functions. An audit record for each of the rows affected will be created in this case.

Use autonomous transactions in database triggers only if the logic of the trigger is not dependent on the changes made by the triggering statement while it is executing.

For more information on how some of these guidelines can be applied in PL/SQL development, see Chapters 8 and 9.

USING PL/SQL IN 3GL AND THE WEB

Use REF CURSORS when passing data between PL/SQL and external (3GL and/or OOPL) environments. Passing a pointer to a resultset is more effective than passing the entire row-set, in this case.

Use Java in the database for optimizing compute-intensive tasks that don't need database access and for extending database functionality not available in PL/SQL. Java also implements a safer type system, automatic garbage collection, polymorphism, inheritance, and multithreading. Always specify the Java class as public and its methods as public static when defining a Java stored procedure.

Use fine-grained access control when accessing resources outside of the database such as operating system files from external stored procedures.

Use PL/SQL within HTML to seamlessly integrate an HTML-intensive application with the database. Using email functionality from within PL/SQL eliminates the need to code external routines for email, thus enabling tighter integration with the database and greater productivity for the application from a functionality perspective.

For more information on how some of these guidelines can be applied in PL/SQL development, see Chapter 10.

Summary

This chapter highlighted some coding standards for you to follow when programming using PL/SQL. Specifically, these standards related to must-follow rules covering various aspects of PL/SQL, including data structure, and data, error, application, and transaction management in PL/SQL. The chapter concluded with some guidelines for using PL/SQL in 3GL and Web environments.

Index

KNOWLEDGE IS POWER
Essential Guides from Charles River Media

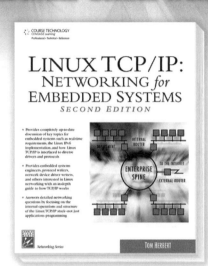

KNOWLEDGE IS POWER
Essential Guides from Charles River Media

**Global Outsourcing with
Microsoft Visual Studio 2005 Team System**
1-58450-445-5 ■ $49.95

Teaches managers, developers, and SQA professionals how to successfully execute outsourced projects with Microsoft Visual Studio 2005 Team System.

The Software Vulnerability Guide
1-58450-358-0 ■ $49.95

Helps developers and testers better understand the underlying security flaws in software and to write more secure code.

SQL Server 2005 for Developers
1-58450-388-2 ■ $44.95

Shows developers how to leverage the new data management, business intelligence, and developer tools in SQL Server 2005.

**Enterprise Application Development
with Visual C++ 2005**
1-58450-392-0 ■ $49.95

Teaches developers how to create practical business applications using managed C++ and Visual Studio® 2005.

**Developer's Guide to the
Windows SharePoint Services v3 Platform**
1-58450-500-1 ■ $59.95

Provides a detailed technical resource for developing applications on the Windows SharePoint Services v3 Platform.

**Programming Microsoft Infopath:
A Developer's Guide, 2E**
1-58450-453-6 ■ $45.95

Shows developers how to generate XML, Web Service, and SQL-based forms using InfoPath.

Open Source for Windows Administrators
1-58450-347-5 ■ $49.95

Provides techniques for using Open Source applications in databases, E-mail, Web content, file sharing, word processing, spreadsheets, and more.

Innovative Cryptography
1-58450-467-6 ■ $49.95

Provides a cutting-edge evaluation and review of current findings in the area of cryptography and explores how to implement these new techniques efficiently.

Text Mining Application Programming
1-58450-460-9 ■ $59.95

Teaches software developers how to mine the vast amounts of information available on the Web, internal networks, and desktop files and turn it into usable data.

About the *Oracle PL/SQL: Expert Techniques for Developers and Database Administrators* CD-ROM

The CD included with this book contains the source code of the examples used throughout the book. This source code is meant to demonstrate or supplement the techniques in this book. Full appreciation of the book requires perusal of the CD-ROM materials. Every effort has been made to ensure that the enclosed source code is bug-free and able to be compiled (except for the code snippets), that the executables run trouble-free, and that the images are freely viewable. Please refer to the book's Website (go to www.courseptr.com and enter the title, author name, or ISBN) to access updates, errata, and any recent details regarding the contents of the CD-ROM.

CONTENTS

For ease of location, the materials on the CD are organized into folders that correspond to the chapters of the book. Source code in each folder has been verified to compile with Oracle 11g and Oracle 10g Release 2, as appropriate.

SYSTEM REQUIREMENTS FOR WINDOWS

Windows 2000, XP, or Vista is required. A document reader capable of displaying Microsoft Word or PDF documents is needed for article supplements. Also for the figures, Acrobat Reader for PDF files is required; it's freely downloadable at http://www.adobe.com.

License Agreement/Notice of Limited Warranty